ENLIGHTEN
THE
F^CK UP

ENLIGHTEN THE F^CK UP

AN EMPATHIC PSYCHIC HEALER'S WEIRD STORIES, TOUGH LESSONS & RESOURCES

WITH

CARINA CARIÑOSA

2020
REGENT PRESS
Berkeley, California

Copyright © 2020 by The Carina Cariñosa Foundation
a 501c3 Non-Profit Public Charity

[paperback]
ISBN 13: 978-1-58790-491-2
ISBN 10: 1-58790-491-8

[e-book]
ISBN13: 978-1-58790-492-9
ISBN 10: 1-58790-492-6

Library of Congress Control Number: 2020934331

MANUFACTURED IN THE UNITED STATES OF AMERICA
REGENT PRESS
Berkeley, California
www.regentpress.net

DISCLAIMER

According to the Buddha, "Believe nothing, no matter where you read it, or who said it, no matter if I have said it, unless it agrees with your own reason and your own common sense." (1)

According to the "Fair Use" clause of International Copyright Law, the authors declare that the use of the photos, videos and information in this academic research are analyzed for purposes of "criticism, comment, news reporting, teaching, scholarship, or research" According to Section 107 of Title 17 of the US Code.

The following information is of an educational and edutainment nature and should not be construed as medical or legal advice. You should consult appropriate written and professional sources to answer questions related to your individual situation. Exercising one's rights often entails some element of risk, and you should verify all information relevant to your situation before acting; the author and publisher disclaim any responsibility or liability for any loss incurred as a consequence of the use of any information herein.

FORWARD

"The Shamans say that being a medicine man begins by falling into the power of the demons. The one who pulls out of the dark place becomes the medicine man, and the one who stays in it is the sick person. You can take every psychological illness as an initiation. Even the worst things you fall into are an effort of initiation, for you are in something which belongs to you."
— *Marie-Louise von Franz (2)*

"Healers are spiritual warriors who have found the courage to defeat the darkness of their souls. Awakening and arising from the depths of their deepest fears, like a Phoenix rising from the ashes. Reborn with a wisdom and strength that creates a light that shines bright enough to help, encourage, and inspire others out of their own darkness."
— *Melanie Koulouris (3)*

"Sometimes the world's sages come from abusive homes, our gurus from poverty, our teachers from AA, our poets from prison, our prophets from the outskirts. Sometimes our saints don't wake up privileged with the intention of making the future better, but focused on how they're going to get through the day. Because god works in mysterious ways. Sometimes freedom is going to come from betrayal, courage from regret, hope from loss, love from disbelief, vitality from horror, motivation from rage, nurturing and beauty from suffering, and something right is going to come from all that's wrong. Because God works in mysterious ways."
— *Tanya Markul (4)*

"To be empowered is to be connected to the guru within. Here, we discover that our dynamic purpose is to share our gifts, collaborate and express pure love in sovereign, co-creative expansion. May beings everywhere become intimately familiar with the truth of their divinely angelic nature."
— *Carina Cariñosa*

"May the agony of my suffering fuel the fire for my love"
— *Silver Ra Baker (5)*

May you be protected and safe.
May you feel contented and pleased.
May your body support you with strength.
May your life unfold with ease. (6)

INTRODUCTION

It's taken more than ten years to finish writing this book, because of fear-based ego, and stubbornly traumatized past lives coming up for healing. I want to be wholly authentic with you, I'm just afraid of telling the whole truth to so many strangers. The truth is that I thought I was so ready to finish this book, and unleash it to the masses, but God told me that I needed to first go home and forgive my mother. Little did I know how much work I still had to do before the time would come to finally overcome my subconscious limiting beliefs. You see, I moved to Panama to escape the aftermath of 9/11. I called bullshit on that whole situation as I watched the second tower fall and our security dissipate. Orwell's 1984 was coming to fruition. (7) In doing so, I also was escaping my former self, my traumatized youth, the consequences of addiction, abuse and jail from outstanding traffic tickets, which I couldn't afford.

In new age terms, I was spiritually bypassing my biggest problems by escaping to greener pastures instead of watering my own grass. I achieved enlightenment in 2012, and started going by the name Carina Cariñosa. Urban Dictionary defines "Carina" as the only way to describe a carina is simply beautiful. She has the full package from head to toe which can make a guy go crazy by just looking at her. Cariñosa in Spanish means, 'loving'. The name suits me well.

The truth is that, during an extremely strong acid trip, God told me to forgive and love my mother, which meant releasing my childhood pain once and for all. Circumstances which I'll describe forced me back to my mother's house. The house was in need of TLC, and it seemed like everything waited for my arrival before breaking down so that I could be available to receive the repairmen who would fix it since she worked during the day.

There were esoteric things to fix too, like the demonic spirit that was trapped in the guest room. A relative had dragged it home after prison. Come to find out, it was the disembodied spirit of an addicted and angry inmate who'd been murdered on the inside. My relative's propensity for crack cocaine made them a perfect target for this spirit to latch onto. My own propensity to addiction made me a target, as well. I was also at the phase in my learning process of working with the paranormal where I was eager to ascend Ghosts and remove demonic or reptilian influences. I shouldn't have done this without the express guidance of a good mentor. My lack of sanctification is what caused the infiltration and totally blocked my ability to work on this book.

I lost the battle for a long while. I'd thought I'd arrived at a level in my healing mastery to where I could combat the reptilian, alien, demonic, and ghost entities alone, but they fought back with a vengeance. I got stuck on a roller coaster of unclean living, living like an American. I would stress eat while battling my unresolved childhood traumas. This lack of sanctification made me a target. I could be fucked with because I wasn't in full alignment. I hadn't completely surrendered my will to God, even though I thought consciously I had. The will of my wounded inner child hadn't fully surrendered for healing.

I came to realize there was a spirit in the house based on the bad dreams that immediately started happening as I slept in the room. Then, one day I hosted a group of people to do Enlightenment Integrations and meditative prayer. The teenager with ESP said there was something in the room trying to entice her to come in. That's when I knew I wasn't crazy. This was an external force acting against my free will. The next day, I did an energetic cleansing of the house with sage, fire and drums. The spirit got angry at the eviction notice and started tapping through the wall. Then, the dreams got worse. So, with more conviction, I did another cleansing ceremony, and made sure to call in the bigger guns. I asked a team of volunteer angels to come down and set guardians over our house. I asked Jesus to come in and help my mom forgive the betrayal of her 19-year marriage gone astray. The entity responded by what sounded like rolling around in his grave up in the attic. It sounded like he was tossing things around and throwing a hissy fit.

If memory serves, that was just before my good friend and apprentice called. She said she was having trouble with something in her throat holding her back. Being the adept that I am, I could see she had a blockage in her throat chakra, the center for communication, speaking your truth, and unleashing your creativity. I offered to work on her immediately over the phone.

"Beloved Ascended Masters, we allow our hearts to connect with your hearts today and every day. To all Masters, known and unknown, named and unnamed, throughout all worlds, times, spaces, and dimensions, if you serve the highest Truth, Love, Light, and Joy, we allow our hearts to connect with yours." In short order, because it takes a bit of time to traverse the multiverse, I saw an angel with its hand around her neck. Then I started dry heaving, and puked out the blockage on her behalf, actually vomiting on my Mom's patio. That's how my gift works – like in The Green Mile, if you've seen that movie.

I told her about the angel, and she said, 'I can see his face.'

I advised, 'Well then ask him who he is and what he wants."

'Gabriel asks what you most desire.'

INTRODUCTION

I told Archangel Gabriel what I wanted, which included more money, sex, help clearing this entity from my Mom's home, and some other goals I now forget. The next day, human Gabriel showed up at my door. He was a technician from a company my mom uses. When I first moved there I'd thought, 'The only way I'm gonna get laid in this podunk town is by meeting someone who comes to the house.' Sure enough, when Gabriel came to fix my mom's cable and internet, he had a thing for me and wanted to visit for personal reasons. Now, here he was on my doorstep, trying to have a quickie while on his lunch break. I saw the coincidence, that Archangel Gabriel is the messenger angel, her throat chakra blockage, and now Gabriel manifested in the flesh to resolve my need for sexual healing. I obliged him and got my kicks for the day.

The problem was that human Gabriel has kids and a woman. So, this was obviously not in total alignment with my standards for dating. Mind you, we have to be really specific with Source because it always brings exactly what we hold in mind and vibration. That's how I manifested him, exactly as my expectation and standards dictated. Apparently, I didn't mind being the mistress; that's how much I still needed sexual healing. How quickly I would forget what my mentor had told me the year before, 'Make sure you have removed the prostitute ghost completely. Don't let her operate in the background.'

Shortly afterwards, I called upon my apprentice to help me kick this spirit out of my house for good. She is particularly skilled at dealing with ghostly entities, and commanding dark forces to back the fuck off. Also, being raised in a home with Catholicism, Rosa Cruz, and Santeria, I figured she was a good candidate for saying the Spanish prayers while I made a huge altar in my office above the guest room. This time, I called on Baphomet (8), the equalizer between dark and light. This time, our combined forces worked. The nightmares stopped, and my mom started going to church again.

Going back home to Mom brought up all my unresolved childhood shit. My eating disorder reared its ugly head again, and my telepathic sensitivities verged on narcissism. In Panama, I had been eating raw vegan, having gone from 315 pounds down to 185 over the course of 5 years. I'd resolved so many of my 'American problems' through God's grace and clean living that I wanted to tell the world with this book. But acting like an American again, bombarded by lower vibes, I began to seek refuge in alcohol, cigarettes, food, and sex. One good weekend of binging, and I'd gain 5 pounds. I gained 60 pounds in about a year. Inflammation wreaked havoc on my brain and destabilized me mentally. Before long, I was taking psych medications to treat mild depression and bipolar/ schizoid tendencies. I'd fallen off the horse again. It took two and a half years to get back on board with true self-actualization.

Shortly after moving back, I finished producing 6 CD's about enlightenment. We launched the Carina Carinosa app, and finished the new website, http://www.carinacarinosastore.guru. I paid my employees and found myself broke again. The money to pay for all this was a gift from God. I had said, the year before, during an intense surrender ceremony (which I'll teach you how to do), 'God, please bring me a big money miracle. I promise to use the funds to further your work and my mission.' The miracle client called within a few days. He'd been referred by my first miracle client. This was awhile back when I worked in international finance and studied the healing arts to reach enlightenment (which we can quantify and I'll teach you about soon). The first client was a miracle answered after my first serious surrender ceremony, in which I'd taken similar vows. In less than 12 hours after the first ceremony, this new client calls. He said he found my information on the web through my former associate, yet, we could never trace back to the exact webpage. Source simply opened a door and made a path where there hadn't been one. The new client and I shared very similar values, and when I told him what had happened, he believed thoroughly that our meeting was ordained.

The money from the second client had gotten sequestered by PayPal. I had him make his sizable deposit through my website about healing rather than my asset protection website. PayPal thought the amount was sketchy, so despite my best efforts, they froze $10,000 for 6 months – actually seven. I'd left Panama thinking the money would be available right at the 6-month mark, but it wasn't, so I was forced to travel down to my mom's house for shelter. I never would have done that willingly with all my childhood angst and unresolved trauma. I just knew her house was the wrong vibe for me. It didn't take me long to realize intellectually that God had sent me back to work out the past, but as the amnesia set in, and I stopped channeling for fear of psychic attack, things got out of hand quick enough.

So, the money was spent to further God's mission, and now I was left broke and horny.

This is a tell-all book. Here you will read all of the higher wisdom I obtained, channeled, and learned particularly as it relates to becoming enlightened. You'll also see my flawsomeness, warts and all. The goal is to be fully transparent so that you can grow from my experience and pain. You're invited to learn what I've learned about obtaining and sustaining enlightenment through the trials, triumphs, and education of my life thus far. This book will give you tools to assist in your journey of awakening.

TABLE OF CONTENTS

Chapter 1:
ACCEPTING YOUR POWER...15

Chapter 2:
UNDERSTANDING 'SIN'...24

Chapter 3:
MY SPIRITUAL NAME...30

Chapter 4:
DIVING IN...34

Chapter 5:
DEVELOPING COMPASSION...39

Chapter 6:
FORGIVING IGNORANCE...43

Chapter 7:
WHAT TO DO?...51

Chapter 8:
KARMA...57

Chapter 9:
ENGINEERED FOOD & CANCER...66

Chapter 10:
WHAT IS AN EMPATH?...71

Chapter 11:
TRUST...78

CHAPTER 12:
SHARING IS CARING...85

Chapter 13:
PEACE VS. PRIDE...91

Chapter 14:
BECOMING YOUR HIGHER SELF ... 94

Chapter 15:
ENERGETIC HEALING METAPHYSICAL MEDICINE ... 104

Chapter 16:
SHAMANISM AND KARMA ... 114

Chapter 17:
LOVE YOURSELF BY LOVING OTHERS ... 137

Chapter 18:
THE MAGIC OF CRYSTAL INTUITION ... 148

Chapter 19:
HEALING THE PROSTITUTE LIVES ... 152

Chapter 20:
THE EXORCISM ... 168

Chapter 21:
FORGIVENESS ... 171

Chapter 22:
PROSPERITY & ABUNDANCE THROUGH GOD'S WILL ... 176

Chapter 23:
CHILDREN VS CAREER & GETTING CLEAR ... 193

Chapter 24:
THE EXORCISM PART 2 ... 211

Chapter 25:
SURRENDER CEREMONIES ... 215

Chapter 26:
PRAYERS ... 220

REFERENCES ... 231

Chapter 1:

ACCEPTING YOUR POWER

Try to suspend your religious upbringing while we discuss the topic of 'What is God.' Please allow me to begin with what God is not. God is not any of the hell, fire, and condemned judgement that many people have been shackled to believe. It's a shame so much of the population has been trained to perceive that God is an authoritarian, a disgusted parent who chooses favor for some and suffering for others. That's called anthropomorphism, an interpretation of what is not human or personal in terms of human or personal characteristics, aka humanization.

It is imperative for you to understand that most religions were tampered with, taken over, by a sinister level of consciousness which was unnatural to our Divine Human Nature. We'll call it 'the enemy' for now. You may ask, rightfully so, to know exactly who the enemy is. Sadly, the enemy has been bred, burrowed, and even implanted inside most all of us through so many different unconscionable methods, often unfathomable ways which could lend your friends to call you crazy. No dear heart, the crazy, is not you. The 'original sin' that preaches about your inferiority to God, or your unholiness, is alien.

The truth of who you are is divine, pure, compassionate, loving, forgiving and intimidatingly more powerful than any oppressive force operating within or around you.

All 'holy wars' are infiltrated consciousness led by the enemy, priestly wolves in sheep's clothing. Now is the time to regain our sovereignty from the grips of overlord- archetypes by reclaiming our divine human powers. We see the enemy in all forms of corruption, particularly government, religion, the FDA, pharmaceutical companies, the military industrial complex, fossil fuel industries, Monsanto, etc. We see the enemy infiltrating our thoughts, actions, speech and behavioral patterns through programming. If there is unrest within us, there is a strategic mass marketing effort for it. These unholy vices and lies are designed to keep us in fear, detached from our true nature and thus under control. However, often the enemy is so covertly programmed into our subconscious minds that we actually mistake these resistant behaviors and thoughts as ourself. We say, 'I'm only human' as if being human meant disempowered or broken. We unwittingly buy into the lies that our minds create through programming that gives the illusion of separateness from Source which is the root of all our suffering.

All feelings which separate you from the truth of your divine nature should be considered illusions. Every feeling of shame, guilt, blame, depression, apathy, anger, lust, even righteous indignation, are negatively charged emotions that separate us from the peace, joy, and flow of Creator's compassion. Our job is to remind ourselves of this, to catch ourselves when we're disempowering ourselves and quickly get back into alignment.

DUDE! You are HUMAN! The next step up is ascended master, like Jesus and Buddha, et al. Stop buying into this human powerlessness game that the enemy created to distract you from being a super powerful badass manifester! The enemy makes you believe you are savages in need of saving from a God whom you should fear. That is bullshit designed to control you like cattle. Just study the implications of your birth certificate, really, for Christ's Sake.

If you believe in human limitation without a proper appreciation for God, the enemy has got you right where it wants you. The enemy wants you to feel disempowered, fragile, frustrated, apathetic and enslaved. It's important to the enemy that you do not realize the physics involved in meditation, channeling, and connecting with higher powers. Once you understand how to connect with your heart and minds, you can tap into every power in the universe. This includes alien beings who keep trying to help us advance the species, which would be a major blow to the oligarchs' status quo.

With this disempowered energetic frequency, we tacitly consent to the destruction of mankind and our planet. We turn a blind eye while the enemy continues to rape and pillage, destroying natural resources and leaving us to pay its debts. Those 'sinful', aka misaligned, behaviors then snowball into major karmic issues and soul contracts with hidden enslavement clauses which are tethered with seemingly unforgivable shame. Some of us carry the shame of our conquered ancestors who converted to the Roman Catholic church to avoid death during the conquests of the 16th century. (9) My life's work has included the unraveling of all kinds of karmic knots. So far, I've remembered a number of past lives which carry lots of karmic stains, bioenergetic imprints and traumas, all of these taking multiple years to resolve. I dedicated my life to allowing God to repair what was broken. It's been an amazing journey, to say the least.

The good news is, you are more powerful than all resistant thoughts when your intention is humbly focused and connected to God. So, if we can just straighten out our appreciation of what God is and is not, we'll have a real fighting chance to save ourselves, our fellow man and our planet. The purpose of this book is to remind you of the enemy's power, as well as your true angelic power, which is capable of defeating the dark forces that enslave our lives today.

God, aka Source, is love. The origin of creation, aka God, embodies the highest truth, the highest joy, and the highest love. The highest truth is our oneness, our inextricable connectedness. The highest joy is feeling connected, safe and protected by Creator. The highest love is feeling deep compassion for all that is. It's a real creamy blissful feeling when we're fully open to receiving God's grace.

If it isn't this evolved form of love, it is tethered with illusions made up by the ego/ mind- a tool we often misuse. Ego tends to separate us from the Truth of Source. I'll not call the mind an enemy, but it is often mistaken. You'll know you are mistaken because it hurts; there is suffering. This happens because ego often acts as if it is the highest truth, irrespective of God, which is a flawed or less powerful way of thinking. An easy way to understand ego is to imagine a toaster. You are the toaster. Ego is the connecting cord that plugs you into the energy Source (God). Without ego, you can't filter God's power into your human body. If you are operating only from ego, it's still a valuable tool, but it lacks all the power of Source and therefore remains underutilized, causing you to feel disconnection. Ego, being disconnected, becomes even more mistaken, resistant, depressed, etc. So, God is the outlet the ego is supposed to tap into in order for the toaster (you) to function optimally. Ego filters energy information, so the more grounded you are, the less likely you are to get zapped.

We live in a world now where people are ungrounded and disconnected all the time. It makes us feel crazy and uneasy. That's why we turn to vices for respite. My desire is to help you reconnect heaven onto earth through your mind/body/ and spirit so that none of the things which cause suffering can control your life anymore.

Attachment & Suffering of the Mind

If you believe that love hurts, it doesn't; hurting is a resistant attachment which causes suffering. Attachment comes from ego's fear of loss and disconnection. Attachment usually occurs when we stop getting our energy from Source and take it from unsustainable energy sources like other people, for example. So, imagine that the more connected you remain, the less things will hurt when they demanifest. Attachment comes from a place of lack. Love, it's opposite, comes from your connection to Source through the heart. Suffering is the actual disconnection from Source (God). So, then, what is love? Love is the forgiving power, the compassion, the conduit by which God expresses itself. If we forget to forgive ourselves and others, we are doomed to suffer in disconnection until the humble decision is made to reconnect, follow and flow. That is because God is forgiveness. We need only to forgive ourselves and others deeply so that we can allow that love in.

Until we recommit to that decision, plugging ourselves into the flow as a daily practice, the enemy will use our ego against us to sell us their product/ agenda of enslavement. I've even noticed illuminati companies marketing to our enlightened desires lately. Make no mistake, those publicly traded companies didn't just have a change of heart. The world's biggest fast food chain may have images of fresh Strawberries and forests in their new designs, but it's still processed crap that doesn't biodegrade. They only offer more green choices on menus because women, who control 95% of the purchases in the States, developed enough self-love to stop taking their kids to eat there, despite the playgrounds and millions of dollars spent on marketing to children. Our voting dollars impacted shareholders who then agreed that it was in their best interest to listen to consumer demands. So, apart from voting with your feet, I'm a firm advocate in voting with your dollars since the election system is so rigged.

The highest truth, love, light and joy is a renewable energy source. The drama that most egos are fueled by is not infinitely powerful. Drama tends to blow up and fizzle out specifically because it is the result of short circuiting energy flow. It's better to get your energy directly from the highest quality Source possible so you can always be connected, right? Think about it, if money was no object, wouldn't you want to consume the absolute best fuel possible at all times? Wouldn't you want everyone else to get their energy from this infinitely powerful Source, as well? Ego and the enemy's fuel are like low octane gas for your car. While Source Prime is like Tesla energy.

I can show you how to improve your connection to Source. The real question is, **are you actually ready to end your suffering?**

A lot of people aren't ready to end their suffering. As Ekhart Tolle calls it, 'The pain body' we create with all our focus on what is not wanted is like a little monster that feeds off the negative fuel. This is our 'savage' brain, or reptilian brain located in the amygdala. The pain body isn't engineered to consume Tesla energy; it's configured to consume low grade fuels like TV's melodrama, war, cursing, making fun of people, putting others down to make yourself feel bigger, and greedy power plays that steal energy from one place to fuel another. An easy example, the pain body is when a relationship breaks up. Most people get their energy by feeding off each other instead of connecting to Source. It can be positive, which is how we fall in love, but eventually the two individuals stop taking energy from Source and begin taking it from each other. When a breakup happens, the pain body creates fears and all kinds of stories about lack, not enoughness, and feeds off our despair relentlessly. It can't sustain itself; it either needs Source, or you.

But since connecting to Source involves surrendering righteousness and will, most egos haven't reached that extreme level of acceptance so it feeds off your energy instead. We usually have to be humbled to our knees before we cry out for help. Still, through the power of ego mind, we quickly forget God's help to unravel the mess and forget Source's involvement when things go right. Ego tends to boast that 'I did this magical thing!" when the truth is, you are a co-creator. Most people and pain bodies aren't ready to end their suffering because it requires surrender to a higher power. It's no wonder that so many people don't want to turn to their higher power because they were taught it's a judgmental, angry, vengeful power, which of course feels disempowering.

So again, it's important for you to understand that this suffering is an enemy that grows from the resistant thoughts we choose to entertain consciously and subconsciously over and over. Before we'll see an end to wars, we must first recognize the treason we've been perpetuating within ourselves and decide to cut that shit out.

Do you decide to be better? If Yes, you **will** beat the enemy. Oh, but trust me, you'll be tested. The shitty truth is that the more you desire to achieve enlightenment or to rise above the enemy, you'll be faced with challenges. Your own shadow will surface, and you'll be caught off guard over and over until finally your immediate baseline emotion becomes loving forgiveness and acceptance of what is. Imagine a bucket of clean water with a little dab of shit floating in it. You'll have shitty water until the bucket is completely filled over with more clean water. Let that analogy keep you humble as you progress in your capacity to consistently maintain enlightened frequencies. Because, once you commit to becoming your highest self, you'll be faced with challenges that can eventually can only be explained by past life karma, or epigenetic karma. Taking responsibility for that and deciding to clear it up is what many of us came here to do at this time. The other thing that will keep us humble is to remember that we co-created the results **with** God. It's our job to evolve into better co-creators.

Nowadays, most of our hearts, minds, and souls have been perverted by multiple aspects of attachment which disconnect us from that original Source of love, aka God. In this way, love, mind, and soul become fragmented. The hologram gets fractured, and varying degrees of truth and awareness come into existence. It's the reason we have such a wide range of human emotions, fractured degrees of the Ultimate Truth. We mistake lust and infatuation for love because it holds grains of truth mingled with desire that comes from lack. We mistake pride and righteousness for justice because our ego is gratified rather than allowing Source to equalize the karma.

Some people believe that they were born bad, that their parents are fundamentally bad people, that God, as it is traditionally mistaught, is like a judgmental hateful person ready to smite them with karmic vengeance for their misdeeds. But vengeance comes from ego. People may have judged that you were born bad, or that once you 'turn bad' you're doomed to stay on the dark side. Once an addict, always an addict, right? Wrong. God made a plant called ibogaine to cure that. The enemy oppresses you from knowing about it. It can be a real bitch to overcome your history, especially in the States if you've been convicted of a crime, had financial issues which affect your credit, or were considered a 'fuck up' by the public education system. You may feel estranged from your family or the people you grew up with.

In all cases, what's actually happening is a fragmented soul acting in amnesia. In religion, spectrums of truth are passed down often by those who speak about systems, techniques and spiritual experiences, but who cannot reproduce or invoke miracles as the gifted prophets they reference. We **should** be wary of following them. Their level of consciousness isn't as high. These teachers forget their own perfection, and, in their own amnesia, they preach not from the same enlightened level as the masters who originally taught us how to live in harmony with God.

They forget the God eternal within the body. We all do. It's part of the human condition of amnesia. God (and Jesus) would teach us to forgive their ignorance, for they know not what they do. I mean, just imagine all the babies we ignorantly raise through fear, intimidation, control, loss of human rights, etc. Ram Das used to lecture, telling a story of this ghost, 'a Spook' as he called it, who described being born into a human body as feeling much like the soul putting on a tight shoe. We wear this veil of human skin by thinking we are humans trying to have a spiritual experience. The truth is we are divine, yet fragmented souls using the human incarnation as a filter to gain awareness and capability until we can consistently remember our divinity and balance our karma in all circumstances. Then, we get to stay in heaven or eternal enlightenment. We won't keep kicking our souls out of the holy land because we'll have resolved all our karma. That's what we're really here for.

This realization is the salvation that religions mean to talk about where your soul can finally be put to rest in heaven (and finally stop incarnating). The quest, while we're here, should be to bring heaven on earth through our bodies and good deeds. My quest is to heal my karma and hopefully that of my ancestors by fully healing myself and you.

You may believe that 'surrender' to God means reaching rock bottom and screaming 'UNCLE', as if you are being strong-armed until you submit to Jesus or some other deity. You'd be entirely justified to reject this notion in search for a higher truth. These uni-dimensional beliefs may represent an aspect of truth that we often must hit rock bottom before we are humbled enough to ask for and accept help, but it's not the highest truth, love, light or joy which is what God truly wants for us. The ultimate understanding is what Jesus and others knew, which is that we are all Gods. They didn't just hear it, however, they felt it by releasing the attachments and sufferings. They released the mistaken suffering of the ego mind to the point that they could totally feel God flowing through their bodies. They also committed to this being their ultimate goal. Allow yourself to evolve into a being of higher consciousness that is able to embody the God eternal within the body. You don't have to take the same oaths that the ascended masters did in order to become an enlightened non-suffering human.

"Mind is consciousness which has put on limitations. You are originally unlimited and perfect. Later you take on limitations and become the mind."
— *Ramana Maharshi* (10)

I hope that, once you feel the exquisite magic of Oneness, the whole truth, you will stop at nothing to achieve it in all aspects of your thought-created reality. In this way, we can learn to accurately harness the authentic infinite power of human solidarity born of our original creator. I wish for you to know the unity consciousness before we all seemed to fall into this twisted pseudo-reality that we unconsciously instigate today. There are as many entrapments and ways in which we enslave ourselves as there are stars in the sky. And I will submit that we have been invaded by some of those star creatures throughout the course of this planet's long history. I would also submit that this extreme cover up helps explain the truth of our origins and the fall of consciousness that occurred in man long ago.

In what ways do you enslave yourself?

In what ways are you enslaved by others?

What are the limiting beliefs that you carry deep inside?

What circumstances must change for you to be freer?

Are you now willing to ask Source Prime for help with that?

To fully understand the ultimate truth, one must become familiar with multiple metaphysical and paranormal disciplines attempting to read between the lines, into the ether, essentially becoming a heart whisperer. This might be too much for the everyday employee with a vested interest in the matrix, but you are not them. You seek far more than a compromised comfort where you are forced to pick the lesser of two evils. You don't settle for spoon-fed lack, not consciously at least, and when you realize a mistake, or misalignment, you have the integrity to adjust your sails for clearer seas. You desire to make amends, even if it means facing unpleasant realities within your paradigm. You desire to reach enlightenment, and you **will** because you will it to be so.

Remember, the ego roars because its message is muddied by the duality of the double-hemisphere brain. Much like how we yell at a football game, it's harder to interpret and process messages over all that internal yelling. Your heart, your truth, purpose, inner guidance and consciousness is so powerfully compelling that it can whisper through your heart, penetrating the mental chaos like dawn. It's simply a more powerful source of energy because it is sustained by God. The trouble is that we've become attuned to focus on the noise instead of the quiet calmness of the heart. That's what meditation is for.

Now, do you have the courage to surrender and listen to God? Are you willing to let the ego evolve, die, and resurrect a million times for the promise of eternal peace? I'm reminded of how a seed must first be planted under extreme pressure and darkness in order to bloom. I'm reminded of how a diamond is made. It seems to me like we have whole nations poised to bloom should we focus our attention on the growth rather than the pressure of current resistant circumstances.

How we view God depends on our level of consciousness

It is virtually impossible to be objective because our level of consciousness is always fluctuating. Our level of consciousness is subject to the myriad of resistant or nonresistant beliefs that we carry. It is scientifically calculated what our perceptions about God are depending on our level of consciousness, at the time, thanks to psychologist Dr. David Hawkins' work. That's really more of where I will focus with you. Basically, everything is connected. Certain notes combine with certain energy centers in the body, called chakras. Colors combine with these notes and chakras, as do emotions, as do the organs in the body. Discordant thoughts and emotions cause illnesses, as do certain frequencies in the air. Subconscious and intentional thoughts are also created by what you consume- TV, food, internet, cell phones, books, etc.

Fortunately, science cuts out the woo-woo. There is an easily helpful tool called the Map of Human Consciousness (11) presented by Dr. David Hawkins in his world renowned book *Power vs. Force.* (12) It's really mind-blowingly simple to wrap your head around the science of spirituality once you've been properly introduced. I implore you to study this religiously as I did. Once you can understand it logically, it becomes much easier to then drop into the heart as your center. We can use this tool to determine what anyone's level of consciousness is right now, or was in the past, regarding a particular situation. You can even use it to calibrate how true this book is, or the bible, as Dr. Hawkins discusses in various YouTube videos. This scale does not define anyone at a fixed level. No level is judged wrong or right. There is simply 'wanted' and 'unwanted', 'allowing' and 'resisting', 'truth' and 'less-truth'.

As human beings, we can fluctuate through the different levels on this scale all the time depending on how focused or influenced we are on a particular thought or emotion. For example, on a scale of consciousness from 0-1000, at this moment, my level of consciousness is 967. It's high because my highest calling is to write this book right now. My feelings towards my mother, however, at this moment, are only calibrating at 765, which is enlightened but still holds resistance. My feelings toward my boyfriend are 855, which is in the state of Nirvana as Buddha described it. However, last night when he said some shit I didn't like, my LOC (Level of Consciousness) was only 181, the level of pride.

My feelings toward my relative are 769. My feelings toward the US government are only 568, which is the level of unconditional love yet still commingled with fear and a lack of trust. What Dr. Hawkins discovered was that there is a critical point (when we reach 200 on the scale) where everything that calibrates below this point makes the body go weak. It represents the absence of truth. Everything above 200, makes the body go strong. It represents the presence of truth. We can use kinesiology to calibrate this level of truth just by sticking out our arm and pressing on it until the arm goes weak (13) because the body knows when something is life giving or life taking.

Because I've become intimately familiar with The Scale, and because I'm a telepathic empath, this helps me sense how I can talk to you in a way that will help you go up the scale logically. Then, thanks to some super-powers from the Big G, we can speed up the time it takes for your consciousness to fully awaken by delving into the wisdom of the heart. I do that through what I call shamanic chakra balancing (14) and *enlightenment integration.* (15) Cool stuff. Liberating stuff; not as hard as your ego says it is, I promise. During my first healing experience, the shaman said to me, "You think this is going to be really hard. It isn't. Just give it to the mother earth." I'm always impressed with how gentle healings are for my clients vs. how much puking or crying I've done on my own. Maybe it's my karma, or the fact that it is usually easier to love others than it is to love ourselves, but that's karmic too. Surely it is my desire to make your transition easier because of how hard it was for me.

Chapter 2:

UNDERSTANDING 'SIN'

It is our purpose, at this time in evolution, to dial down the volume on our contrived 'sinfulness' and tune up the frequencies that heal and repair sin's damage. Just know, you are not the sin, nor are you the sinner. The sin is a simple misalignment from Truth. You are the innocent, ignorant, misaligned and misprogrammed child of God. Sin isn't a word I use. It's just a convoluted concept with a label, a word, that I am using because it is part of the common vocabulary of misconceptions. If we remove the traditional judgement from this word, sin defined is a thought or deed which is out of alignment with oneness which therefore invites suffering.

Here are some extreme, yet common examples of sin in today's society. Let's say someone you know is celebrating the holidays. They throw caution to the wind, and break out a bottle of whiskey knowing that this has always led to further substance abuse in the past. After a few shots, they find themselves taking a whiz in the bathroom calling the cocaine dealer saying to themselves, "I know better than this." Two weeks later, they come to my office experiencing low energy, self-defeating thought forms, and would ya looky there – yep demons, etheric parasites, and medusas are feeding off their mind, body, and spirit. Meanwhile, they are suddenly possessed to post memes like, "Don't blame the holidays. You were fat back in August." What has gotten into them? They have estranged themselves from God, aka love, and invited those rowdy succubi into their being through a lack of self-determination. It's a misalignment from truth. We need to be vigilant about who is on our guest list at all times and get some incomparable spiritual bodyguards to keep in alignment. Therefore, we must call upon resources from Source for help.

Trust me when I tell you, I'm not judging anybody in the least. I have been there, done that, and burned plenty of bridges. I just get tired of suffering and have become an expert backtracker to the point that my spiritual bodyguards are on speed dial. In fact, they are with me 24/7 helping make sure this book gets published and reaches the ones who need it. I've fucked up so much it's gotten to the point that I have become my own spiritual bodyguard, or at least, I keep trying to be that. I've gone to battle thousands of times thanks to my friend, that lazy demon named Inconsistency. Something in me is pretty dense, greedy, and emotionally broken. Mmm yes, Dante was right about greed being a root to evil. All I can do is find ways to pull the weeds and burn the seeds lest I condemn myself to death by ego. Will you allow ego to be the death of you?

Mind you, you'll still have an ego when you become enlightened. ANYONE who thinks they are enlightened and DOESN'T have an ego is full of crap. Jesus had an ego; just look at how pissed he got at the money changers. You'll still have a personality, but you won't find yourself thinking in such resistant ways. You'll act more holy. The volume on your mind will be dialed down so that you can just set course like GPS and go with the flow. When 'life stuff' gets in the way, you'll be able to accept it and rise above it with greater and greater ease and grace.

When we are in the act of flirting with an unhappily married person, saving their number into our phones, about to take a naked selfie, photoshop it, edit it, send it, or masturbate to it, we are innocently, in our ego-driven amnesia, looking for happiness and relief through a fragmented portion of God's love. But that quiet wisdom inside knows suffering is on the way; the pleasure cannot be sustained. Until now, you might not have been aware that such actions actually invite your body to become a host for etheric monsters to feed off your energy, but it starts to make sense when you find yourself masturbating uncontrollably like a caged animal, for example. Now you must meditate ten-fold to clear the infection and develop the self-determination to delete that succubus from your friends list.

A caged animal. That's a good analogy for what happens to our soul and our purpose when we aren't striving to live in alignment with the highest truth, the highest love, and the highest joy. We chain ourselves to this matrix because it seems so real as we feel so separate from Oneness, Wholeness, Source, Universe, God. Trust me, I'm not judging anyone. I fall prey to it often. This book has taken 4 years to write because I kept learning from my persistent and ever-evolving ego. A girlfriend said to me, 'Girl, remember the devil will stop at nothing to keep you from doing good, but you are stronger. Let your light shine.'

I like nice things, but I don't like paying full price. That pirate past life still has influence within me. I like to look pretty, and I'll use my looks to influence people.

That past life as a prostitute is still operating within me to some degree. The 'devil' (resistant energies) likes to feed off my greed, vanity, and fear of poverty from past lives. So, to counterbalance that, God and I decided to learn from being fat, and, at one point, homeless, and at another point an escort, even though I may not have been fully conscious of it at the time. I don't believe that I have to be a bald hermit sleeping on a bamboo mat, sheltered from sin, in order to be a spiritually enlightened teacher in modern society.

Even though I've learned that I am a Divine Spirit far greater than my body, more majestic than my tresses, resistant forces will stop at nothing to play off of my ego's amnesia, vanity, gluttony, greed or righteousness. Those are traits which I've inherited, or been raised with, or feed into as I enjoy my reflection lifetime after lifetime. That is the karma that my past lives' amnesia brought into this incarnation and continues to foment. Those are my crosses to unbare as I walk the balance beam of life. Thus, I smile at you, a pretty, quirky, multi-talented, and intellectually confident young lady dedicated to purifying herself. I'm not waiting for my elders to die and pass the torch before claiming my authority and stepping into my power. I'm showing you my bloopers and self-help library in the hopes that it will bring you closer to oneness.

Don't miss what Dr. David Hawkins has to say about the lower realms seeking to subvert truth. (16)

The only vaccination I have against 'sin' is a moral compass that gently guides me, like GPS, away from disdainful suffering every time I take the wrong turn or miss the next exit. God isn't the judgmental spouse dogging you from the passenger's seat. That's ego. God is the GPS voice recalculating the quickest route toward your programmed destination. You are the driver, and can always switch the coordinates. Just don't listen to the demonic hitchhikers trying to scam you into giving them a free ride on the highway to hell.

Discovering the Goddess--Personality Disorders

Suggested reading: http://thespiritscience.net/2014/06/16/what-a-shaman-sees-in-a-mental-hospital/ (17)

The higher consciousness which has been quietly grooming me away from suffering, me, [birth name hidden for protection of privacy and sake of legalities for my publisher], the girl from Texas, is now known as Carina Cariñosa. To help you picture this, let's say that Carina is me version 2.0. Once I finally found a mentor, he assessed, "You are the avatar/incarnation/instrument for a particular Goddess. Find out who." Turns out it's a Celtic Goddess named Brigitte. She'd been quietly operating in the background like an invisible, yet essential piece of software. Like most software, sometimes the clarity of this Goddess' voice gets infected by malware, trojans, malicious viruses, and plain old human will intercepting or crossing signals.

It wasn't until my body and brain were ceremoniously programmed to recognize the different systems operating within me, that I was able to turn down the volume on ego and tune into the frequency of authentic-heart centered oneness. Much like we tune into the radio, I would often dial into the frequency of Hopeless 101, Anger 105.1, Cynic FM or Sugar Coma 98.5 FM, figuratively speaking.

Drinking, eating sugar, gluten, and smoking pot short-circuits my entire electrical system, much like throwing a cat into the shower. I especially can't drink beer anymore. My supposition is that I'm allergic to the glyphosate the beer ingredients are sprayed with, which affects my gut microbiome, and thus my serotonin levels are gravely affected. When old me, or unascended or unenlightened me manages to overcome all the obstacles and exercises her Higher Will, she makes the decision to let herself, as Carina 2.0, become a clear channel for Source to flow through. Thus, you are experiencing Goddess Bridgette 3.0 as I write or do energy work. To some, what I just said may resemble multiple-personality disorder, or again, spiritual bypassing. It's really just an awareness and observing of pieces of my consciousness at different phases of evolution expressing themselves. Those aspects of personality have been given names, although Goddess Bridgette made it clear who she was and that she's always with me.

From a scientific perspective, what is happening is a molecular change of the carbon atom transmuting from Carbon 12 into Carbon 7. This YouTube link is quite insightful explaining the glow represented in religious artwork as it depicts holy persons who are transmuting carbon. The glow is caused by an excess of carbon 7 neutrons. (18) So you see, according to physics, chemistry, and the ancient art of alchemy, this 'multidimensional personality' can be explained logically.

Similarly, symptoms of bipolar disorder, which I've been diagnosed as, are actually just necessary releases of trauma coming up for healing the way you would pop a zit. I relapse into the pain body, become aware of its falseness because it feels bad, and then I 're-mind' that mistaken aspect of my soul to the highest Truths. In minutes, I raise the consciousness of those thoughts and feelings and voila, back to happiness. Like most zits, the hormonal fluctuations can be controlled by a diet that is in vibrational alignment with nature. I typically think in a more bipolar way after drinking alcohol. So it's a result more of inflammation, dehydration, and possibly the 'spirits' of alcohol causing my bipolar symptoms more than it is a genetic predisposition. Although, I propose that the genetic predisposition is actually me carrying the bioenergetic memory of my father's traumas.

That's why I've been so resistant to having children; I want to clean up the karma before passing on my genes. Most of my fluctuations are due to a lack of determination about my diet because I have a hard time subconsciously accepting my human vessel. As an empath, it's very hard for me to stay grounded, so I smoke quite a bit instead of doing breathing exercises to ground the energies all day. Growing up, I always wanted to get out of my body. I was too sensitive for my environment, so I packed on weight in a failed attempt to block my environment. It's taken of a century to heal that longing to return to Source. Now, when the amnesia gets thick, I take psychedelics to remind myself of the Great Universal Oneness of all that is.

Nowadays, it takes me anywhere from 20 seconds to 2 minutes to reintegrate back into enlightenment. It took me 18 years of applied study to get to this point. Now that my "junk DNA" is activated, and I practice frequent surrender into higher power, people often will say to me, 'You look like a Goddess.' or 'You look heavenly.' or 'You're so radiant.' I could be wearing pajamas, or in some cases have been high on LSD wearing a bandana on my head. That heavenly angelic expression, is a vibrational frequency being transmitted through the physical body radiating outward like a fukushima of angels. It's the reason people can hug me and experience great relief because I literally try to make my body a vessel for angels.

I'm not saying you have to take the same oath I did in order to achieve enlightenment. Your Truth will look different than mine. Your lens, or way of processing, will lead you down different paths than mine. However, the same basic oaths to achieving enlightenment are universal. Enlightenment happens when we set aside ego (aka fear filled control in all its forms) and allow the highest truth, love, and joy to radiate through our total essence. We allow God to steer while we co-pilot instead of the other way around. Enlightenment involves taking an oath to become your highest ascended self, the most fully self-actualized version of yourself humanly possible.

There are degrees to enlightenment, which I'll explain further. Achieving those higher levels of allowing God to flow through you requires benevolence toward others. The gates to achieving enlightenment involve becoming a heart-centered person, and realizing that it is always safe, that God is always protecting us. Oh, how the profit-driven industries would hate for you to feel safe. It's so easy to manipulate us when we fear for our safety because once the body is in fear, below that critical level of 200, it can be fooled and fueled by unsustainable energy sources like sex, drugs, and TVs melodramas.

Think of your 10 favorite things. Following those passions will lead you to enlightenment.

How long does it take you to surrender back into your peaceful place?

Can you honestly say you've ever felt enlightenment? Maybe you were enlightened as a child, before you could be abused and ill-programmed. I can quickly evaluate that answer with you in a private reading. Enlightenment offers a glow that most of my clients emit after listening to just a one hour meditation. In some cases, depending on the magnitude of their desire to release suffering and allow peace, I can hug enlightenment into people in under 60 seconds. For those who practice constant surrender, we can think of each other into nirvana from an effortlessly higher dimension of consciousness that displays itself in delightful coincidences like, "Oh hey... yeah I was just thinking about you too. That explains where the warm fuzzies came from. " Awareness [love, light, compassion, God consciousness] penetrates beyond the dark veils of separation, fragmented by the reptilian brain we are evolving away from, and changes form in a kaleidoscopic return to prismatic light. So here I am remembering and experiencing that I am Divine Truth, and by reclaiming the God-given authority to remind you of our sameness, you inherently are beginning to remember your own divinity, as well.

In this space of remembering oneness, experiencing higher realms of enlightenment, miraculous healings occur. We sat at the Cafeteria Mess Hall during a festival in Asheville, North Carolina in October 2014. A young man had cancer twice. Ouch. Awareness to the pent-up hatred and frustration was empathetically and telepathically brought to my consciousness. The decision to release the hatred was made, born out of a refusal to suffer any longer. Having just attended my workshop, he believed in our combined powers as individual children of God, in my compassion and belief in him, he was convicted to relieve himself of this self-hate once and for all, aka self-determined to do whatever it took. By calling upon any Source of healing support available in the galaxy, Bridgette pulled the residual cancer frequency out through his arm in under 3 minutes. Surrender is epically easier than ego makes it out to be. He'd just attended my enlightenment integration workshop, meditated, made a decision, and poof — no more suffering was needed. He enlightened the cancer in his mind which had manifested in his body. Cancer is a staunch resistance to life. It is unforgiveness.

He learned the value and power of forgiveness. It just took the creation of a tornado to land him in front of the great Wizard of Oz so that he would surrender his will to God. Then, Bridgette advised him to "Drink lemon water as part of your daily protocol from here forward. Everyone who has cancer has acidity. Lemon makes your body alkaline. Obey your body's nutritional cravings. Get educated about what you're consuming. Remember how you aligned and surrendered here today. Keep doing that instead of holding in your frustrations or egotistically creating grudges while pointing the finger outward. Practice forgiving yourself in order to forgive others."

Chapter 3:
MY SPIRITUAL NAME

arina comes from the Italian word meaning 'cute' and Cariñosa from the Spanish word meaning 'loving'. By addressing me as Carina or Bridgette, you are essentially activating those highest versions of me. Old me has a long history of suffering, and can be easily triggered because there's still unresolved resistance conscious and subconsciously. My birth name is reserved for my closest friends who support me through those personal struggles. Of course, my family still calls me by the birth name, but they're the only ones. If you know someone who has adopted a spiritual name, calling them by it is a way of honoring that newer version of them.

Now, granted, if they are acting from the resistant or wounded self, it might be completely necessary to address them with that original name. It will most certainly catch their attention. If it catches resistance, you've hit the ego on the head, but most people don't respond well to such confrontation. Have no fear about 'breaking the illusion of enlightenment' when the person is trying to evade the truth or triggers. In that moment, you may be serving as an anti-enabler.

I have a long history working with 'sacred wounding.' Sometimes, a spiritual name is a way of ghosting or masking. It's best to ask permission to call someone by their birth name, if they use a different one, because proper timing, and consent, are crucial to healing.

A lot of wounded people may find themselves taking a spiritual name as a way to escape the karma involved with their names. In a way, I was guilty of that for a while. It hit me hardest when I returned home after 8 years of living in Panama. I'd created this blissful new identity for myself, and then swan dived right back into my deepest childhood wounds by going to my mom's house. To be called by my birth name all the time, by the person whom I most resented for my wounding, was a real punch in the gut. The good news is that, if you're truly on a spiritual path, you'll flow through the escapist tendencies, dive in, and resolve those traumas when God says you're ready.

I seem to get bipolar every time my wounded child becomes ready to release more of her trauma. I've been releasing childhood trauma on behalf of my dad's memories too. You see, as it remains an active trauma within him, and we are so closely made up of the same stuff, it is also active within me, especially since I choose to be heart centered. So, as I heal my mommy wounds, I can set the intention to also heal my Daddy's wounds, if he will so allow. Thankfully, he does. One night, I put a note on the fridge so that as my child opens the fridge she'll be reminded, "That moment is healed with love. I love myself and others unconditionally. I forgive myself and others." Mom's wounded child, unwilling to observe herself, took it down. My wounded child went upstairs and sobbed for 10 minutes. Then, I was fine again. The next day, I avoided temptation in the fridge 5 times.

It can take a while for a person's total thinking to reach enlightenment depending on how often you practice being triggered, how deep the wound is [genetic karma takes a while] and how much consciousness you breathe into those resistant thought forms. It took me a solid 5 months to stop feeling bipolar with my consciousness in the secluded safety of living overseas. My biggest areas for self mastery involve unraveling the illusions my child mind told itself in order to cope with my parent's divorce at the tender age of 4. I'm releasing the anger and abandonment from my mom's dismissive lack of nurture while I was a teenage middle child unable to win her positive attention. I'm also working with Freud's explanation for why I have oral fixations and promiscuity issues.

I'm pretty amazed at how it seems the mess will never fully heal. And then, my high self parachutes me into my mother's home so that this boil can finally be lanced. This woman is drunk on merlot disrespectfully yelling my birth name from across the house, and now I have to meditate and cry out some trauma in order to avoid kicking the cat or eating all the brownies. [It took an additional 2 years from the time I wrote that paragraph to finally heal the above three issues. It took multiple surrenders as I chiseled away the walls of my heart, forgiving her deeper and deeper.] But what finally helped, was leaving a toxic situation, and accepting the situations without attack or defense.

Calling someone by their ascended name is also an effective manipulation/ communication tool to speak as if you are calling upon the higher version of a person, lest you activate the ego or 'pain body', as Eckhart Tolle calls it. Yes, I speak of manipulation and enlightenment in the same breaths because essentially, we're all still trying to get something. One simply must determine if they wish to get the best or the worst out of an individual, experience, opportunity, or set of possibilities. Do you choose suffering or love? I'd like to unconditionally love my mother out of her drama, but instead of moving that mountain, spirit is teaching me to surrender and go around it; to be less empathetic and more self-determined. While the mountain is still there, I'm referring to her as "The Beautiful Ms. [Last name]", the self-image she chose to embody which enabled her to lose half her body weight. I know that eventually that mountain will bloom flowers and orchards of unconditional love, just maybe not in this lifetime, but hopefully. I see new blades of grass grow daily as I fertilize it gently.

Even the Buddhist ideal of Nirvana, which is a sort of coasting and flowing patient feeling, still holds a desire to remain in Nirvana. Higher consciousness above this level of Nirvana includes the desires to heal your family bloodline as well as all of humanity and the planet. So we can desire to manipulate toward the highest truth, love, and joy. Just remain aware and willing to be vigilant with your own corruption first and foremost.

Desire doesn't expire.

It just grows more steady, calm, omniscient, gaining an unstoppable inertia the more self-determination we focus upon as we clean the mental attic. It's like saying we take our foot off the pedal so that we can stop breaking abruptly, and the vehicle's engine is simply propelled forward as if on cruise control. The question is, where are you going? If your brain decides the destination, you can bet that eventually you'll find yourself in Oz even though your heart was set on Kansas. Eventually, all roads lead back to Kansas so we might as well teach our kids to follow their hearts from the beginning. Just focus on what you sow today, seed by seed, and you can expect an abundant harvest.

Another real world example of enlightened manipulation through name calling would be that instead of thinking or calling that girl an [expletive], call her a Goddess or queen. Instead of calling that guy an [expletive], realize he's your brother. You might be real caught up in your frustrations and think, 'Yeah, my retarded brother....' but just keep working toward forgiving his ignorance as you would forgive your own or that of a child. In this way, relief and joy are released. Most of the time, we are all ignorant children suffering from amnesia of the mind. That's the human condition we're evolving beyond.

The degree to which you are committed to consciously seek a sustainable highest high, combined with your willingness to look inside to resolve unsustainable beliefs or traumas, determines the velocity at which you will ascend the scale of consciousness and experience true self mastery. Bipolar people are just really good at ascending the scale by releasing resistance quickly. I reached enlightenment by 32, and invested 15 years of active truth seeking to get there.

Though I can now do supernatural 'miracles', I still have my Clark Kent moments. As a telepathic empath with tons of personal and ancestral karma, Superman strength is required to take on and heal most of my crap. In a world full of asshole behavior, it's common for empaths to suffer with addiction problems. Years of using food for comfort or to "add a layer of protection" against the bad vibes I constantly feel, and lifetimes of being the wounded warrior, messed up the clarity of my being and resulted in a plethora of obstacles to overcome. I piled on too much fertilizer and kept burning the seeds of my good intentions with all that anxious glutenous impatience. **Chasing the high of enlightenment just seemed like a more sustainable and fulfilling addiction.** I'd rather chase an angel than chase the dragon. The trick to catching either is making peace with the angel and dragon within. As we say in New Orleans, "You gotta learn to dance with the devil without gettin' your toes stepped on Sugar Child."

I've tried moderation, but my empathic telepathic monkey mind resists it. Maybe ego perceives moderation as boring. Thus, we prefer to live on the edge- of creation. Moderation and enlightenment are two different things. Enlightenment is extreme. The lesser evolved me prefers to swing from extremes like a gorilla while the enlightened me just focuses on balanced nutrition like a panda. Panda is more careful yet remains still in the trees, still agile, just more focused-breaking fewer branches- able to maintain balance with less velocity- falling less in the forest of life. It's the chaos, the edge of creation, that gives birth to epic new discoveries about yourselves. Some people fear that enlightenment is boring; I can assure you it is quite the adventure to master your thoughts and creations like a skilled chemist. Since you don't want to blow up the proverbial lab, 'tis better to learn the formulas for enlightenment and prepare to pass life's tests with prismatic multidimensional flying colors.

Chapter 4:
DIVING IN

I remember the public pool, at 9 months old, diving off the deep end into my Daddy's arms squealing out in a nervous and excited fit of giggles. I'm still like that. I know it is always safe. It's just that somewhere along the way, life programmed us to fear instead of teaching us the formula toward self-actualization. The only difference is that now, I know that the internal guidance, the Godfather, is going to catch me. I trust myself to recognize when thoughts are out of alignment, and know how to correct them towards the highest Truth. And like any Godfather, you better respect it, or suffer the consequences. It's not a matter of favoritism, punishment vs. rewards. It is simple cause and effect. So, let's commit to living on the edge of creation without blowing stuff up, shall we?

This book provides a number of tools that I've developed to personally circumnavigate the caveats of life more gracefully. If you are evolving into levels of peace and above, I've tried to create a guide that accurately depicts, maps out, and provides a sort of GPS geared at achieving very high sustainable levels of enlightenment. For now, I think this is one of the few resources that will talk to you at that level, like a real person, in a language and style that is relatable to the millions of cool cats out there today. In other words, I'm a sexy bilingual blond with tattoos who cusses and meditates from North America. I'm not old, haven't physically traveled to the traditional Holy Lands, haven't lived in an official ashram, and didn't use a bunch of holy objects, spells, or altars in order to reach or sustain enlightenment. So, you don't have to be a poor bald monk sleeping on hardwood floors isolated on a mountain or one of these ultra spiritual people with spiritual objects all over the place in order to express self mastery.

In fact, the formula is quite simple. Here it goes:

If you Trust, you can.

Decide. Commit. Succeed.

Let nothing stop you, not your lower self, not the limiting image of who you think you are.

Reframe, recontextualize, revisualize who you want to be and allow it to be flowing to you, through you, as you.

Got it? Great. Now you can skip the next 200 pages and just move on to the audio recordings.

Giving credit to Divine Guidance, thanking free will, and thanking my willingness to be awesome at all costs, it has taken a lot of courage to show you my life with little-to-no-filter. In fact, courage is a critical level of integrity characterized by the ability to supersede prideful ego by humbly admitting inwardly, and outwardly, that, "Hey look. I mess up. I make mistakes. Now, how can I do better?" It's level 200 on the Scale of Human Consciousness. It's taken a long time to become free from the fear of ridicule. To be honest, mushrooms and ayahuasca helped me get there.

Haters are going to hate. If you try to teach people to become more aware, expect viscous resistance. The majority of the population has trouble hearing "No. You're wrong." because they are not willing to point the finger inward and take radical responsibility for their thoughts and actions. A less resistant way of thinking would be to realize that "No. You're wrong." equates to "That's not entirely True. I call bullshit on the part that's bullshit." Most of the world's problems happen below this critical level, where we are willing to admit that our shit stinks too. You could be Jesus incarnate telling a 'sinner', "Uh, noooo. There's a better way." and they are going to persecute you. Oh wait, that's exactly what happened to Jesus, isn't it? From their filter of resistant consciousness, which again has a frequency much like a radio station, they simply cannot tune into your perception unless they've experienced that level of consciousness before and are willing to do so again. Their matrix of resistant beliefs have them stuck on a hamster wheel of thought frequency like a broken record that repeats whatever critical song and dance they are habituated toward. You could show them a bouquet of roses, and they'll be stuck noticing the thorns.

I think everybody should 'take the blood of Christ', in the form of some hallucinogen, in a ceremonious environment, where an enlightened shaman is holding space for their illusions' ascension. In fact, evidence from the Rosetta Stone suggests that this 'blood of Christ' actually came from the amanita muscaria mushroom. (19) We should take a strong medicine that forces us to our ego's breaking point, so that we must let go and let God, so that we can taste the true bliss of God's love, so that our brains can be rewired to allow the messages of the heart to be heard more clearly. At our worst, in many cases, our beings have actually been hijacked to prevent this crucial level of integrity which introduces the power of Higher Will. I'm talking about etheric implants which are the result of being born into the matrix. (20) This is one of the 'woo woo' subjects I'd avoided mentioning for the longest time. But now that I'm free from needing your approval, I'm brave enough to risk you thinking I'm crazy. Bear with me; at least it'll be entertaining.

A critical point I like to make very clear is that you are not the resistant beliefs. You are not the negative mantras repeating inside your head. If you have broken records of hateful thoughts, feeling drained all the time etc, that is not you. YOU are divine, pure, and totally badass. You are not the pain body or the crazy monkey mind. Forgetting our divinity is the cause of our suffering. Own that the resistance is there instead of resisting or fighting against it. Example: Never try to kill or destroy your ego. Instead, take ownership for your garden and decide to cultivate it. Radically accept it. Move on ASAP to solution seeking. Call upon the rest of your divine awesomeness and guides to blaze awareness through your aches and pains. The sooner you get on board with reclaiming this power, the quicker you'll succeed at breaking free from the dark forces of the shadow side.

Allow me to point out that I will never call it 'the shadow self' because that side is illusion. Yes, it is there, and it seems very real, and it is definitely operating within your expression, but the highest truth, love, and joy is Divine Pure powerful lovingness. So, I don't want you to confuse the shadow as who you are even though it is currently a part of you. The shadow will likely remain pervasive but also will dissipate since you chose to incarnate during this difficult time in our ascension process. But rest assured that your next incarnation will be bliss by comparison. If you really do your homework this time around, you could even avoid another incarnation all together.

You Deserve Angels & Guides

Angels and guides are always on your side. We all have them. Unfortunately, most people don't believe they can connect with angels or spirit guides or ancestors. Most people don't feel worthy of miracles or God's attention. Most people gave up on that as a possibility because of their misunderstandings on God. That is mostly just due to the fact that you don't open dialogue with these entities, often for fear of seeming crazy. Once you start talking to God or actually communicating with your guides and angels, through your quiet little heart, you'll quickly become convinced they're real. I get it; trying to communicate with a Celtic Goddess named Bridgette really made me question what people would think of me, what I thought of myself.

Can you see that I was just projecting my own judgmental mind onto an imagined audience? Because it is limiting and feels bad, that kind of thinking isn't sustainable, and therefore, is not the highest Truth, so I got over it.

The other primary reason people don't communicate with their spirit guides is simply the strength and size of their egos. Ego tends to take credit for all the good stuff and points outward blame on all the unwanted stuff. This is the most critical paradigm shift in consciousness needed on our planet today. We have to stop taking full credit for our co-creations and give credit more to God. The more we are open to that awareness of invisible, yet tangible, forces working on our lives, the quicker we'll be able to surmount life's challenges. If you had told me in 2010 that 4 years later I'd be writing a nonfiction book discussing enlightenment, demons and ghosts, I'd surely have LOL'd. I mean some of this stuff is far out, but truth is stranger than fiction. And let me just say, I am not a movie buff. Nor do I engage in pop culture. All of my ideas and experiences have come from the field in Panama, not Hollywood. I didn't watch TV for 8 years, lest I'd probably have admitted myself to a looney bin or never put in the time to study the science of what I'll share with you.

For the sake of creating a body of work that is digestible in mass, I've attempted to keep some of the stranger things out of this manuscript. Friends say my life's story should become a TV series. As these situations have come across my path, I strive to keep an open, scientific, discerning mind about the drama of this incarnation looking for reasonable explanations as I'm guided mostly by intuition. Something crazy will happen, and I'll ask Source, "What was that?!" and boom, the explanation pops up in my news feed.

All I ask is that you ask yourself, **"Could this be true? What is it about my beliefs that feel so threatened that I must indignantly resist what she is saying?"** Therein, you'll probably find an illusion of separateness ready for a return to Source.

As a healer, often still surprised by what can happen when clients report an angel dropping in, or when a dark force is scrambling my dreams, or when I feel 'Something has gotten into me,' I often ask, "Holy crap! What on earth is happening to me!? Is this seriously what my life has become? Can science explain that?!" My work is often anecdotal and based on newly provable science, mathematics, or physics. I'll not take the time to attempt to 'prove' my claims beyond the occasional sharing of links. You'll have to do your own research. However, I have developed a weekly enlightenment newsletter which you're welcome to join if interested. It hosts a number of YouTube videos from experts in their field, much like guiding you through the psycho-spiritual supermarket. Those are the videos I've used to go higher in my mastery and understanding.

Abiding Faith

All of my attempts to understand the Universe and my role in it aim at taking the woo-woo out of the metaphysical supernatural, making it explainable. However, in the final analysis, you don't need to understand physics to achieve miracles. You just have to have faith in your highest essence and feel the proper conviction as you follow the alchemical formulas for releasing resistance. This is known as "abiding faith". You are encouraged to utilize that spiritual tactic. Heaven knows that growing up in the buckle of the bible belt I struggled to surrender to abiding faith. My ex would say, "You're always looking for the 5th paw on a 4-legged cat," an expression liars use in Latin America. I always want to understand, but sometimes you have to just let go and realize that the answers will come when they come. Like how you piece together a puzzle, it takes a while for the whole picture to form. We're just going to be really careful about whom and how we're going to surrender.

If I had only been less stubborn, and offered more abiding faith, my journey would probably have been a lot easier. But I didn't have a frame of reference for what Oneness looks like or feels like. I wasn't raised in the ideal loving family. In fact, my Mayan birth chart says I am "the payment". While at the Geo Paradise psytrance festival on the Caribbean coast of Panama, Suki, the bilingual daughter to an elder Mayan shaman, said to me, "Your Mayan symbol is 'Toj'. You are the payment because you can handle it." In reviewing some of my testimonials, one in which my cross-to-bear resembles that of Jesus, I thought, "What a fine mess I have chosen to clean up... the spiritual janitor who will empathetically suck out all the world's suffering to evolve our hologram into the 5th dimensional utopia. I must have been nucking futz to sign up for this mission. Or coerced. Or seriously egotistical to think I could take on this challenge." Probably all are true to some degree. The fact is, we're all here inhabiting this time/space/dimension, and it's time we cleaned up our act. **Are you Willing?... I mean are you really willing to stop causing yourself perpetual suffering?**

Remember: Decide= commit= succeed. It happens in that order.

Dear Me as My Highest Ascended Self,

I'd like to bring an end to my suffering now. I allow you to help me in this now moment. Please, and thank you very very much. Thank you, thank you, thank you, thank you for helping me transcend my ego's illusions. Thank you for guiding me towards the highest truth, love, and light. Thank you for helping me expand beyond imagination. I allow this day to turn out more magical than I can imagine. Thank you, thank you, thank you!

Sounds too simple? Try it. Repeat from your heart. Focus on this for at least 1 minute and 20 seconds.

Chapter 5:

DEVELOPING COMPASSION

Living a very mobile lifestyle, I pop in and out of people's lives. People continuously comment that I appear to have reinvented myself, to my relief, usually in a good way. It's true, I evolve and transform pretty quickly. Every 6 months, something is very different.

Because of this oath to become that highest ascended version of myself and to save the ones smart enough to save themselves, as you can imagine, my life is pretty intense. I mean, can you imagine having a close personal connection with a telepathic empathic indigo starseed shamanic healer singer? I run around the house doing vocal exercises making monkey noises while naked midday. I can't imagine holding a corporate 9-5 job. I'm cool with God seeing me, because I know I'm not being judged by It. Monkey noises are simply what it takes to have a strong singing voice.

By the way, God is omnisexual. Not male, not female, but IT. I'm reminded of the meme that says, 'God is watching even when you're masturbating!' Fortunately, I can only imagine that God and my guides have a sense of humor. In fact, the topic of spiritual sexual healing is major, and I invite you all to explore the truth that "God is omnisexual." and that Jesus had sex. (21)

My "control drama" (22), according to The Celestine Prophecy (23), is the role of interrogator. When my ego is not in alignment, the role of the interrogator is to pick out what's 'wrong' and bring it to light. My Higher Self wants to return it to oneness. My ego self, however, just comes across as a self-righteous, controlling, condescending dickhead. In a professional setting, this seemingly necessary coping mechanism, as an empath, is quick to intuit where the false belief, illusion of separateness, or trauma resides. In a personal setting, it can be hard for me to just 'let you be with your bullshit' because if our hearts are openly connected, I can feel the weight of your resistance, which is pretty fucking uncomfortable compared to my enlightened state. The weight of people's resistant thoughts can be very overwhelming in social settings or especially at home, since I'm heart-connected with those people. It can be pretty tough on my loved-ones because, as an empath, I feel their evolution and devolution within me. So, it's hard for me to stay focused and not try to change them narcissistically.

As an empath, it can be hard to separate the wheat from the chaff, to distinguish what is my b.s., versus what's their b.s., and how to stay conscious enough to transcend and transmute it all. I can understand why clergy are often not allowed to marry. I can't be a clear channel, removing past-life traumas from your timeline, without concern for something 'sticking to me' if I've just had an argument with my lover, you see.

"Compassion hurts. When you feel connected to everything, you also feel responsible for everything. And you cannot turn away. Your destiny is bound with the destinies of others. You must either learn to carry the Universe or be crushed by it. You must grow strong enough to love the world, yet empty enough to sit down at the same table with its worst horrors." — Andrew Boyd (24)

For this reason, a measure of narcissism and selfishness is necessary in our modern society just to cope and focus on our own needs. But we've taken it too far by blindly giving the government our money to perpetuate unwanted wars. We see homeless people suffering and look the other way. When I've not done my spiritual practice, I look the other way. When I'm in greater alignment, at the least, I'll pray for them. It is as if, in our lack of awareness upon re-entry onto the planet, we signed new birth contracts full of disempowering fine print. It is the karmic imprint of our ancestors and our former selves in a world full of conquests and stolen birthrights. Depending on our level of awareness and point of attention at the time of re-signing, it seems we have unwittingly agreed to a horrendous lifestyle based on lack, fear, and dualistic false beliefs of separateness. These are the matrix/ contracts which stretch beyond your conscious free will.

Fortunately, everyone entering the planet at this time also has signed contracts for evolution. It's your job to become aware and reclaim sovereign ownership of your life and get a move on with raising your consciousness. I can also show you how to renegotiate the terms of your karmic contracts toward your birthrights, your inheritance of well being. The biggest issue I run into with this is our inability to forgive ourselves for the betrayals we were forced to commit against ourselves in order to survive during this or past lives. Many former soldiers are reborn full of shame. Many casualties of war are reborn with a sense of entitlement. I was very invasive because I had been very invaded. Forgiving that, and having self-compassion for that, since we don't tend to remember our past lives, is pretty tough, but not insurmountable.

Reclaiming Sovereignty from False Gods

Who wrote the contracts? A false God and his legions of Archon Angels – the God of judgement, anger, and spite whom we were admonished to beg forgiveness to once the consequences of our devilish sins became too much to bear. You know, the Archon Angel Gabriel who stands at the pearly gates to review your life's choices and decide if you're 'worthy' of entry into heaven. Yeah, all bullshit. That was created by man under the influence of unholy agendas. People came to believe it, so it became written into their soul's framework. So, let's be clear, that's not the god of whom I am speaking.

Read Cameron Day's revelations entitled 'Tell the 'Lords of Karma' That You Are Sovereign-Why I'm No Longer a Lightworker". (25)

Unfortunately, in our innocent ignorance, upon entry into 3D, the messages of truth, abundance, and love are often hijacked, scrambled and fragmented, making it difficult for us to turn on and tap into the most loving intergalactic awareness. When I asked Brigitte why she was working with me, she replied "to guide you through the underworld". What is the underworld? Ah, the realm of disembodied spirits creating a veil between truth and humanity feeding off our energy. We must learn and practice piercing the veil with loving precision so that heaven can descend into earth as Christ taught. Reading Cameron's article was cathartic because I remember how true the teaching of Jesus felt compared to how untrue the machine of the church felt. I wondered, "Why don't they teach more from Jesus' direct quotes?" Answer: The bible was hijacked by the Lords of Karma and their minions. Jesus' words don't serve most church's agendas.

Watch 'The Truth About Angels' by Tobias Lars. (26)

We must realize that the only way out of the illusion is from within the heart by exploring and clearing the fragmented hologram. In the future, earth ascends into heaven; heaven descends into heart, and it manifests a supernova of co-creative awesomeness.

Here's a simplified explanation of it all thanks to Tobias Lars. 3D, 4D, 5D- Spiritual Judgement Against Body, Sex, and Emotions. (27)

Hay Dios, what kind of a mission did we sign up for, and can I get a renegotiation to this contract please? The short answer is, yes we may always revise our contracts, vows, and agreements. The Lords of Karma is a perversion of the Truth, so it's negotiable. Think of it as a balancing of karmic forces. Here, we're looking for that Buddha balance, lest we are continuously tipping the scales out of whack making life wonky. Here, a review of the DNA lineage, the genetics and consciousness active within your genetics comes up for review, like in a board meeting, only you as your highest self are the ultimate judge and decider of your fate.

The Lords of Karma would hate for you to decide your own fate. The degree to which a renegotiation is successful would be similar to having legal representation and intermediaries using a standard code of ethics- only in this court, everyone wins because are shedding the limitations imposed by the Lords of Karma, piercing the veil, and reintegrating back to the highest truth, love, and joy. While you're doing that, I recommend adding a clause where you shine your powerful light onto the Lords of Karma so that they can be returned to Source for healing and reintegration. It's easier said than done, of course, because the Lords have something to lose- all the energy they were harvesting from you. Of course, now you know that the energy they can get from God would be infinitely more powerful, so do them a favor, as if they were ignorant mistaken children, and ascend their resistant asses. Are you ready to reclaim your sovereignty and renegotiate some contracts?

Chapter 6:

FORGIVING IGNORANCE

Now, obviously, I'm not yet a saint, but I think the future of sainthood is going to look pretty cool moving forward. Too bad we won't be honored in the history books. It'll look more like how we look and with less 'religious photoshopping'. Jesus will manifest through us in Facebook memes looking like how you look- like black Jesus or Hipster Jesus, all the while retaining his originally pure energy signature. I bet there will be hipster looking saints, motorcycle riding saints and siren sexy saints. Heck, aren't most of the Ascended Masters depicted as men with long hair crossdressing in androgynous chiffon robes with Michael Angelo proportioned features? Religious photoshop. In fact, I had a Betty Boop sexy angel sticker on my car. She's my avatar.

My work is not watered down in an attempt to be politically correct. I'm open to your constructive remarks. In this way, we all grow. That's simply how expansion works. What bugs me, however, is how I might never get a Guru sick day. That's a lot of pressure, and makes it harder to step up. People make it seem as if all people who are reclaiming their divine authority should never get a day off or be allowed to have a drop in consciousness. I promise, you can be enlightened and still get angry. Of course, while angry, you are not being enlightened. That's why the path can seem a little bipolar when you're first starting to sort through your shit. Anger tends to become less intense- more like peeved, annoyed, irritated or frustrated when you master it from a higher perspective. **The degree to which you are willing to forgive my ignorance, error or innocence is a reflection of the degree to which you are willing to forgive yourself, or not.**

A colleague from Dallas, a Latin Indigo healer/contractor was leading a workshop at the Envision festival in Austin, Texas back in March 2014. He said, "Think of your worst enemy, or the relationship most in need of healing. See yourselves as ignorant little children. Stop abusing the innocent ignorance within you both. Drop your fists. Put down your weapons. Forgive and hug your mutual ignorance." It's a shame he forgot that one day while experiencing a resistant level of consciousness that I pointed out. His pain body interpreted my text as being condescending, and he cut me off. Pain bodies will make you react in very explosive ways. Try to regain consciousness as soon as possible and work with your shadow so you can clean up the messes it makes. I try not to make decisions until I've regained consciousness. If I catch myself arguing in the mind, it's time to meditate.

Reclaim Your Power

"Nature loves courage. You make the commitment and nature will respond to that commitment by removing impossible obstacles. Dream the impossible dream and the world will not grind you under, it will fill you up. This is the trick. This is what all these teachers and philosophers who really counted, who really touched the alchemical gold, this is what they understood. This is the shamanic dance in the waterfall. This is how magic is done. By hurling yourself into the abyss and discovering it is a feather bed." — *Terrance McKenna*

Accept responsibility

Surrender in a commitment to the authentic truth of your divine power.

Forgive everything about the past so that it stops tainting your present and future.

"Let go of your history to make room for your destiny." — *Bishop T.D. Jakes*

Allow your imagination to work for you, not against you.

Paint the picture you most wish to see.

Set goals. Know the difference between a goal and an objective.

Get out of your head. Focus on the present. Take it day by day. Make today count.

Take it easy. Be light about all this.

Give yourself naps when you get cranky.

Trust that the rest will take care of itself. The Universe will continue to fill in the details as you continue to show up and play ball.

I had to learn all of that the hard way. I hope you can be more graceful with yourself than I was. I hope you can allow and call upon all of the light working for you. Humans just like you have done this in order to assist in this epic etheric clean-up. Your work will lead us to that 5th dimensional utopia where Tesla's free energy technologies make it possible for us to pay the bills with hugs. (By the way, did you know Tesla channeled his ideas? They were given to him by E.T.'s.) In the meantime, yes, we've got our work cut out for us. Try not to get discouraged.

You'll be forgiven of your past if you can forgive yourself because the Truth is, you're already forgiven. There's nothing to forgive because it's all part of how we grow.

God loves us with an overwhelming intensity. There is nothing to forgive, yet once you connect, you'll feel an overwhelming sense of forgiveness. I'm referring to all the people, situations, our karma and therefore our future outcomes can all be given a miraculous grace just as soon as we allow it to come in. In this way, the cycles of pain will end. You know, like when someone 'strikes a nerve' and touches a painful old memory or fear.... notice how easily the pain surfaces and scream for attention. If only we acknowledged, listened and filled the pain up with the highest truth, love and joy, it would subside. The fragmented memories become stuck as the emotion creates twisted knots of resistant thoughts within the body.

You know how when you ask someone how they're doing today, and they start complaining or going into the story about their pain? We can erase that from our mental and cellular memory. I don't mean to sound insensitive or naive. I know it's hard. It's hard because it's broken and requires superior vibes to heal which can be hard to muster in a broken heart with a fragmented resistant perspective. Certainly, we are all entitled to feel horrible about the horrible things that have happened to us. My response is simply, **'Who could you allow yourself to become if you could allow yourself to grow beyond that fragmented history? Who do you want to be now, moving forward? How do you choose to write the story today?'** How empowered do you want to feel? Remember, you are not a victim: you're a volunteer. You must focus on the positive or else the resistant thoughts will become resistant knots which can grow and mutate into cancer.

My husband died of a drug overdose. I was widowed at age 29. At 280 pounds, my body hurt all the time from that codependent, addictive, abusive relationship. I was filled with rage, and I was tired. In the 4 months before we married, I stress ate, like a typical American trained to stuff my emotions with 'comfort food'. Well, it was processed food, and I gained an additional 35 pounds. If you do the math, that's 315 pounds. There's something about being in my mother's house that unnerves me and makes me want to binge. I've healed so deeply now that I can't even pull up those memories of abuse and hardship anymore. How? I mentally erased it, or as one lover would say, 'I cancel that.' There's a difference between blocking or bottling a traumatic event versus allowing the emotions to come up and then, with a more empowered sense of self-love, you cancel or erase those traumas from your body's memories. If you don't clear it, the unresolved karma will continue to circulate through your force field until an equilibrium is found or a disease is created. Achieving that equilibrium means acceptance and forgiveness so the ties can be severed and healed.

There are people experiencing genocide or whose homes are being swept away by typhoons and hurricanes. There are mothers unsure of how to feed their children, and wealthy people whose investments have gone bad. There are rape victims, parents whose children have special needs, people victimized by the 'healthcare' industry and 'the system' or 'the man'. The list goes on and on. Give your wounded ego a moment to realize that you're not alone. It could be worse, as it is for thousands of others less fortunate. This is a stealth way of pivoting out of depressive resistance. Reminding ourselves of how much worse others have it is an effective way of remembering to be grateful for what we do have.

Plenty of people are victimizing themselves, though. It's easier to point the finger outward than inward. This book is to encourage you to gain the courage and skills to go deep inside so that you can work out the demons, raise your inner child, erase the pain body- whatever it is you've got to do in order to raise the consciousness on your pain and eliminate the suffering. We deserve to experience limitless abundance, no matter how 'horribly wrong' we've been victimized or behaved. But you've got to realize the two can't coexist harmoniously. Abundance and suffering just don't mix. So, shed some light on it.

Our job is to find the perfection in it all, even in the toughest of circumstances. Our job is to let it be what it is, accept that it happened instead of resisting, so that we can move into a place of healing through self-compassion and higher perspective. When tripped, I ask, **"Now how is THAT perfect?"** Every choice is an opportunity to polish the mirror until we can see clearly, omnisciently, as Christ saw, the perfection in all things, including our folly. You've got to look for the positive lesson instead of fueling the negativity with more resistant thinking. In the clinically proven Map of Human Consciousness by Dr. David Hawkins, pure consciousness has no judgment, only compassionate wisdom and omnipotent understanding. You can see/feel/know how everything is connected and perfectly designed to foster your growth in awareness and capability.

The awakening process is one of great human achievement. I won't lie, it hurts, but it only hurts until you learn to use the event as a springboard towards more personal achievement. Obstacles are put in our path to make us grow. Very little growth tends to happen when everything is going well because it gets comfortable. We need contrast to get us up off our asses. It's the overcoming of struggle that makes us more powerful. From a higher consciousness, because you feel compassion for your own struggles, and joy for your own triumphs, through the power of a healed heart, you can see that we're all united. Because we're all united, you don't want anyone to struggle through that same pain. So you surrender it to Source for healing and transmutation and for the benefit of all others. You give it up. You stop grasping onto that story of pain, and make space for a more abundant truth to flow to you, through you, as you.

Pure consciousness feels like you'll be sitting there and can't tell the difference between where your face ends, the air begins, or whose heart is whose. Only a tenuous omniscience or distraction can help you distinguish the difference between you and your friend, lover, or the client I'm doing a healing on. In pure consciousness, everything FEELS totally connected, one in the same. In pure consciousness, your perspective is expanded to a bird's-eye-view so that you can see how your whole story, including all the down turns, is connected and was necessary to get you to grow in awareness and capability. If you want that kind of perspective, you've got to stop closing off your mind to make space for the expansion. It won't happen without your consent. Benevolent energies might be in the celestial realm subtly guiding you, but major healing can't come through until you ALLOW it to with your consenting consciousness. You've got to ask for it. **Do you now consent to experiencing miraculous healing in your life?** Say yes and watch the magic begin to unfold. When you see things loosen up, becoming less resistant, be sure to give thanks for that, rather than ego always claiming responsibility. That's how you stay connected to Source, through gratitude to It.

If you have trouble believing you can achieve this, I'd submit that is ego arguing for its limited control. Ego tries to convince you of all the logical reasons why you don't have time to work that hard on yourself. I mean, you've got to go bring home the bacon. Others are counting on you, right? Well, I'm pleased to announce that if you want it, I mean really want it, in some cases, I can do an enlightenment integration in less than 5 minutes. That means you can now walk away connected to the totality of your highest ascended self, with 'junk' DNA activated and chakras flushed clean, in the time it takes to click through the TV guide or make mac and cheese. That's how much God wants us to get it together and return to Source!

Unwitting Attack

I used to interfere in people's business without being asked. Sometimes, it is not obvious that we are attacking. I thought I was offering a less resistant perspective to help them 'see the light'. I was just trying to help end their suffering. Unfortunately, however, if the advice, opinion, fact, or observation is not solicited, the person won't be open to hearing your wisdom, and they'll think you're being condescending. Much of the time, our attention to a problem is an attack because people think we're judging them the way they are judging themselves or others at that time. Or worse, our level of consciousness is low and we're actually judging them like assholes. From these resistant suffering perspectives, they can only see that you're judging them critically, even if they know you to be a compassionate person, because their will is stuck on that frequency. A phenomenon is noted in science, that merely observing an object causes it to behave differently. If they think you're observing them the way they are observing everything with resistance, then watch out! Let your focus be light hearted compassion that projects the light of God onto them, and ask God and their guides to take care of the rest. That action rates 778 on The Scale of Consciousness.

People can only be helped when they are willing. This willingness, on the Scale of Human Consciousness, ranks 349 out of a possible 1000. It is just above pride, just above the level of neutrality where you decide to let go. That surrendering is the magic key to pivoting out of resistant suffering. It's when you ask, 'Now how is THAT perfect?' It's when you say, 'I fucked up. I make mistakes. How can I do better now?'

I needed to heal people because the discomfort of others makes me so uncomfortable. It's the partial reason I'm writing a book. I need to just express it, lead the horse to water, and surrender so that folks won't feel directly attacked by these pre-recorded observations. Having challenged virtually every ego of my friends, colleagues, and mentors, and having been bitten by a dog, face broken by my relative, and investigated by various international agencies it made me question, "What's the safer more effective way to 'fight' injustice?" Answer: Don't fight it. Send it love bombs with the mind and stay out of dodge. Love bombs are truly the weapons of the new millennium. However, don't rub truth bombs in the ego's nose unless you still need suffering as a teacher.

My job before enlightenment was as an international private asset protection logistics strategist.. Thanks to FATCA, working with banks became unenjoyable and dangerous as a US citizen. They even sent a spy from the United Nations to come check me out at one point. Feeling the strain of this battle, I sat down my wounded warrior and asked, "Well if this isn't the best way to help people, then what IS the greatest and highest calling for me? How can I help the world in a big way using all my skills and talents?" The root of the answer was that I had to allow myself to shine at full wattage (even if that were going to piss off a lot of dark egos). Being angry or highly principled about injustice was dimming my light. It kept my consciousness divided like republicans and democrats.

Come to find out, anger invites energy theft from disembodied entities. Now, I not only surrender to God's will when it comes to assholes, I also pray for them. The cracked cheekbone was a reminder to pray for my relative who was overcome by dark forces. The cheek was also a reminder not to rub my righteousness in anyone's face. Over time, the prayers have been working. For his birthday, I gave him a nice bag of really great mushrooms. He reached into enlightenment that day. Remember, with The Scale of Human Consciousness, using kinesiology, we can calibrate where someone is on that scale just using a simple muscle resistance test with your arm. The conversations with my relative have gotten a lot more spiritual. This coming from the same guy who hit me after blowing up about me trying to answer his question, 'What is spirituality?' That demon had a strong ass hold on him. It wouldn't even let him listen to the answer to a question about spirituality! Now, I'm convinced that the guardians I placed around his home have been doing their job. The trick is that now he allows me to pray for him.

How can we get even without stooping to their level and giving away our power? We've got to lift them up patiently by leveling the playing field step-by-step. We must bring them up, leading by example even if no one is following, and always remind ourselves to let God chisel someone's ego in divine timing. **Focus positive vibes towards all your enemies. Make it a point to meditate on your enemies until you can reach into the healing space of loving them so much that you wish no suffering upon them.** The divine master in you commands it. That's a powerful way to transmute the karma. You also might like to do a little binding spell by chanting, 'I bind you from doing harm. Harm to yourself and harm to others.' Spend an hour praying for world leaders, corporations, the banking cartels, the media, the politicians, the public servants, the military industrial complex, the employees of oil & coal companies, etc. Then spend an hour meditating on all the critical moments of unforgiveness with your family, friends, spouses, children, etc.

This is a Herculean task because it can be hard to observe the injustice without starting to mimic it. We beat match with the bullshit, to a degree. We allow injustice. We eat meat and drink cow milk. We don't recycle or compost. We don't lobby congress incessantly to kick out Monsanto. Our taxes pay for wars that we don't believe in but allow. You see what I mean? We get complacent.

If we somehow believe that we don't deserve to enjoy abundance while others still suffer, then we empathetically become a vibrational match to what we focus attention onto. You know, like how we start bitching about a problem instead of working to resolve it. What good does that do? We tend to plummet right down from our high flying disks sinking into pride, anger, apathy, or shame. It is the conflicting duality, the catch 22 of having just entered into the heart, on the cusp of unconditional love (500-540 on The Scale), yet not quite the space of peace and abiding faith (600) where we oath to allow God to be the director. The enemy wins the battle through our tacit consent as we fall out of love back into the mind and are humbled by our failure to sustain those high vibes- by the failure to tame our own ego. What is outside is a reflection of what's inside.

So, we must resolve to stay in our integrity- the loving divine nature, as Christ did on the cross. I do NOT want to get into politics here other than to say that my covert strategy for protesting the NWO and all that other bullshit is not to protest at all. My plan is to lovingly cast compassion's dissolving light onto their internal demons until the systems collapse. I call upon higher power to help, which they are- trust. The collective anger has been draining our resources and here we are paying for it. We buy into and perpetuate the injustice. So, we really need to focus on realizing how the external enemy has corrupted us, and repent. On an esoteric note, it's also 'evil spirit' forces keeping us on life support. We act as if we're just strong enough to feed off of, but too weak to fight back.

Some habits die hard. I was praying for the cleansing of my family bloodline because I can't stand to be around my mother's resistance perpetuated by grandma's lessons in poverty consciousness. I got cocky and tried to deactivate and dissolve the etheric implants (28) injected by 'The Lords of Karma', and whatever other energy harvesters. I was seriously attacked. It made me start puking and felt like it was strangling my heart. Admittedly, I became alarmed and called my healer 911 hotline for help. You can access them through my app. To which, Jeff said, **"Send it love. I'm going to send love to the source from which it came."** Within seven minutes, I was better, but that demon had harvested about 35% of the energy from my organs. So, don't get burned foolishly protesting on your own in anger.

Be aware: Do not try to reclaim your sovereignty by attempting to remove etheric implants on your own. Only an initiated professional should attempt the protocols. I had been warned and was told that my job is to provide a physical spiritual counseling role instead. Two phenomenal healers who have helped me escape the matrix's stronghold are now available to you by downloading the Powerful Energetic Medicines A pp for Android (29) & iTunes. (30) Review our services catalog of professional psychic healers. Alexandra, Jeff, Wolfgang, Teresa, Mujin, and Rachel have truly healed me. You can also listen to my world peace prayer on the app's Free Gift section. These are all examples of how to effectively fight fire with Christ Consciousness.

Chapter 7:

WHAT TO DO?

THERE'S A SAYING IN SPANISH, 'El que brille mas, atrae mas bichos' which means: He who shines the brightest attracts the most bugs. As a lightworker, this is the story of my life. I've had a very powerful healer tell me, in response to this belief, that if you believe that, it will make it true. She, and the guides from my original birth family, always encourage me to know that the light shines more powerfully than the dark, all the time. I find that hard to be true given all the shit that is coming up for healing right now, but that's because I still have trouble maintaining that focus.

I didn't know I was a 'lightworker' when I was defending injustice as a teenager in the 90's. I'd become the scapegoat while defending the underdog in ways that no one ever defended me. I'd try to fix people's problems when I couldn't fix my own. I'd empathize with their pain. Subsequently, I'd attract negative attention, making myself vulnerable to attack by absorbing their psychic junk because of my lack of self worth. I just knew that it hurt to be picked on and that I was strong enough to stop it. But a piece of me was fighting in anger. I would 'teach people a lesson'- usually at some cost to myself.

Then, one day, I realized a balance of becoming the ultimate bug zapper, which is to let light shine in all circumstances, especially in the face of heinous crimes or personal attacks. **In the face of demonic attack, always always love back.** I'm also learning how to stop taking it upon myself to do God's job, which allows my life to be easier than imaginable. I just focus my attention on surrounding them with light, and putting them in communication with their guides. Picture the Buddhist monk who allows his limbs to be chopped off one by one in the face of the tyrant warrior. Sometimes, it seemed I was giving them the blade and making myself easy bate. After so many experiences (present or past life) it's little wonder that I was wounded. I was wounding myself. I was stuck in a cycle that only Higher Love could save me from. I was attacking my mother and grandmother's karma from a place of resistance rather than forgiveness.

So I breathe... patiently... giving myself time to remember the truth of my divinity in the face of her well-meaning amnesia. I breathe in patience, and practice forgiveness, remembering that the divine truth of all that I am can never truly be attacked so there's no reason to fight back. Ego fights out of fear and a lack of forgiveness, of which I AM.

In what ways are you wounding yourself through the illusion of attack?

In what ways do you perceive attack? Could it be your mind creating the outward circumstance? What would feel better? As Abraham Hicks says, 'What's the highest feeling feeling?'

Where are you stuck in fear? What cycles are you tired of repeating? What are you tired of experiencing in others? Tell God what you want and start walking in that direction.

If you are here, at this time, to heal the status quo or if you are simply tired of suffering, the way out is by healing the hypocritical attack through the inside out.

To win the kingdom of heaven on earth is to practice compassion for yourself (particularly our bodies) and everyone else (particularly those that trigger us). Compassion is what holds things together. Compassion is defined by Webster's Dictionary as the sympathetic consciousness of others' distress together with a desire to alleviate it. Now, doesn't that sound like the definition of a truly loving God? I guess that's why God made me so darn empathetic, and why I find it so important to express compassion inside and out. As a healer, I find it really easy to embody that Christ-like compassion. It's a simple evolution of consciousness, and we're on the front lines at this time. Have compassion for your own 'flaws' first. Recognize our collective humanity, fallibility, awesome capability and overall 'flawsomeness', (32) then love into it.

I know that's easier said than done when we're in the thick of an argument. This is where Eckhart Tolle's training about 'The Pain Body' becomes a valuable practice to implement. Utilizing compassion gracefully is facilitated by mental rehearsal. This concept also draws from the book Psycho-Cybernetics (33) by Maxwell Maltz.

Exercise:

Imagine you are observing your last big fight.

Review the script, and identify the language of your control dramas. (34)

Catch yourself emotionally before the snowball of suffering begins by breathing forgiveness into the situation.

Reframe what you said with less resistant-more loving thoughts. Try several times, allowing yourself to pivot up into a higher feeling feeling (35) over and over. Write it down to help focus and improve quickly. Change the script to a loving one.

Make the decision to respond with a higher perspective next time, next breath more awareness. Breathe now. Feel yourself saying that new loving script.

Seek refuge in higher consciousness materials for support and proper preparation.

Remember the British army adage of the 7 Ps: Proper planning and preparation prevents piss poor performance.

I've survived the depths of despair and experienced the heights of heaven. These are the messages I've had to learn the hard way so that you don't have to. Please know, wellness and harmony will always thrive no matter how much we resist. The big question is, **how much suffering do you need in order to learn the lessons your soul intends for you? How graceful can you be with yourself and others? How much compassion can you express in your next breath?** Wherever there is light, there cannot be darkness. Learn to shine the light onto your darkest parts, and you'll heal every situation beyond what your mind can imagine.

Victimization

Most of the time, we don't see our suffering as a choice. Certainly, when we're trapped in the vibration of suffering, we tend to see ourselves as victims of circumstances outside of our control. We often fail to explore how that circumstance was fully created by us (or our Higher Selves) as an opportunity to grow in awareness and capability or as a result of karma from this or other lives. Ego is full of amnesia. Victim mentality is a cute covert manipulation of the vampire-mind that steals energy from others rather than owning mistakes, repenting, and reclaiming power. Many illnesses can be traced to victimization. This link shows a list of ailments and their metaphysical cause. (36) Once it is accepted logically, the counseling technique of thought reframing is good. Those of you who know Louise Hays, owner of my Publisher, Balboa Press, may recall that her first book was a metaphysical physicians' desk reference to illness and disease.

Using one of my 10-40 minute guided meditations will provide relief to the extent that you desire it with all your heart. You CAN accept your present reality and see the greater meaning of how that experience stands to serve you if you are willing to push through ego's apathy, victimization mentality, or pride. In order to change the dis-ease favorably, you must desire that change. There are so many frequencies on this planet telling us that we're all unworthy, alone, or what's the use. In our naivete, the brain tries to accept responsibility, it says you deserve the pain that you get, or that life is suffering. You accept the limiting belief that the struggle is real, forgetting that it is all an illusion within your control to change. Ego says you brought this upon yourself, misunderstands karma as judgement, and then the 'parent' aspect of ego punishes the ignorant child. Can you feel the duality of the double-hemisphered brain? Wouldn't the one-love heart centered perspective feel better?

The angry, vengeful victimized powerless-to-have-prevented-this perception you may be holding with respect to a particular life trauma, was fully designed as a result of many small consequences over time. Nothing happens by chance or accident. Everything is by design. If 'mistakes' and 'accidents' were real, surely by now the world would have blown up, you see?

Whether you buy into the notion of past lives or not, humans have poor selective memory, often at the expense of objective self-reflection. This may be the number one reason for sitting down with a pen and paper forcing yourself to answer a long list of questions like "In what ways could I be wrong here? List 10." "What mistakes might I have made? Can I forgive myself?" Write a letter of forgiveness to yourself. The purpose is multifold. Gaining the willingness to look at all those potential flaws is set up for you to witness yourself more objectively. You can do this once you better understand the Universal Laws and Principles, have a breakthrough moment, and then pull the trigger on your self-defeating habits. But we simply can't do that on our own through the self-centered perspective. Allowing higher power to flow through is mandatory to complete the equation. For atheists and skeptics, this can simply be your highest ascended self, the most awesome version of you imaginable.

Imagine the limiting speech that was taught to you by a cruel environment. How can we act in opposite ways? Consider the homeless. Enough people have made them disbelieve their own worth. Along the line, they've given away their power through a series of disempowering choices, and now they are starving for love and begging us to see the pain we've inflicted with our egotistical indifference. Could we practice the power of abundance, flow and compassion by saying, 'How do I commit to being better?' and trust that God will return our abundance? Think of it as accruing good karma points. I read somewhere it said that many of those who helped the Jews in concentration camps incarnated as Hollywood stars. Imagine that. Imagine the ripples a duck makes on the pond as it journeys. What kind of waves do you choose to make?

When was the last time you tithed, gave, were generous, shared without fear of abandon, gave to those who could do nothing for you? How can we receive if we don't give? How can God fill our cups if we don't make space to receive it? The Highest Ascended version of who we are is always with us. Would tithing really take away your happiness? Science says sharing and volunteering actually increases happiness and self-esteem. We feel like better people by tithing because all people are hardwired to help one another. Obey the guidance, and ask your guru within, "What is the right amount to share?" Open your heart and allow yourself to expand beyond mind's limitations. Open your mind and allow the rest of who you are to flow.

Have I mentioned that only 1/3rd of you is in the body? The other 2/3rds of you is energy that can reside outside the body, like your aura. Parts of you are existing in higher dimensions, or the magnetism that attracts all that is wanted, that's you. Victim mentality stops you from harnessing all that extra energy to your advantage, and then shit just seems to keep going wrong.

You can accept that we come to this earth as diamonds in the rough. Life's purpose is to polish and reveal the multiple facets of our True Divinity, our Highest Ascended Selves. The University of Life polishes us through contrasting experiences, rough waters, and hot fires pressuring the carbon into diamonds. Without the contrast, we wouldn't be able to evolve. This University of Life buffs us so that we learn how to live in harmony. The more we resist, the more life persistently sands us down and rubs us until we become willing to surrender and flow with the tides, downs and ups, bad and good, thin and abundant. **My question is, "How much more do you need to suffer before you'll surrender to the flow and allow yourself to shine?"**

Exercise:

Sit back and think about some of your most painful life experiences. The ones that come to mind first are the ones that still need the most attention and healing. Give it some.

QUICKLY write down the most painful memories that come up. Have a cry if you need, but don't get stuck.

Repent- PROMISE yourself, on each memory, that you will attempt to heal those memories with a higher consciousness, and promise to make a change toward the highest truth, love, and joy.

Recite this prayer: "Dear Highest Ascended Self, I allow you to deliver me the higher consciousness necessary to heal my heart of these wounds. Erase these memories and give me a fresh start. I call upon a team of volunteer angels and allow you to find all, clean all, and clear all the fragmented darkness throughout this or any other time space continuum or parallel lives throughout all worlds, times, spaces, and dimensions for all of eternity. Please help me cancel this event from the karmic timeline with love, ease, and graceful compassion. Thank you, thank you, thank you. Bless me, bless me, bless me. Bless me, bless me, bless me. Bless me, bless me, bless me, bless me."

Chapter 8:

KARMA

THE REASON WHY the past keeps repeating itself is because there's still some important lesson to be learned and trauma to be resolved. History is only destined to repeat itself unless it is looked at from a higher perspective. So, let us go back and look at the recent junk in our life, while it's fresh, before it rots and turns into an inflamed physical wound. Allow the highest truth, love, and joy to infuse and reframe your thoughts, and the body will respond. The incident may be long gone, but if we're still chewing on it, it's infecting our present reality and our bodies. Healing acceptance and forgiveness is needed. Only then, can we stop tainting the future because our present will be cleansed.

Would you like to increase your abundance today? Then look at a potentially self-defeating attitude you exhibit. For me, it's impatience and discipline. A solid culprit is when we say, 'I know.' or if you're like me, getting impatient because I'm certain I already understand. I have to develop patience and listening skills, aka compassion. What do you have to develop? We are so full here, yet spiritually bankrupted by our big heads. There is so much room for us to inject compassion into the situation and create an opportunity to get paid back by sharing or acting upon our knowledge in some way. The degree to which you are purely giving determines how infinitely more powerful your good karma is when it's time to redeem your rewards.

Exercise:

1. Appreciation avalanche: (37) Think about the best things you love most about your life. List 20-50 things you love about life. Yes, get out a pen and paper or type it out.

2. Write out some things you want more of, feeding off of the good feelings already established above. Merge the satisfied and gratified feelings of what you already have into the things you want more of, so that there's no place for feelings of lack about what you have yet to manifest.

3. You've got to get deliberate about making room for that abundance, replacing the 'I know' mind with humble open arms. Don't worry about how you're going to get it. Let God handle the how, while you continue to bow and allow. The 'don't know mind' is easily filled, and God wants us to know he's filling it.

4. Include positive expectation and belief in your deserving to have your heart's desires. Any places inside you that don't believe they deserve, send it healing and raise its awareness. You've GOT to work on your deservingness. All abundant people know they deserve it. If this means you need to become a better person, commit to acts of kindness.

5. When things aren't working, we can't just throw the baby out with the bathwater, so we've got to look at the times when things were really working and take note of the formula. When you reach a phase that is working in your life, take note, like physically write down the circumstances and actions you took. Look at the elements to the alchemy of your life's successful recipe. You've got to decide to remove certain ingredients like harsh speech, abusive people, jobs that don't fulfill you, people who don't believe in you, friends with bad habits, non-income-producing habits, income-taking habits, resistant beliefs, and the 'I know it all' mentality.

6. With your mind, write on a chalkboard all the resistant things you need to change in order to live a more abundant life.

7. With your mind, erase the chalkboard clean three times. Each time the chalkboard gets cleaner and cleaner.

8. Breathe in a contented sigh of relief.

When I did this exercise, I busted out the soapy water and used a toothbrush to clean the mental/ emotional cracks. That's how diligent I am about making room for abundance. By mentally, deliberately, focusing attention toward cleaning up the negativity from our life, the subconscious can begin doing these chores for us on autopilot while the Universe responds to our focused intentions.

Did you do your homework yet? Congratulations. You have just applied the science of alchemy and metaphysics! Way to go! You are now becoming a more precise co-creator for your abundant future, and you didn't even have to get out of bed! That was easy.

Enlightenment

Did you know: If you desire to reach enlightenment, then you are destined to achieve it?

Sometime around 1998, I read in a Buddhist book that you could even achieve enlightenment in this lifetime if you desired it enough. Nirvana is the feeling of having enough, plenty, whole, satisfied, and confident the buffet of life will continue serving up your desires. Christ's teachings (I'm not speaking about the bible, strictly about his words) attempted to show us the power and dominion we can have over all these earthly situations by embracing and allowing pure consciousness to flow through us.

I feel like a Christed being and allow God to flow through me intensely when I take acid. There is much evidence to support that Moses' burning bush may have been encrusted with magic mushrooms. There is further evidence to support that the Vatican, and all religions, for that matter, are shrouded in history using intoxicants, like hallucinogens, to induce spiritual experiences. (38) Natives of the Amazon use frog poison, snuffs, and ayahuasca to improve their consciousness and extrasensory perception. Even Ram Das' Guru, Majara Ji, called LSD medicine. A fascinating documentary called *The Pharmacratic Inquisition* (39) studies the use of intoxicants in religion based on the Rosetta Stone translations. Recently, two dozen religious leaders (40) took acid in the name of science. Certainly, in my case, hallucinogens were the stepping stone to escape the matrix, allow pure Tao consciousness to flood through me, and accelerate my healing process. I didn't know how to live healthy, because it had never really been demonstrated in my life. But LSD showed me a higher consciousness so that I had something to strive towards. Admittedly, during the course of this past two years, upon making the decision to be all that I can be, LSD is my medicine of choice for kicking fear's ass and reclaiming my power since my goals are so much bigger than I am.

According to Dr. David Hawkins, and several others, up until about 1987, not so many people had reached enlightenment. Fewer still had reached full consciousness. However, in just the last few years, many millions have done so without fully realizing and understanding the magnitude of their personal and social achievement. Basically, it's the feeling beyond peace. Enlightenment is the integration of higher powers running through you as you take an oath to serve, listen, obey, and act as your Highest Ascended Self.

Full 100% consciousness IS actually acting as God. Enlightenment took me 13 years to achieve once I decided that was a goal. Paradoxically, the transition happened while I was homeless. In February 2016, I did enlightenment integrations on two young fans in about 10 minutes. For those who have never heard of or known me, but whom are really willing, I can guide you to touch that level usually in less than a day, maybe even an hour or less. At the festivals, I lecture and it just takes an hour or two of guided surrender meditation because those people definitely want it and are willing. I've made a pre-recorded enlightenment integration CD available to you through the app, on iTunes or on the foundation's store at http://www.CarinaCarinosaStore.Guru/ (41)

These days, we have indigo, crystal, rainbow, and even star children. The indigos are a hybrid evolved version of the consciousness from the boomer and hippie parents. We come in with a certain level of consciousness that is generally more evolved than the consciousnesses of our parents. It's basic evolution, and as the would-be-parents become more enlightened, so too will their offspring enjoy a higher level of consciousness, as well. The circumstances of our birth and family were all perfectly designed to help us increase that consciousness and to clear our soul's karma. Likewise, our raising of consciousness directly affects our family. You not only are setting a better example, but your heart is emitting a stronger frequency of higher intelligence. If you will open up your heart to connecting with mankind and offer it healing, then your high vibes can affect more people because you will it so.

In one respect, enlightenment is actually something we are learning from the children's evolved consciousness. My first energetic shaman, Jason Kerr, was only 34. That just blew my mind. It was very encouraging to know that all this sacred wisdom could be accessed and implemented at such a young age. Jason used to party too, but he got serious, got a mentor, and got beyond the fear of being different. I remember the first time I went with him to the hot springs in Panama's canyon valley along the edge of the volcanic mountain Baru back in 2010. He stopped his white jeep to pay homage to this dry land with a rattle, a leather pouch, an eagle feather, and his sacred scepter. I thought it was weird and made me a little uncomfortable, but I kept curious and respectful.

In perhaps my third healing Jason laid small crystals along my chakra system, and after some serious crying, I felt an expansive release emanating from within, filling the room. Jason said, "Remember this feeling. This is harmony. Hold this with you as you carry on." I can calibrate that moment of consciousness at 567 out of a possible 1000 on Dr. Hawkin's clinically proven Scale of Human Consciousness. (42) Harmony is not quite peace, which reflects a deeper trust in the perfection of the Universe. That's the step above harmony. However, harmony is definitely located in the heart where we are feeling unconditional love, and almost utterly beyond worry. Feeling worry is an indicator that your consciousness is below 600, the level of peace and the gateway to enlightenment. It was the first time I'd not been angry at my deceased drug addict husband in about 5 years. Instead, my heart was filled with acceptance. As I took the bus home back to my little cottage at the foot of the mountain, I watched a rainbow (my favorite) and smiled into the sunset as a painful feeling was finally erased.

I continued to work with Jason. He told me that he'd been 'holding space' for me on his altar, and showed me his room which had pictures of various Ascended Masters. He had a preference for Jesus, aka Yeshwa, and respected his altar objects with deep reverence. I believe in holding THINGS lightly, but he understood what it means to hold things SACRED. He was very protective of them. I won't say he worshiped them, but more like a carpenter caring for his tools, he didn't want another person touching and messing up their energy. They were all serving a purpose, holding his intention. I'd not gained any appreciation for crystals at that time, but the power of his faith that they worked warranted my respect. I was certain there was a science behind it, a logical explanation, but I surrendered my need to know. It was a combination of abiding faith, respect, and my desire to stop suffering. I wanted to be a better person and stop thinking those nasty thoughts about my ex and his family. Plus, the proof was in the pudding; no doubt, I was a widow suddenly able to appreciate life again. Pills couldn't do that, but a shaman could.

At the tender age of 29, I marveled to think that by 34 I could reach his level. It wasn't that I wanted to be like him, nor could I even picture myself doing what he did. I just knew that I wanted to save anyone willing to save themselves. I wanted to share the harmony I felt. I wanted to do whatever I could to prevent others from feeling the sorrow I'd known. This is a typical level of empathy for when people are vibrating at the level of unconditional love, 540 on the scale. Not everyone has the luxury of being a hermit on the side of a flower covered mountain in Panama. People have debt and dependents. So I figured I was lucky, and the first thing I could do was hug my peace into them, but since I lived so far away from people, I had to hug them with my mind. That's how I began practicing what became a powerful psychic healing gift.

The one thing we all want in common is to be happy. Happiness means different things for different people. Ultimately, happiness means fulfilling your purpose. To get there, first we must have peace of mind that we'll always be supported in the pursuit of our passions. That requires trusting and listening to our hearts, and this requires overcoming the limitations of mind. So, we have to surrender the mind's fears to make room for abiding faith in God. Once you've tested your faith, and seen how the Universe supports you, feeling enlightened is the natural effect. You feel like you have a safety net. The way to test if it is safe to fulfill your passions, however, is by first holding space for that reality within your body. This is the secret, the physics, to manifesting exactly what is wanted. As Bashar says, you must first open space for what is wanted within your mind and body in order for it to become apparent in your reality.

To be enlightened we must practice being in joy. In an exercise from The I-Ching Handbook: Getting What You Want (43) it says to practice joy for 30 minutes a day.

What makes us happiest is knowing that we are in the process of fulfilling our highest calling using all the skills and talents we've cultivated along the way.

Enlightenment manifests in the body as the transmutation from a carbon based atomic structure to crystalline base. We decide to stop compromising our awesomeness, and that activates our DNA, inviting our bodies to vibrate on a different level, or dimension. We take an oath to let all of our power flow through our human body. This includes celestial powers vibrating within other dimensions of reality outside our traditional 5 senses. We honor our flawsomeness (and the flawsomeness of others). We accept our struggles as opportunities for growth in awareness and capability. The more enlightened you become, the greater your ability is to call upon all of the God life force available in the multiverse and allow it to flow to you, through you, as you.

In order to make happiness last longer, we must remain willing to sit with uncomfortable thoughts until we can accept them and love into them. Then, they will no longer trigger us because the thought's negativity as a baseline emotion won't be there anymore. In this way, we work them out, and close the chapter (or even erase it) instead of inadvertently letting those stinky chapters continue to vibrate in our present experience. You should never vehemently reject what is not wanted because what you resist persists. Please understand that all humans have the power to amend, erase, and write a new chapter for themselves, freeing themselves from the sorrow of the past. You just have to become willing to forgive the past and then do the homework of allowing each unwanted thought to arise for healing.

I don't mean to advocate lengthy hours of tearful self-improvement reflection. I've been through all of that, and while it holds value, people tend to get caught up in the emotion, rather than surrendering it, and are often unable to shed light on their situation. They aren't in a position like I was where I could escape into a $100 per month home in rural Panama to cry for 1000 days. That's why we take psych meds to act as a band aid. The reason psych meds often don't fix the problem is that psychiatrists aren't offering spiritual solutions to help you resolve the trauma. So, let me have suffered enough for you. God gave me a gift to speed up all that process for you. We'll do counseling, but mostly we'll get there through the energetic work and follow up CDs. Like all things, it works if you work it. I'm just trying to give you the energetic Cliff's Notes to end your suffering.

Enlightenment promises that once you've gone through the destruction of your ego's games, which no longer serve, life will become increasingly magical and fulfilling because you'll have learned to flow with Source which is far more powerful than flowing through the constrictions of the ego mind. Destruction still happens, though. It's like deciding to remodel a house; some degree of demolition is required. This can be a daunting task if you're faced with ending certain relationships or feel trapped by your uncomfortable creations. A chakra balancing will help immensely. (44)

The ultimate spiritual goal is to bloom wherever we are planted and, in every moment of each day, cultivate the ability to remember love, gratitude and unity. It is a practice. You could be atheist and still become enlightened, but I think that's going about it the harder way. In a way, atheists can be very spiritually advanced because the general belief is that you yourself have the power, which is true. I'd submit that most atheists are spiritually advanced in their basic understanding of physics. It just requires further study. Most atheists, on the Scale of Consciousness, rate in the 400s- a level of understanding, the domain of science. I'd like to meet an enlightened atheist, or a heart centered atheist willing to integrate as their highest ascended selves. I'd look forward to the challenge of speaking to them in a language we can mutually agree upon based on the science of spirituality.

Personally, I find it very relieving to know that we all have angels and spirit guides. It's nice to know I'm not alone. Personally, I find it comforting to know that there are legions of ascended masters and aliens chomping at the bit to help us overthrow dark forces and reclaim the utopia of this ancient planet. For me, believing in benevolent omniscient entities that wish to assist me is a faster way to receive grace than just trying to fumble through on my own. Angels know how to love me the way I need to be loved, people not so much. It's like accepting help even though you are a strong person. I certainly didn't believe in angels as part of my reality until recently. It had to be experienced. I'd ruled out the obvious logical possibilities, one-by-one, like a scientist eliminating variables, until I was left bewildered and begging for grace beyond my mind. I may have surrendered to Jason Kerr healing hands a few times, but I most certainly was indignant enough to have spent 2 decades asking 'why' and searching for the experience of ultimate truth. I can be so stubborn that divine intervention is consistently required. It's as though I make God prove Itself to me, and in that indignation, I create situations that are out of alignment to the point that divine intervention is absolutely required. Save yourself some time and frustration. Just know you are loved on the other side of the veils and standard lines of deviation..

If you're really far from feeling love and gratitude in every moment, no worries, it'll come. Just give me a dishonest or irresponsible Panamanian taxi driver or some malfunctioning technology! It's total sandpaper to my nerves. All of my bitchiness flows out. Then I realize, "He's my teacher; he caught me. I got upset. There was something in need of healing here. Do I want to give away my power here?" Breathe, breathe, breathe, observe. In this way, I can quickly return to smiling graciousness rather than chewing on my discontent. Unfortunately, wisdom is often what we get just after we needed it. That's why enlightenment is a practice. We all have our workout situations.

Instead of condemning what life is reflecting, stop and do the homework of acceptance, reframing, forgiveness, reclaiming of power and clearing. Don't be afraid about making the wrong decision. As long as it feels better than what you were already doing, and harms no one, it's beneficial. Just keep reaching for that highest feeling feeling, (45) as Abraham- Hicks would say.

Be patient with yourself and others. The human body, for example, takes time to process new codes received in a DNA activation, or from the time you make a true commitment to change your worldly experience. New habits take time to become ingrained. Outward appearance is a projection and culmination of internal thoughts and habits which have become codes. Decoding, defragging, analyzing the code, downloading new programs, and the unfoldment of those new activations takes time. One must do the protocol and then wait for the unfolding. It's like planting a seed and waiting for it to bloom.

In the physical third dimension, a gestation period is required. In the 5th dimensional reality we now all have access to, if we so decide, things happen as quickly as you can think about them. It just may take a while for you to get on board with your decisions emotionally/ physically/ logistically/ etc. Or, you may experience a 'miraculous' transformation in moments and be permanently healed of an addiction or old resistant beliefs. Either way, there will be an unfoldment to the consequences of your decisions. The more activated you are, the more swiftly you can process human emotions like a boss. Use a journal to measure your progress and process out all that mental trash that makes you live in disharmony. Write out all the trash and give it to God, releasing it up for transmutation. Ask God for help forgiving. That's really key. With practice, you'll be able to do this more and more quickly and won't need the written technique. Just have faith that you can.

If you trust, you can.

Doubt creates a static dissonance that muddles the vibration. Let's say you've set an intention. If you doubt the power that gives energy to that creation, it's like having a slow leak in your tires. Pretty soon, things will get wonky and you'll be thrown off course. If you have real faith, it's like a jet pack propelling you forward with speed and precision.

My grandpa's greatest gift to my mother was to say "If you want to be better, BE BETTER, because YOU can." My mom tended to take that meaning from a position of pride, but I'm sure he meant it from the loving perspective that the force is always within you. Of course, you can achieve your dreams dear star seed. You are a little star descendent from the big stars. The seed of your Divinity is within you. You just have to practice opening up to that divinity. That's what I call the Guru Within. Our connection and role within the totality of mankind is the most important connection left for us to practice understanding. Once you feel it emotionally, beyond the intellectual, you'll be enlightened as long as you keep practicing surrender to Source.

The Key is Within.

The biggest challenge we face is in learning to stop running, stop seeking gratification from outside consumption, stop pointing the finger outward. We must reclaim our power. Courage is required to point the finger inward. We must say, 'Look, I mess up. I make mistakes. How can I do better?' What we need to feel alive and happy are tools to help unravel the glory that resides within.

Imagine you are a star about to explode into its full brilliance. You've got to call upon your power, the power within, and the power that created you.

We must constantly practice calling upon that power in order to let go of the distracting melodramatic frequencies being transmitted by the billions of minds on this planet. You've got to have grit because other people are full of energy leaks, and they become vampires. We need that energy in order to hold and sustain enlightenment. We need that energy in order to fulfil our total awesomeness. Any decisions to 'let it be okay' that you're not being your most awesome today is either A) True surrender to your current reality, B) Compromising your excellency and/or C) The result of energy leaks.

Chapter 9:

ENGINEERED FOOD & CANCER

I REMEMBER BEING THE CHILD of a single mother growing up in the 80's. I'd look at those colorful cereal commercials, which still make my mind salivate, thinking, 'They are really trying to target me emotionally.' McDonald's has spent billions of customer dollars researching how to get your children to nag you for their Frankenfood. Coca Cola programs you to believe that its products are a regular part of enjoying a social lifestyle. They play off your desire to feel connected rather than alone. Funny how sugar is more addictive than cocaine. The more you buy, the more they advertise, the harder it is to step out of this sick cancer-causing social norm. After 9/11, I put down the TV. Now, I use my extra time to fulfill my passions and purpose instead of allowing the TV to program and market to me.

Little by little, we have to empty our cup of ALL the illusions that split our energy. They take up space within the body, confusing our vibrational offering. There are several 'radical' ways of deprogramming those deep personality quirks you may have falsely accepted as who you are. Western medicine has sold us a long line of surgeries, pills, and no known cause for our debilitating dis-eases. Imagine if heroin had its own commercials telling you to ask your doctor for more details. It's the same thing when colorful marshmallows are marketed to your kids, and we wonder why they have ADHD. Here's a radical idea; how about commercials educating my family on the benefits of apples and broccoli. Yet oncologists will tell you it's radical to expect nutrition to cure your cancer. Cleaning our vibrations from the toxicity begins with censoring the negativity and misinformation. For deprogramming, that's where metaphysics, shamanism, quantum physics, magic, herbalism and all the other spiritual sciences converge. It's not "new age". Ancient cultures have experienced and participated in enlightening practices for thousands of years.

Energy = Inner G

As Deepak Chopra says, 'The genes are there, they've just not been activated.' A proper diet that doesn't suppress your energy is key to keeping your DNA activated once it comes online through enlightened practice. Nourishment prevents sugar and salt cravings which are actually just vitamin and mineral deficiencies. This is why juicing is so great for the body. The live enzymes and direct nutrition to the gut will not only provide proper nutrition, but that microbial balance in the gut will positively affect serotonin production. Remember, there's no substitute for raw food nourishment. It is alive information that adds instant energy to the body.

The myth about protein we've been sold to believe is that the body breaks everything down to amino acids. The body uses amino acids to make protein. By eating animals, we are adding a middle man to what plants already provide. The cow eats grass, or at least it is supposed to. I can't tolerate pork (even bacon) anymore because they are fed GMO grains, not grass. If you look at cows in the wild, they are not puffed up and swollen, like the ones used for milk production, or the massive chickens. It's no wonder we're swollen and inflamed with chicken titties! Milk causes mucus which prevents essential nutrient absorption in the guts. Your gut microbiome accounts for 70% of the serotonin production in your brain.

Dead or cooked foods slow the body down and waste energy to process the dead data. As you activate your extra sensory perceptions through enlightened intention, you'll notice that you become more sensitive to animal-based foods. For example, we were enjoying a buffalo filet mignon at a famous steakhouse in Dallas. I could feel the spirit of the buffalo. I could see through its eyes and feel the vitality of its essence as I ate it. Now, imagine eating a piece of animal that is stationary, and never experiences freedom. That's the data you're unconsciously programming into your Inner G.

Consider using live plant medicines, oils and essences. For the less adventurous, there's meditation, yoga, and other forms of exercise. Remember that pharmaceuticals are generally synthesized from plants and that nature can do some miraculous things that marvel western science because it is fractionated data which CAN be patented and profited from. Guanabana fruit (a.k.a. soursop), for example, is 10,000 times more effective at killing certain cancers than chemotherapy. Big pharma knows it, but they can't synthesize it, so they suppress you from knowing about this deliciously satisfying curative fruit.

Nothing external can replace the sustained good feelings we get from learning how to be positively charged, trusting in our super powers as awakened beings and manifesting our hearts desires. Enlightened practices will help you achieve all those things. Eating things that eat the light is key. Eat the sun through plants.

Curing Cancer

At the risk of a lawsuit or death, I'm going to share with you all the natural remedies I know of for curing cancer. First, let me say, I'm not a medical doctor, and you can see the references to articles and facts that prove what I'm saying by liking the foundation's page on Facebook Powerful Energetic Medicines. (46) We have created a body of work called Cure Cancer At Home. It is a digital directory of all the known alternative cancer cures from around the world. You just click to buy the products. I've researched for you which brands seemed to have the best reviews, and also found all of the products referenced in the acclaimed documentary Forbidden Cures. (47) The documentary leads one to believe that the cures cannot be accessed unless you travel overseas constantly for treatment because the FDA pushed them out of the States. So I found where to buy the treatments online. We humbly ask for your help to finish packaging and promoting the product. There's a number of videos that need to be produced for optimal efficacy. If you truly care about donating to cancer research, we'd really love to focus on this level of help to our guests at the private retreat center. We are ready to put together a certified medical staff for alternative treatments in cancer, addiction, trauma & relationship recovery, as well as enlightenment retreats and ceremonies. It'll be called The Safe Space.

To access the Directory please visit https://alternativecancercures.org (48)

The list below is not exhaustive, but here are some highlights.

- Graviola or Soursop fruit- 10,000 times more effective than chemo. Get it on Amazon in a big can. Blend with Ice or milk of your choice. Drink religiously if you have cancer for 2-3 months.
- High Grade Frankincense & Sandalwood Essential Oils. Ingest high quality essential oil. 3 drops, 3 times daily. Apply topically over affected area (example: breasts or on stomach or above ovaries etc.)
- 1 part cottage cheese to 2 parts fresh cold-pressed flaxseed oil. Eat daily if you have cancer. The woman who discovered this was nominated multiple times for the Nobel Prize.
- Forgiveness- Practice the Ho'oponopono (49) technique on all your resistant thoughts. The discordant frequencies of stress, and inflammation or infections caused by a weakened immune system need the peace of forgiveness to heal.
- Thank your body. Thank your cancer. Love into the cancer instead of loathing and resisting it. Talk to it. Ask it why it's there. What purpose is it serving? What does it want you to do? The cancer is an indication that you are living out of alignment. Ask the cancer to describe how y ou're living out of alignment. Listen to the quiet voice and correct your course.
- Surrender to God, and let the light come into your body for healing. I've known several prostate cancer patients who were either disconnected from God, or their mother, and who felt emotionally castrated by their wife. Surrender to God really opened up those areas and made space for the cancer to heal.
- Shit tons of Vitamin C- Preferably in the form of fresh lime juice, orange juice, or Vitamin C shots. Notice the FDA is trying hard to phase Vit C shots out of the USA. Our retreat studio will provide these by a licensed nurse. Drink liberally and religiously. You need about half a cup a day of lemon or lime juice to cure cancer or 1 lime per day for prevention.
- Lime- Drink religiously to prevent illness. This will alkalize the body. Cancer can't grow in an alkaline environment.
- STOP SODA POP. STOP DIET SODA. QUIT IT!!!! The pH in Soda is 3.8. Cancer territory is 5.0 and below. The body wants to be at about 7. Lime juice is 11. Check out alkalinity charts on Google Images to see what foods are alkaline or acidic. Make sure you are getting alkaline foods and cutting out acidic ones.
- Watermelon- It's very alkalizing & helps the neuropathy caused by chemo & radiation.
- Dandelion Root- Kills cancer cells in 48 hours.
- Baking Soda (because it makes you more alkaline)

- Bitter Melon
- Chaga Tea- super high in antioxidants
- Energy healing sessions with myself or telepathic healer Mujin Choi (50)
- Cannabis oil, aka Rick Simpson Oil- (51) For skin cancer, apply directly to the lesion or take internally 3-5 times per day for 6-10 weeks. We can refer you during a counseling session.
- Remove sausage, processed meats, dairy and packaged foods. At MINIMUM you must switch to grass fed, no-hormone, no nitrate, humanely raised etc, and you must increase your vegetables to more than half your daily consumption to reverse cancer.
- Here are two amazingly delicious and healthy juice drink recipes that will save your health across the board. https://carinacarinosa.com/release-fat. (52)

I have produces a Delicious Cancer Tea and a Cure Cancer supplement and micro-dose formula that is jawdroppingly effective and deserves grant funding for further testing and research. Download our app and check out the ingredients in the farmacy.

Chapter 10:

WHAT IS AN EMPATH?

An empath is a person with the paranormal ability to feel other people's thoughts and emotions. We are extra sensitive to energy. We're like super antennas. Better yet, we're like awesome routers with a super fast Wi-Fi connection. A trained empath has a direct line to Source intelligence, like the Google of all Googles. This ability to connect is very similar to accessing The Book of Life, (53) as described in the Bible, though the Bible has distorted the meaning. The now accurate interpretation is the ancient one of the Akashic Records, (54) which we discuss in an audio. I've recorded a little lecture about empaths to help highly sensitive people better understand WTF is up with all that dis-ease you may be feeling if you are highly sensitive. We pick up on your discord and feel past people's walls and in-authenticity. At the bottom of my website is a great resource called The Empath's Connection, (55) if you think you might be one.

As an untrained empath, intellectually, it was like a Rubik's cube trying to undo past life karma, break the invasive imprints from an abusive childhood, and muster the discipline to create consistently positive thought patterns. Being highly telepathic and empathic, I sometimes had a dismal time separating what thoughts and feelings were mine vs. what was imposed upon me. I'd also have a tendency to argue telepathically with people. I'll be talking out loud to myself arguing with them. They'll feel it because I'm reading their minds and able to get into their headspace. I would jump into people's space the way an untrained psychic would enter your space.

Detox

The psychologist told me at the tender age of 17 that he wanted me to go to rehab. He said, "I can't properly diagnose what is you and what is a side-effect of your cocktails. You need to detox so that we can clear the table and make space to work things out emotionally."

Detoxing is a constant part of life now. To reach enlightenment, I had to stop drinking. That lasted 18 months until it was time again to celebrate my birthday month. Therein, I tried 'moderation' like everyone who argues for their human limitations would advise. I can't call it peer pressure, just caving in and not respecting my boundaries, feeling bored and a bit anxious because I'm picking up all those stressed or drunk vibe. It is said that empaths have a tendency for extremes, addictions, bi-polar, manic depression, etc. This is also a common issue with Indigo Children who are evolved. We are the revolutionaries who have inherited a mess and put up a stink about it. We came to push the status quo to be more empathetic.

A point to make about bipolar and addictive personality types is that you are actually a really good proponent for reaching enlightenment. 'Bipolar' means that you can go up and down the scale of consciousness a lot at one time. You might have trouble sustaining higher frequencies, but you do the mental homework of processing out the resistant and false beliefs. As long as there is a decision to BE BETTER, or even to BE YOUR BEST, then you will surely make it to higher levels of consciousness. Part of the gift of empathy, when one commits to serving the light, is that you can transmute the suffering of any space because you can osmosis into it. The trick is to practice on yourself first. To do that, we must develop an awareness of what energy is yours by eliminating the energy of others.

"I now release all energies that are not mine and return them back to Source for healing and reintegration."

I have studied countless hours on nutrition. So many of us need help transitioning from toxic habits to more allowing and flowing ones. Understanding how detox works is necessary. I began using the ionic detox machine (56) as part of my monthly health care and weight loss plan. It is a staple in my practice now. For empaths, detoxing energetically through creative expression, movement, showers, and dietary protocols seems crucial. Empaths have to take care of what goes into their bodies and move every day to breathe out the stagnant energy they may be processing from their environment. Remember, we're like Wi-Fi routers. We pick up signals from all over. We pick up the energy from the earth, the sun, the political scandal of the day, the suffering of those ravished by war or natural disasters, the protests around the globe as well as the thousands of prayer groups who are sending light to the planet.

Of course, on a mental level, to detox properly you must take ownership. We have to accept responsibility for undesired karmic effects that come into our experience. In one of my favorite books, *The I-Ching Handbook* by Wu Wei (57) it has us practice an exercise of accepting responsibility for everything, including the weather. Next, you accept the situation for what it is as though you created it for the benefit of your expansion, and practice going with the flow, turning it to the positive, doing the best you can to be happy with wherever you find yourself in the moment. Use adversity, or a change of plans, as a chance to practice taking responsibility. Allow yourself to be guided by your higher self. Don't overschedule your life. You need to make time for detoxing.

Internalizing Orgasms

We must learn to love ourselves completely. There is nothing better than being in love with yourself and life all the time- it even feels better than sex. Sometimes a good dry spell can even help us grow spiritually. It may even be a result of karma that we must work with the lack of a sexual partner. Unattended, this can manifest as masturbation as though one were a caged animal. Harnessed, this energy that creates life can most certainly generate sonic booms of joy in your life. The Indian Guru Nithyananda recommends 6 months of celibacy for men and 3 months for women. This gives the body time to adjust from the misappropriation of energy, which is typically discharged through the root chakra, and rather, encourages us to train the energy upward toward the crown. Easier said than done, right? Think about it. From a biological perspective, the body can learn to move this powerful energy of creation in any direction we choose. I will show you how to do this in the pre-recorded enlightenment integration CD. (58)

Society has marketed sex because it's so powerful and feels so good. However, we are prostituting these powers if we only train our bodies to harness the force for a few seconds of orgasm. Imagine, you can 'blow a load' from your root chakra up to your crown. Certainly, we can learn to work those creational forces into the heart and pineal glands where it is able to produce extended periods of orgasmic bliss. We work frantically to ejaculate for that three second taste of bliss. Why not make some time to breathe the orgasmic feeling throughout your entire body?

Iconic author, Napoleon Hill, argues that most highly successful businessmen are also highly sexed. What they've learned to do is harness this sexual fire, aka Kundalini energy, whereby they pick women as muses to energize and focus their creativity. They direct the instinctual procreation energy into their endeavors. The technique, according to Hill, is to stop masturbating and start creating, instead. You can still have sex, he says, but not masturbation, as the body can tell the difference. I practice

Napoleon Hill's technique as well as some ancient breathing exercises like the breath of fire, the wave, and various grounding meditations. I actually prefer going to the gym at peak hours because on an animal level, the sweat and pheromones inspire me. More importantly, however, I'm cultivating a delightful relationship with myself, enjoying my own company, and that makes me self-reliant when it comes to my own happiness. As a healer, I can blast through a tumor effortlessly because I've learned to discharge the energy through my heart and hands rather than just out my vagina. If our orgasms have the power to create the miracle of life, it stands to reason that rerouted energy can produce miracles through the heart, hands and mind.

So, if you love how sex gets you high, you're going to love it when you discover how to harness your Inner G, which is a sustained vibration of ecstasy and joy. To hit the spot, we must cultivate our relationship with 'God'. We all have a different G Spot, or perception of what God is. I'm just saying; the Big G is you- your true Divine Essence, your Guru Within, your fertile ability to create life. You harness it through deep breathing meditation just the same way as you breathe deeply while harnessing the creation of life as you are focused on an orgasm. Think about it. Visualize yourself moving the energy from the sacral chakra pushing up through the heart and crown. The seed of our divinity is God eternal source wisdom within the body. Practice creating supernovas of abundant peace and joy on earth through breathwork next time you're about to cum. Then give thanks for all that is wanted while you are in this least resistant state of allowing and flowing.

Our purpose is to embrace the God within us and to express it in all our deeds and thoughts. Remember, Snoop Dogg was an OG and then he went to Jamaica, got grounded, found his roots and started calling himself Snoop Lion. Imagine if you were to give your star the space to really shine. Every 'mistake' of creation holds the codes for divinity. It's just that the answers lie at the opposite of the misaligned action. We must look to the source. When we get to the root cause of any 'miscreation,' we can harness those electrons to cancel and balance any karmic contracts, to erase and heal, to clarify and stop anything which is not serving the greatest and highest good. All chords, hooks, attachments, genetic defects, karma, disease and curses can be erased from the timeline past/present/ and future. You are that powerful. You can reprogram the bio-energetic memory of your genetics to heal yourself, your family, and every other living being on the planet. We just need to stop jacking off and redirect that energy.

When I go into a deep meditation or visualization, my mind can now produce sustained heights of ecstasy. The feelings of peace are naturally transmitted to anyone in the vicinity. If one should consciously choose to dedicate their joy and share their abundance of love vibrations to all of humanity, during meditation or orgasm, the intention needs only to be set, and it will be so. Dr. David Hawkins, and I'll elaborate on this in a separate lecture, shows us how the paradigm of power and our ability to affect others becomes exponentially more powerful as we raise our consciousness. One enlightened person at the beginning of enlightenment, number 700, has the vibrational power to affect 75,000 others. At level 800, you can influence the energies of 7,500,000 people. When you reach the 900s, you can influence 7.5 billion people. I find this to be very true, as I step up into the 900s from Buddhism's state of Nirvana, which ranks 850 on Dr. Hawkins' scale. The 900s level of consciousness is one where you know and can clearly see how you are creating your reality. You are fully owning your experience. To consciously project healing toward the radiation of Fukushima, or to visualize the banking elite having their hearts filled with love and touched by angels, is truly a service to mankind.

It's really a trip. It's heaven on earth. I remember when I was first able to sustain this joy for extended periods of time. My student truly thought I was faking it. That was at levels 650-750, 600 being the gate of enlightenment, the seat of joy, the beginning of allowing my Higher Self to flow through, where you believe that you are always safe. The light had wrapped me in a blanket of protection so that I could only shine and not be a sponge for his toxicity. At a biological level, my DNA was activated beyond the traditional double helix strand. There are actually twelve helixes creating 6 strands which wrap into a tube shape which is like a big straw for light, or your Higher God Self, to flow through. In this way, we are evolving from carbon base to a crystalline base. Like it says in the Tool song "46 and 2" chromosome upgrade. (Like it says in the Tool song "46 and 2" chromosome upgrade.)

Please stop for a moment. Try to imagine how infinitely more powerful you could be if you only harnessed your energies in a more productive manner. At some point, your imagination finds a limitation to fixate on because it can't imagine the miracles God has in store for you. That is called arguing for our limitations. Flip the switch and turn down the volume of the excuse-making disempowering devil on your shoulder. Turn up the volume on that quiet little consciousness that whispers 'You can be so much more.' Have faith, and make space for miracles, flow, love, joy, peace, and abundance beyond your wildest imagination. Let your faith roar so loud that you can't hear what the doubt is saying. You deserve it. Even if there are dark spaces inside that still don't believe you deserve it, keep feeding it the light to dissolve it.

Exercise:

Try this. Take a few minutes right now to connect your mind with someone you love and have a good relationship with. Call them tomorrow and see if they were thinking about you around the same time. See if they could feel you. Watch as you start connecting automatically in the physical. I say to people all the time, 'Oh you must have heard me thinking about you.' It happens to me regularly. Observe and give thanks for it. As Abraham Hicks says, 'Ask and it is given.' GIVE THANKS FOR THAT. Law of attraction dictates that you'll become more and more powerful the more convinced you become of your power. Just practice. Do that now. Now, in all honesty, this ability to know when someone's about to call, or attracting perfect timing for calls, and even knowing who is calling me as they are dialing- that all began after I tripped really hard on Ketamine for the first time. Saint Kitty Meow Meow, we would say half-jokingly. I'll save those stories for a different place, but essentially, my point is, though I don't go using hallucinogens all the time, I really do get a lot out of them when I do.

How do you know when it's time to switch shores, jump ship, bail, or shift gears? The hardest decision in life sometimes can be knowing when to stop versus to keep going. I suggest not to focus on all the logical observable facts. Rather, instead, listen to what your heart says, even if it's a whisper compared to your mind's logic. Decide what you want, what you are NOW willing to do. Ask yourself, 'Is this really fulfilling my passion? Am I in love as I think about this? How can I feel in love about this?' Regardless of what decision you make, logic will fill in the empty space with reasonable evidence and facts to support your decision. This is true whether it's a resistant pain-causing decision or an allowing pain-relieving decision.

Shoot, I had to experience homelessness for several uncomfortable months before I would stop digging in my heels and could humble myself to accept help from others, especially Source or 'God', whatever that Truly meant. I had to get on my knees and surrender, open up completely, and allow God and his crew to move in. I didn't know how to trust that Source was always going to provide for my needs. I had no other choice but to surrender my will. I didn't know how to trust Source or anybody else. But I was stuck, and had no choice. It took mere hours for God to come through like gangbusters.

One day, I read something that said women are strong. Women who realize this are even stronger. But the strongest women allow themselves to receive help. Thus, they have plenty of strength to give. I allow myself to be given every gift or act of kindness. I allow others the joy of sharing. A beautiful Goddess nutritionist said to me that she now enjoys the food so much more when sharing because she knows another is about to absorb the love offering she has joyfully created from her Inner G. In this way, she raises the vibration of the food, thereby fomenting healing to all who enjoy her nutritious creations. Imagine that kind of high vibe service at your wedding.

She also reminded me to smile through yoga. I make my patients smile throughout a healing. It's a technique taught in Buddhism and reiterated by my mentor Wolfgang Arndt. (59) The energies flow into a smiling heart, and fortunately, we

CAN fake it 'till will make it. In this way, we are practicing the vibration of joy which attracts more joy.

Exercise:

You are now invited to practice the vibration of gratitude. Smile. Look around and find some reasons to be thankful. Now, claim your inheritance of wellbeing. Call it into you. Own it. Trust that you are a powerful abundance magnet. Decide in this moment to attract abundance beyond your wildest imagination. Surrender each naysayer thought, sweeping it out of your mind's reality one by one. Commit to do the preparation needed in order to handle that much wealth and beauty in all its forms. Take some deep breaths inhaling abundance and exhaling scarcity consciousness. Let that dissipate into nature somewhere for recycling. Know that you are powerful. If you need support, I've got a number of guided meditations available. You can also schedule a private session and I'll record a personalized meditation specific for you to work out on.

Chapter 11:

TRUST

Faith is the same as trust. Law of attraction states that if you trust bad things will happen, then you'll surely attract more bad things. To fully understand this concept, however, requires first a level of courage and integrity where we are willing to realize, 'Hey I make mistakes. How can I do better?' The problem with accessing this higher level of consciousness is that one has to make a distinct choice. Determining to accept that you may be mistaken somehow requires humility. Humility is necessary for trust or faith. Often, pride stops us from being flexible, which leads to suffering, which leads to desperation in which one can only surrender to a higher power for support. How many times must you fail, suffer, and flounder around before deciding to always ask, 'How can I do better? What's the highest truth in this situation?' What would love do?

Most people don't know what pure love is. Many people believe love is suffering. It isn't; that's just co-mingled with mistakenness. Most people know all about hate, suffering and attack, though, so they project these qualities into their experience of love, therefore muddling the vibration. It is this practice of hating, constantly reassuring themselves that they are right, which is such a huge issue to be worked out on. The solution? True Love bombs. Each time someone trespasses against us is an opportunity to practice loving forgiveness and non-attachment.

In my first energetic healings with shaman Jason Kerr, he said to me, 'Before one can become very invasive, he had to have been very invaded.' That was certainly the case for me. What healed me? The patience of higher consciousness choosing to demonstrate unconditional love healed me. The gentle discipline of trusting in the goodness of others healed me, appealing to the highest aspects of who they are and can become- the chosen belief that the Universe is always supporting me. I chose to believe in this and allowed time to prove me right. That's abiding faith. Look at how people live today with video cameras everywhere. They watch TV buying into fear/ scarcity/ lack and attack. They are slaves to the fear. They believe in a painful world of suffering because that's what the news always portrays with its fear agenda. And I simply ask you, 'Do you like how that feels? You are free to choose a happy reality. It requires reprogramming. The only thing you'll lose is the suffering.' You see, the reason TV tries to keep us in fear is because we can't access higher frequencies as easily when fear and doubt are present. So it's a distinct choice to ignore the fear and doubt.

The next area to be addressed in this case is the attachment to things, objects, beliefs and identification that this 3D reality is all that exists. For this, I humbly suggest hallucinogens as a quick way to snap people out of believing that this matrix is the be-all-end-all reality. Sometimes, there is a secret 'YES I like attacking. I get off on suffering.' The addicted drama queen feeds off the adrenaline like a junkie 'chasing the dragon'. Have you ever started a fight and felt your pupils dilate from the rush like a savage animal? Ever notice how your body gets off to watching horror, drama, scandal or a fight? That's our reptilian brain, our animal instincts which we are evolving away from to become our highest ascended selves.

I, Ram Dass, Terrence McKenna, and a huge host of others owe our higher consciousness to the responsible use of hallucinogens. It's like breaking the Berlin Wall of resistant belief. Desperate to feel better, to understand my world more, I began chasing the love high discovered while under the influence of these medicines. I heard it said that the body can reproduce any emotion or feeling discovered under the influence on its own. So I tried to recreate that amazing love juice in every situation. I had a memory of what unconditional love felt like from the drugs, and began meditating on how to access those feelings while sober. The trick is non-attachment. Attachment feels bad. Another way of saying 'bad' is to say instead, 'unwanted.' Make it less resistant or judgmental. What are you attached to? How do you know you're attached? The thought of not having it/them causes suffering. What external sources of happiness are you depending on? Whenever you're ready to let that go, remember that love will help you by filling in the space. Self-love will save you. Meditating on filling your body with God's love can replace any external stimuli. Resistance is futile as the universe supports creative expansion. Attachment constricts that expansion. Remember, what we resist persists, and that causes suffering. What we accept, in love, transmutes to a higher level of awareness which of course feels better. Do what feels better. Release yourself of the resistant beliefs, people, and things that no longer serve your new determination to love thyself first.

So stubborn, determined, resistant girl that I was, it took some serious divine intervention from the University of Life to show me self-love. Thankfully, enrollment is free, but sometimes tuition is hell to pay. Especially if we're not paying attention, aka awareness. The quicker we can get on board with learning and working through the lessons, the easier and faster we'll move on to graduation. We'll know we've graduated with our proverbial 'associates degree' when we feel loving. Love on the scale is 500. So, the fastest way to get there is to ask, 'What would love do?' and act accordingly.

Now, try feeling loving all the time regardless of the circumstance and especially in the face of resistance. A 'bachelor's degree' is when we cultivate unconditional love for everyone all the time (level 540 on The Scale). The master's degree is when we feel peace and harmony (level 600). We stop asking God 'How?' and listen to the heart's subtle signals for the answer. We trust, with abiding faith, that God is handling everything. This is the gate to enlightenment. The Ph.D. is when we are allowing our highest passions, aka purpose, to flow through us as a channel (level 700-849). Then there's double Ph.D.'s when circumstances don't bother you (level 850-899). It's a deep, core, acceptance of what is combined with the realization that all is by design. All is supporting our expansion. The ultimate human mastery is seeing how you are the creator of EVERY situation in your life (level 900s). You see how every unwanted situation lead to a realization that brought you closer to your highest desire or purpose.

Remember, we may have felt these distinct vibrations a lot and worked with them a lot, enough to earn the title of 'sage', but it is easy to slip back into old habits. That's why enlightenment is a decision to practice listening to the power of your heart. Like they say in Alcoholics Anonymous, take it day by day, and forgive yourself quickly.

A documentary I highly recommend for help visualizing these quantum and metaphysical principles is called Thrive: What On Earth Will It Take? (60) You can watch it for free.

Non-attachment

How did I become reduced to homelessness? I needed to be humbled. I needed to be stripped of my attachments. My life needed to be reduced to the point where I only had God to carry me through so that I could learn to trust that it is always safe. I needed danger and fear to cause enough suffering that I would surrender to God to see It's majesty- to see that It was greater than me. I had to learn to waste not want not. This taught me mindfulness. One learns to get closer to the earth, to appreciate all that is. One learns that the Mother Earth always provides. Our planet's natural state is abundant. We have fruit everywhere in Panama. We only have to learn to work in harmony with earth to get off the cash system. Right now, earth is evolving.

She's a reflection of all the changes happening within us, and vice versa.

We must learn to go with nature's flow, the seasons of abundant times and thin, the changing of tides and astro-physical shifts. I experience a constant evaluation of how much rest is too much, how much work is enough, and what kind of planning will produce desired results. As I grow, I just stress about it less and less because I've learned to trust. I've evaluated what is my highest purpose, in alignment with God's desire for my evolution. I trust that all outcomes are leading me along that path, because I've firmly set my intention to be guided. I daily practice reminding myself of those higher ideals. So, it's easier to let go of attachment to outcomes because I trust that all things are working out. All things are perfectly designed for me to grow in awareness and capability. The simple answer is just to relax and do what you want to do while keeping your eye on the prize.

Going with the flow as a resistant Type-A business-woman was especially paradoxical. I finally realized that if I'm following my bliss, I'm following my purpose. If I'm really allowing myself to be in the vortex of abundance, and letting the day turn out more magical than I can even imagine, then Source is going to write the story far better than I could, which is far more delightful. It will be done on Source's timeline. Learning to trust and obey God's timeline over my own still takes practice. Our job is to get up, dress up, show up, and go with the flow. Be present for life and then go with the impulses that come from the heart and not the mind. Luck is the combination of preparation meets opportunity. Learning to trust the goodness of God flowing through my life and realize that there will be lots of opportunity still takes practice, for me. I need to work out the fragments of trauma still carried from childhood that don't allow love into its reality.

The gestation period for my career is going slower than I would have imagined. That's because I'd stopped most of my daily practices of enlightenment. I stopped meditating and started acting like a regular American again. I wasn't filling up on my Inner G which propels me toward my highest bliss. I'm pretty impatient. I'm attached to instant reward. Subconsciously, I'm attached to the idea that I'm entitled to have anything I want because I've been so deeply wounded. My ego thinks God owes me. This resistant disbelief creates all kinds of miscreation. It's most evident in my driving. I tend to think everyone should get out of my way, when it's really me who isn't going with the flow. So, I started using driving as an enlightenment practice. I put a sticker on my steering wheel that reminds me to be patient. "I deserve greatness" should be reframed to "I allow greatness". Can you see the subtle yet powerful difference?

I want Christmas every day yet I keep kicking and screaming like Veruca Salt. I attribute the velocity as being directly proportionate to my focused desire and the amount of abundance that I can responsibly handle at any given time. But obviously my ego is mistaken because if I were truly being responsible for that abundance, I would practice responsibly embodying those higher ideals with more diligence. It doesn't seem to matter how hard one is willing to work if one is not allowing, if one is coming from a place of lack within their hearts. A person can work very hard at cultivating something in the wrong way and bear no fruit. I guess that's where fate comes in. We have to wait for all the proper causes and conditions to form in order for the puzzle pieces to fall into place. God is being patient with us, so we should practice being patient with God. And then, we must be present to win. Remember, there is no manifestation without action. Get up, dress up, show up, and go with the flow.

As we learn to cultivate the guru within, it's a lot like cultivating a garden. When you plant an apple tree, you don't expect it to bear fruit the next day. But you keep an expectation of a positive result. The trick is listening to God, to love, to your heart and nature's subtle cues. So there must be a conditioned willingness to listen to your heart more than your ego mind's logic because it just can't calculate the outcomes at God's level. This is a daily practice of tuning into your heart. Our job is to follow the impulse and ride the waves. We give up our attachment to the expectation of a bad result in favor of trusting higher power. The more we relax into this truth, the more tuned in we will be so that when an impulse arises, when our gut instincts kick in, we'll just know that we're supposed to jump up and fertilize the lawn, or mow the grass or whatever chore intuition is guiding your attention towards. For example, my guides told me to finish this book before the end of the year. My intuition started really guiding me back to this at the beginning of the year. I had put myself in a living situation that became limiting. As I continued to allow myself to expand, it became a nagging feeling to work on the book. So, I micro dosed some mushrooms, which released resistance, and here we are.

I just love knowing that every time I clear something logically or energetically, that it is logged in the subconscious of the Universal Conscious mind. There have been a number of tests to prove that as one group becomes aware of particular facts, that the intuition of seemingly unrelated other people is also increased, thereby making it easier for people to learn. This is to say that, as you and I practice enlightenment, we are holding a supportive frequency, a beacon of light, which magnetizes the subconscious of other humans. This makes it easier to 'convince' people of the truth because the truth is already magnified inside of them, no longer dormant. They feel the resonance of the highest truth more easily. The desire to know one's true self is innate. People will listen to you talk about the recent planetary alignments' effect on your moods, sleep, and relationships because we can all relate. That is my hope by writing this tell-all style book. I want you to know that enlightenment is not just for celibate bald monks in the Himalayas anymore. The face of enlightenment is changing to look just like you do with all of your painful backstory and years of suffering. We are reaching a time where everyone can be transformed a little easier thanks to every individual decision to end suffering.

If you are attached to your story, to your history of pain and suffering, to the limiting belief that you're only human, that you are what you've always been, then, well, you're probably not reading this book. If you know someone like that, try getting them a copy as a gift. Angel, you are so much more than you've allowed yourself to believe in the past. Trade those limiting beliefs in for a shinier set of possibilities. Realize that a lot of your old beliefs will break down, and it might make you feel bipolar or even multiple personalities. Just keep committing yourself to being more than you've ever been and you will become more than you can imagine.

Getting started on the path to enlightenment

I began on this path in 1997 when my Mom had a stroke. I felt like my Super Man was suddenly paralyzed. My external source of security was destroyed. I had to find security now. But where? Migrating from the Disciples of Christ (Christianity), to Buddhism, the I-Ching, metaphysics and quantum physics, to the Hindu religions and you name it; I've found that the seed of Truth in spirituality exists everywhere we are willing to look. There goes that concept again- FREE WILL. Seek and ye shall find. Basic law of attraction. That's why there are so many versions/ understandings of God. We are all having a personally contextual experience with the guru within, mingling with the mind, depending on the various cultural heritages and family traditions. There is a grain of truth in all of it as well as a pile of mistaken ego illusions to boot. It all depends on what vibrational frequency you are operating within at the moment. Your view of God depends on your level of consciousness.

It's kind of like how you can never hear a song the same way twice. You can focus on different elements of the tune in different ways depending on a world of varied perspectives or focal points. What you gain from hearing the song the first time causes you to observe it differently the second time and so on. So, this work of enlightenment, and observation, of reevaluating beliefs and ways of doing things will constantly be in revue as we seek the highest feeling feeling. It took me from 1998 until 2012 to reevaluate my thoughts enough to reach enlightenment. But now, we have such easy access through the internet and the Universal Consciousness, that it can be achieved much quicker. No two persons' logical and emotional perspectives can be the same because we process our observations in so many different ways. Enlightenment is a physiological/ mental/ spiritual decision to deal with what is perceived in a graceful non-suffering way, a way that is full of peace for as many parties as desire peace.

Perception is only reality in the eye of the beholder. When we know that what is right for one person is likely not true for another person, simply because they cannot share our same emotional and logical perspective, then it becomes easier to be less indignant or stubborn with our demands of others. So, study it all and see what resonates with you. As long as one is not completely possessed by ego, our internal guru will be able to tell truth from non-truth. Remember, spirituality is a personal practice on a deep individual level. It's like the Buddha said: "Believe nothing, no matter where you read it or who has said it, not even if I have said it, unless it agrees with your own reason and your own common sense." In this way, we cultivate the divine seed within. Nourish it with education. Apply critical feeling, using your body as a truth monitor. Seek refuge in good books. Observe the tension or relaxation that any particular experience brings. Process and release whatever comes up. This is how we become familiar with what tickles our G spot and remain open to newly expanded ideas. If you haven't yet had a deeply spiritual experience, or if it has been awhile, we invite you to consider attending a surrender ceremony. (61) Your Super G might be in a different spot than someone you love; learn to let that be okay. Cultivate your own garden. Don't worry if people disagree. If you trust, you can. There is plenty for everyone. If you are open, you'll get the healing you need. Open your heart to these truths.

"All things are possible for those who believe all things are possible."

— *Wu Wei, The I-Ching Handbook*

Chapter 12:

THE MAP OF HUMAN CONSCIOUSNESS

I resolved that my suffering would not be in vain, that my hard won lessons would not be lost in the abyss of time. Once, when I was 14 at church camp, I saw that this wisdom and compassion I'd gleaned from living through multiple divorces, childhood depression and a suicide attempt helped relieve the suffering of another little girl. For the first time, my pain felt like it had served a purpose. I was able to have deep compassion for the suffering of others. The power of that compassion and empathy has grown into super energetic hugs and smiles now that the Masters and I have erased the bio-energetic memory of those traumas. Light just radiates from my being.

Without money as power, I learned how not to view my power based on my bank account balance. By sharing the same economic status as people with no similar educational background as me, I learned how to view no one as special, just everyone is beautiful. My heart was opened as I saw that it is always safe to trust God completely. To find my next meal, I had to rely on divine intervention, following my intuition, keeping my word or being consistent. Seeing the impact I was having on these kids and they were having on me, the firm dedication was made to be a servant. Deciding to use the power responsibly to do whatever it takes to be a good instrument, I opened my heart one day inside a cathedral and reached the first levels of enlightenment (peace). It was the moment that I allowed myself to believe that I was safe, loved, and protected. I felt this way because I'd agreed to flow. I'd agreed to give back what I was being given.

Over the course of several months, I was delivered to levels that avatars like Jesus and Buddha are known for. Maybe you've never enjoyed the experience of receiving unconditional love from a stranger. I can tell you there is something magical in helping someone who can never repay you. Try it. The happiest people are those who volunteer and give gifts. Sharing really is a great way to practice the abundance mindset. When we know that there will always be more, we are free from attachment, able to share the magical gift of plenty. We may not go to church anymore or tithe 10%, but in so many ways it's a beneficial practice. My guides told me that 20% is right for me to share.

Love is the weapon of the future.

Love can be transmitted throughout all worlds, times, spaces and dimensions. Love is light. Where there is light, there cannot be darkness. Love is infinitely more powerful than hate. Hate is the absence of light. Do you want to end conflict? Wave a white flag within and cultivate more self-love, acceptance, tolerance for your flawsomeness and forgiveness of self. Once you've infused the light back into your own darkness, you'll stop seeing darkness everywhere.

Let Us Understand
Dr. Hawkins' Scale of Consciousness

Observe how people act when they are stuck in a particular paradigm of consciousness.

The 500s

A magical thing happens when we compassionately begin sharing our knowledge and engaging in interesting discussions. We can think of it like Blue-ray technology. 'Convincing' others becomes so much easier because the light and truth within is open to receiving. Truth resonates. Subconscious memory is activated. The seed of divinity within wants to remember more, believes that it can, and trusts that more good things are coming. As momentum builds, the subconscious appreciates the nourishing divine truth as fuel for further growth, which helps resolve divisive thoughts. Our soul's true essence is reflected to us as Source Wisdom shares its knowingness, compassion and benevolence. This is the power of true love. Life becomes easier to deal with. We flow through situations with more grace, less resistance, more accepting of what is, and more faith that we CAN have exactly what we want. We feel satisfied for the first time. Our hearts smile, and hopefully, now awake

THE MAP OF HUMAN CONSCIOUSNESS

Clinically Proven "MAP OF CONSCIOUSNESS"

View on God	View on Life	Level Name	Level #	Emotions	Process
Self	Is	Enlightenment	700-1000	Ineffable	Pure Consciousness
All-Being	Perfect	Peace	600	Bliss	Illumination
One	Complete	*Spontaneous Healing* Joy	540	Serenity	Transfiguration
Loving	Benign	Love	500	Reverence	Revelation
Wise	Meaningful	Reason	400	Understanding	Abstraction
Merciful	Harmonious	Acceptance	350	Forgiveness	Transcendence
Inspiring	Hopeful	Willingness	310	Optimism	Intention
Enabling	Satisfactory	Neutrality	250	Trust	Release
Permitting	Feasible	Courage	200	Affirmation	Empowerment

POWER ↑ **STRONG** — CREATIVE

Levels at or above 200 have Truth, Integrity and support life.

Levels below 200 are False, Lack of Integrity, do not support life. — DESTRUCTIVE

View on God	View on Life	Level Name	Level #	Emotions	Process
Indifferent	Demanding	Pride	175	Scorn	Inflation
Vengeful	Antagonistic	Anger	150	Hate	Aggression
Denying	Disappointing	Desire	125	Craving	Enslavement
Punitive	Frightening	Fear	100	Anxiety	Withdrawl
Disdainful	Tragic	Grief	75	Regret	Despondence
Condemning	Hopeless	Apathy	50	Despair	Abdication
Vindictive	Evil	Guilt	30	Blame	Destruction
Despising	Miserable	Shame	20	Humiliation	Elimination

FORCE ↓ **WEAK**

POWER is self-sustaining, permanent, stationary, and invcible.
FORCE is temporary, consumes energy, and moves from location to location.

Logarithmic Energy Field Increases: 1=1: 2=10: 3=100: 4=1,000: 5=10,000 6=100,000....etc

All levels below 500 are "objective" and all levels from 500 to 1,000 are "subjective".

Enlightenment Integration Workshops

www.carinacarinosastore.guru

info@carinacarinosastore.guru

512-539-2952

FREE HUGS
United in Love
The Carina Cariñosa Foundation
512-539-2952

Copyright © 2019 · The Carina Cariñosa Foundation

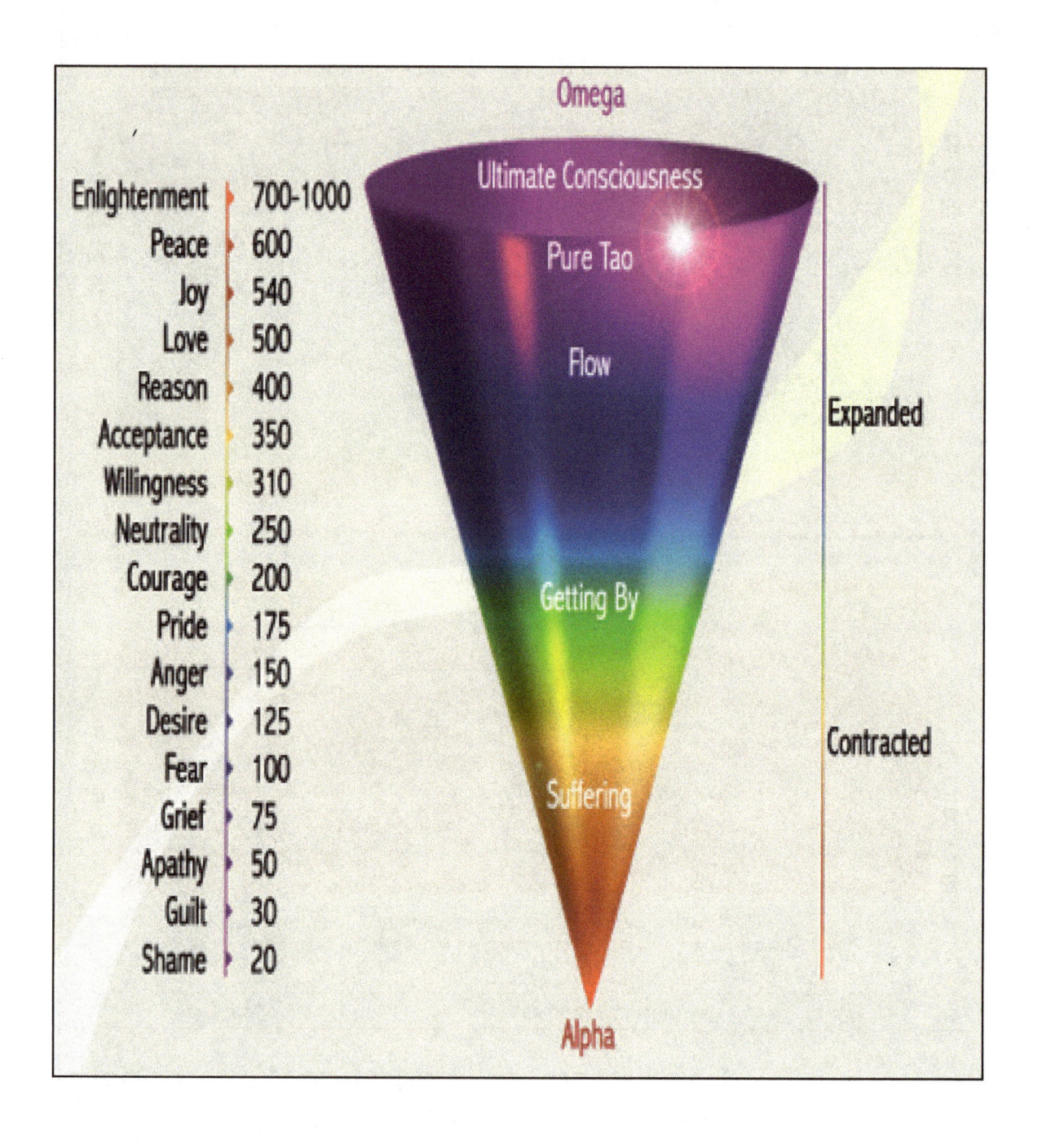

Enlightenment	▸	700-1000
Peace	▸	600
Joy	▸	540
Love	▸	500
Reason	▸	400
Acceptance	▸	350
Willingness	▸	310
Neutrality	▸	250
Courage	▸	200
Pride	▸	175
Anger	▸	150
Desire	▸	125
Fear	▸	100
Grief	▸	75
Apathy	▸	50
Guilt	▸	30
Shame	▸	20

Omega

Ultimate Consciousness

Pure Tao

Flow

Expanded

Getting By

Contracted

Suffering

Alpha

and hungry for more truth, we decide to further develop the connection.

However, most people stop evolving once they've reached the level of love (500 on the Scale of Human Consciousness). Many people taste the power of loving consciousness only a few times in their lives because they do not believe they can achieve it 100% of the time. They let their minds stay in control instead of shutting up and listening to the heart. They are too vested in the mind-controlled reality that society perpetuates to allow for the heart to reign supreme. Perfect love challenges the socially divisive constructs we've bought into for so many years. The majority do not want to put in the work. There are too many distractions; so many excuses to keep turning focus outwards. We'd rather blame than take responsibility. We'd rather believe 'I'm only human' rather than reclaim our divinity. People have become over invested in the matrix of material things and routines. To realize that you have invested so much energy into something that wasn't in alignment with the love or peace that is felt in the 500s can be like a major earthquake. Friends and drinking buddies don't resonate anymore. We can become repulsed by the system, by the people around us, and even repulsed with ourselves for living in such amnesia. How can one forgive themselves and the rest of the world for so much failure to love? We must cultivate the will to stop suffering. Decide not to suffer. Realize that suffering is a sign of immaturity. Allowing ourselves to suffer is simply a lack of self-love. Resolve to love yourself no matter what.

Of course, it is a daunting task to say, "God, I release my attachments to all of this material world for a bounty of perfect love in my heart. I trust you to lay the path before me. Make me an instrument. Thy will be done and only thy will." We're worried that means we have to become paupers to live in the glory. We mistakenly think giving up attachment for objects means having no more objects. That's just not true because Source is abundant. However, you may need to release those attachments to worldly objects so that Source can guide you toward your highest bliss. What we're asked to do is not covet objects more than we covet a connection with God. We mistakenly believe that God's will for us is different than our will for ourselves. We don't trust the power of our hearts' desire. We still view ourselves as separate from God. Part of our will is still operating from a place of fear, in the mind. At this level, we still see God as separate from us because we haven't yet learned to let God flow through us more completely. We're acclimated to having all energy flow through the mind, from outside sources instead of breathing in God through the heart.

The 600s

A complete surrender to God is the gate of enlightenment or the 600's on The Scale. (62) At this level, 600s, we feel peace because we can now feel the safety and protection that Source and ourselves Will for us. When you commit to embodying your highest will, that IS God's will. So, the next phase toward enlightenment is to commit to becoming your highest ascended self. That commitment is the bridge between reclaiming your power as a divine human being and allowing the divine powers of God to flow through you. To stay at such a level of mind requires practice. We must practice relinquishing resistance in exchange for God's grace. This will cause non-serving habits to fall by the wayside. You enjoy your own company and the presence of celestial harmony more than you crave the dramas constantly perpetuated by those trapped in the more resistant paradigms. They can't imagine what you now know. And so it is, that one retreats to the God eternal within the body, seeking refuge in good books and attracted strongly to enlightened company.

Chapter 13:

PEACE VS. PRIDE

Upon further examination, we can clearly understand that someone who is thinking in the paradigm of pride does not think the same as someone who sees the world through the perception of peace. Pride is a very resistant and closed consciousness. Peace is a very open and allowing consciousness. Unless the prideful person has experienced peace before, he cannot fathom thoughts of unconditional love, harmony, and safety. It is out of his world of possibility. It is too far of a vibrational leap to comprehend or access. The primary difference between these two thought patterns is that the prideful person attempts to control in response to external stimuli. The peace-feeling person lets go of trying to control in favor of allowing help from his Higher 5th dimensional Self and guides.

Protecting yourself from resistant people

For protection, the peaceful person's strategy, then, is to beam thoughts of love, harmony, light and peace onto the prideful person. The enlightened person calls upon help from guides and other higher-dimensional beings for assistance. He does so 1) to dissolve the virus' power 2) thereby creating a protective bubble in which 3) he will attempt to relieve the suffering of his neighbor through the expansion of love and light in that direction.

A further enlightened being, in the realms of pure consciousness from 700-1000 will have the power to instantly forgive the prideful thinker, which automatically creates a shield of protection because it is so infused with light that the darkness or resistance cannot exist. Unless of course, the resistant individual touches a nerve that is yet to be healed in the enlightened person. In this case, the enlightened being realizes he must clean that stain within himself. For this reason, the contrast arose. He immediately takes responsibility for creating the situation and resolves to learn his lesson. The longer it takes him to resolve, the deeper the karmic stain, the more profound the resistance is throughout the person's chakra system, the more enlightenment needs to be practiced.

For self-preservation, it is important not to press our view upon individuals below the level of courage and integrity, no matter how badly we want them to think less resistantly. This is known as blasphemy. If we press our views onto others, we are negating their free will, which is not benevolent, it's 'righteous ego'. It's like firing random bullets into a dog kennel. The disturbance would cause all the dogs to bark, therefore causing more suffering and unwanted consequences/ karma. The proper tactic is to pray over them. Ask for a team of volunteer angels and guardians to watch over them. Release your attachment to the outcome. Trust that the light you are commanding for them will penetrate the darkness in God's good time.

Once, after being attacked and falsely accused of something from my former sister-in-law, I realized, "She does NOT understand my point of view. She can't possibly fathom that I think a different way than she does. She thinks everyone is as critical as she is, so she plots and lies to protect herself from all of her imagined divisive projections. She honestly believes everyone else is the bad guy and plays the innocent victim who absolutely has to lie for survival." Telling the truth would have literally killed her, or rather, her ego's illusions to which she was inseparably identified and attached. This is a classic thought process of projection for those below the critical level of 200 on Dr. Hawkins' Scale of Consciousness. Mind you, I was not so high on the scale at the time either. However, I had experienced less resistant thinking and was much more Self-aware. I was willing to take responsibility for my thoughts, actions, and experiences. I was willing to trust in something greater than myself.

Critical Mass

Remember the process of critical mass. As we transmute fear and have the courage to ask for what is wanted, we are gaining more and more momentum toward enlightenment. The nervous system relaxes and prepares to fully integrate the Higher Self more into the physical body. This is the point where we must say, "Thy will be done and only thy will." Whose will? Your highest self as a Christed consciousness. Picture this person now. S/he loves you unconditionally, knows everything about you, and is your best friend. What does s/he look like in their most perfect form? You just gotta listen and remember to talk to your best friend for guidance! In an instant, our High Selves can resolve fears on all levels, regarding any subject, and thus allow more of our Higher Power to shine through us, until there is no more mental separation between us and God. We become fully integrated like Jesus and Buddha.

Activations & Protocols

A series of activations and protocols is usually necessary as there are a lot of biological changes that must happen in order to constantly hold this much energy. I personally have done all kinds of YouTube videos that have seriously moved some energies. One time, I was sitting poolside listening to an activation. Thank God no one was around. In this 30-minute activation, I peed, puked, sneezed, cried, and nearly pooped my bathing suit. Talk about removing some blockages! The video is available in my enlightenment newsletter.

The most important lesson

If I can impart only one message of encouragement to you, let it be that we are all unconditionally and infinitely loved. Anyone who ever told us differently was mistaken. God has no human qualities of vengeance. Mother Nature doesn't get jealous. Karma isn't a matter of favoritism. It's a universal law. Therefore, who am I to judge where you are right now on your path?

Our job is just to remember that everything is divine and learn how to get out of our own way. When we learn to stop beating ourselves up, or holding ourselves down based on the false outdated guilting, blaming, or shaming of our subconscious programming we can be healed because wellness is a more pervasive natural state. Even if you temporarily forget, it is always safe to come home and rest in the infinite power of Creator. There IS a safety net. It IS safe to fall. There WILL be an angel there to catch you. The sooner you believe enough to ask for help, the less you fall because you will be allowing more help from your super guides. Less suffering is good, yes?

It is safe to be vulnerable. In fact, when we have completely given up all of our defenses, that's when we are the strongest. We are so desirous for things to go right that we surrender into allowing ourselves to be carried downstream toward exactly what is within our souls' highest good to experience. You can trust that your soul wants to experience peace and joy. Don't give up; give it to the masters. Surrender your doubts and fears. It's so much easier to let Source work it's magic than to try and do it alone. Let go and let God. Now, practice patience/ abiding faith/ trust that it is all coming together perfectly as it should. It is easier to allow than to create. Allow Source to create for you. After all, it's listening to your heart's desires.

Chapter 14:

BECOMING YOUR HIGHER SELF

Give yourself time to contemplate

Meditate

Visualize who you want to become

Listen to your inner dialogue

Write down the negative and resistant thoughts that you hear playing over and over in your mind or subconscious so you can get them out of your head.

Pivot those thoughts, by offering least resistant opposite thoughts.

Reflect upon the mistakes of your past

Resolve to do differently moving forward

Pray to God and your higher self for assistance to make these changes.

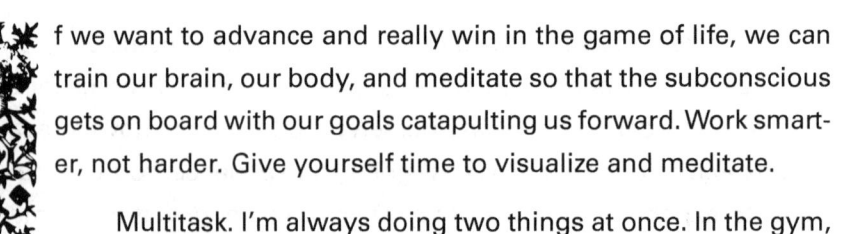

If we want to advance and really win in the game of life, we can train our brain, our body, and meditate so that the subconscious gets on board with our goals catapulting us forward. Work smarter, not harder. Give yourself time to visualize and meditate.

Multitask. I'm always doing two things at once. In the gym, I'm singing. While cleaning, I'm doing vocal exercises. While winding down for sleep, I'm praying and giving thanks. While having sex, I'm channeling kundalini energy through my chakras and attracting money into my bank account through visualizations. I'm relaxing on the couch while delegating authority to employees in the Philippines. They are working while I'm sleeping. I cook once or twice a week, making big bodacious humus packaging it for later, or a huge salad to eat for 2 days, or making a hellacious smoothie bomb to last the whole morning. While massaging a client, I'm doing reiki.

When I let it all go and am ONLY with myself, the third eye opens and I see a circular ring vibrating up into the ether. In the car driving long distance, I'm rehearsing learning songs. When I hear a song I like, I'm on my phone looking up the lyrics to download and practice later. When I'm leading myself in a guided meditation, I'm recording it for you, as well. I can do so much more, with more ease and grace, now that I've taken the time to ring out my personal sponge of all that old painful crap. My DNA is activated and online. In order to give myself the space to focus on radical self-care, I moved to the country in Panama in order to lower my overhead costs. Being in the country helped curb spending on outside stimulants, forcing me to go within. Try living without a computer for a while, expand your horizons. My chi (vibrational frequency) is so high now that I am constantly experiencing technical difficulty. Eventually, I learned to accept it, and take it as a sign to go do something else. The 'procrastination' experienced, gives me a stronger deadline, so I actually get more focused on the task and get it completed quicker. This gives me more time to enjoy my own company and work on my other goals.

Give yourself the space to make the upgrade. Going through the process of enlightenment and setting up the perfect life for yourself requires lots of rest. Trust me, I get more done, more efficiently, with higher quality and consciousness when I give myself the space to rest. If I'm honoring my body's health requirements, and listening to my intuition, then I end up saving myself a lot of time and money. I can work in 1 hour what might take an employee 3 days to do because when the timing is right, everything lines up, and I just follow and flow into the feeling place with ease and grace. Intuition guides and the heavens open up over whatever you're doing because multiple dimensions of intention are bringing things together FOR you.

Remember, there is no manifestation without action.

According to Abraham-Hicks, the formula is to:

Ask for what is wanted

Surrender knowing it is coming

Keep on moving forward in faith.

If you're going to orchestrate an incredible life and future for yourself, remember that, as the Beastie Boys said, 'Every thought in the mind is a planted seed.' Since all things come from thoughts, it is best to give yourself time to cultivate detailed allowing thoughts of abundance and wellness. Practice being specific, generating the good feeling of having or accomplishing what you want. Then, practice being general with the thoughts and feelings surrounding what you want to create. Just generate the good feelings you want to experience around your goals. Just hold the good feeling and open your energy to receive abundance beyond what your mind can imagine. Remember, you are a magnetic frequency that attracts what you hold in mind and heart.

I used to not be able to follow my intuition's own good advice. It's pretty common that we know we should do this or that, but we dig in our heels and just don't. We hold ourselves back by not holding ourselves accountable. Rather, the ego personality makes excuses. Please understand, you are not your personality. You are an eternally divine being of light. You just forget and let the personality take over. You can break that cycle gracefully by relaxing into this truth through meditation. In my upgrade process, I was renting an apartment for $350 in Panama City's historic district of Casco Viejo where there are many non-profit clubs. When I first moved back to the city, within 24 hours of arriving, I managed to manifest a great job paying $2k per month. $2k in Panama was great money, and about 30% more than what the best bilingual Panamanians were making at the time. Thanks Source! I would spend all of my spare time singing and looking up YouTube videos for DNA activations. I just laid in bed and slept a lot while my body changed from carbon to crystalline based. I'd go dancing to move the energies so my body could regenerate a new, freer me. It totally worked.

Now, granted, this was a fairly volatile time for me mentally, because as an empath, I could really feel other people's energies. The area was full of poverty consciousness. But the excitement of discovering that I could read my friends' minds, and the unrelenting KNOWING when a particular person was about to call, experiencing that heightened ESP is addictive. Then add to that seeing synchronistic numbers as a guide whenever I was 'in limbo' or rather, in surrender waiting for God to work his magic. That was/is like heaven saying 'I'm with you. Hang tight.' Seriously, seeing the numbers when I felt tossed by the winds was one of the few things that kept me from losing my mind.

The consciousness of my beliefs was rising, so a lot of beliefs had to be reevaluated. This caused several bipolar symptoms, because I'd think a resistant negative thought, and sit there working on pivoting the thought or trauma to the highest truth and love. I'd cry hard about once a week. Or, on some days, I'd just cry out a whole series of unresolved issues.

But this time, I could tell the pain of the past wasn't going to come back. I was erasing it from my bioenergetic memory. YouTube videos are great for receiving free healing, gotta love it. Just type in the words: DNA activation, binaural beats, solfeggio healing, sound healing, shamanic healing, Dr. David Hawkins + subject, Abraham-Hicks + subject.

For those who are curious, or who have answers on what specifically the numbers mean, I typically see numbers on the clock like 02:02, 11:11, 10:10, 08:08, 04:04, 03:03, 12:12 like this. During my integration process, it was more like 3:33 and 4:44.

Let's refer back to Dr. David Hawkins' Map of Human Consciousness (63) for a moment.

What was happening during these activations to my physical body was reflected

Map of Consciousness
Developed by David R. Hawkins

The Map of Consciousness is based on a logarithmic scale that spans from 0 to 1000.

Name of Level	Energetic "Frequency"	Associated Emotional State	View of Life
Enlightenment	700–1000	Ineffable	Is
Peace	600	Bliss	Perfect
Joy	540	Serenity	Complete
Love	500	Reverence	Benign
Reason	400	Understanding	Meaningful
Acceptance	350	Forgiveness	Harmonious
Willingness	310	Optimism	Hopeful
Neutrality	250	Trust	Satisfactory
Courage	200	Affirmation	Feasible
Pride	175	Scorn	Demanding
Anger	150	Hate	Antagonistic
Desire	125	Craving	Disappointing
Fear	100	Anxiety	Frightening
Grief	75	Regret	Tragic
Apathy	50	Despair	Hopeless
Guilt	30	Blame	Evil
Shame	20	Humiliation	Miserable

in my mental state- the psychology- the paradigm of my thoughts began to significantly shift. In the chart, you can see that the 300's are the level of comparison. The 400s is a level of understanding. The 200's is the level of courage and integrity where we can see beyond pride and become willing to admit that we make mistakes. Perhaps we become neutral and let go thinking, 'What will be will be.' It's the level where we stop digging in our heals. As my consciousness dropped out of the duality of the double-hemisphere brain, down into the heart, thoughts began to reach into the 500's, the level of love and 540 as unconditional love. My compassion expanded to where I found myself really interested in playing with the little 'poor' children in my neighborhood.

Achieving the 600's, for me, was a time of poverty. Two months later, I lost the $2k per month gig because the guy's company was in trouble, and he couldn't pay me. I had to rely completely on instincts, trust God. I lost the apartment. I was fortunate that somebody let me store my stuff on their nearby property. I began bouncing from hostel to hostel, all within that little historic district. I was learning to let go of the importance or attachment of material things. Mind you, I still had a house full of stuff 8 hours away at my country house. Most poignantly, I had to become humble enough to accept help from strangers, from 'poor people of color' who seemed to have nothing but compassionate hearts and mutual respect for my struggle. Previous to this, I'd been raised somewhat racist. Here I was, this super educated, capable, and powerful white woman relying on the help of folks earning less than $300 per month. Then, I read something saying that the strongest person, though s/he can do it all on their own, is stronger when s/he allows others to help. God was teaching me by forcing me to ask for help. I had to learn how to surrender my very stubborn will.

I decided to let myself receive help. This taught me that we're all one. As the days would pass, I'd wake up in the morning without a dollar to my name. I had to rely on my smile and hugs to find someone who could share a meal with me. I'd meditate to stay relaxed. I learned first to waste not want not, which curbed my American greed issues. Secondly, I learned to know that it is always safe, that we are always protected. The relief and joy were so overwhelming that I walked into one of the many churches in this beautiful Spanish/ French colonial district, and I promised to be a servant for the light. In other words, I took an oath to become the highest ascended version of myself. That's when I reached past the 600s. The 600s is the level of peace, where you know that it is always safe and have surrendered your fears for the future. You put yourself in God's hands. You surrender your ego and plans and put all your chips on dedication to the highest path, whatever that may be for you.

The 700s was a commitment to becoming my highest ascended self. A ceremony to connect with that highest version of myself happened. Mind you, this is not a mental process. It's experiential. We'll talk about the numbers more in detail later, either in this book, or in a lecture or webinar. Dr. David Hawkins wrote several books explaining consciousness, which you should definitely read or learn about on YouTube. So, I can't really do it justice here in a couple of paragraphs, but hopefully you are beginning to get the idea that 'spirituality' has a definite science, and that this isn't just woo woo wishful thinking. I was so relieved to find that my mental health issues had a rational scientific explanation. Those issues always subside after I guide myself through an enlightenment integration and reconnect to my higher power.

While living homeless in the city, squatting at a friend's apartment with no electricity, a friend from Canada came to visit, giving me a much-needed break. I took him on a spiritual tour throughout Panama. We were sitting back at my country cottage one afternoon when he handed me Dr. Hawkins' book The Eye of the I: From Which Nothing Is Hidden. (64) That book was giving the play by play of my evolutionary process. From that moment on, like so many others, I was hooked on Hawkins' work.

Further, we discovered that I could use his kinesiology technique on myself, alone, to get accurate numbers. He was astonished. He and his girlfriend had been trying to use the kinesiology method but were unsuccessful because, while together, their levels of consciousness were below 200. They were locked in resistant vibrations together and couldn't surrender their egos or inherently doubted themselves. I knew I could do the technique because I'd not been raised to doubt myself. I also knew it was because I was making the effort to clear doubts and fears. Additionally, it's a gift because as an empath, I'm like a super sensitive antenna. But for example, if I'm stuck in fear, desire, or shame, I can't use the kinesiology method on myself because my mind is trapped in the world of illusions, aka suffering, where life seems to happen by forcing it.

Mind you, I still have all kinds of fears to this day. Mostly, they are about getting trapped in relationships, and gaining the courage to share my gifts and message. There will always be something to work out on. Life evolves. There's always some new level of consciousness or personality to work out on. It's just that now, I have techniques of getting it out of my head, putting it on paper, reframing it, clearing and erasing it, and setting some new intentions. Stuff works like magic, as long as I show up for life and take the steps.

What is Meditation vs. Contemplation?

Expert definitions will vary, and I'm certainly not an expert on meditation, but I do know a lot about surrendering meditations that raise my consciousness from the depths of despair up into full oneness. This link describes the scientific benefits of meditation for your brain. (65) Contemplation and prayer are talking to God.

Meditation is what happens after you peel back those layers of chatter, getting into the void where you can ask a question and listen to God, aka your Guru Within. Or, you just coast, like on cruise control, through the astral realms while surrendering the thought forms so you can go deeper and deeper within. In my head, this looks like a tunnel emanating from my third eye that I travel through. Or, I'll focus completely on my breath to the point where I can't tell the difference between my breath, the cells in my body, the air, the couch, the ground, the sky, the core of the earth, and the expansiveness of the Universe. Usually, we are better at talking than listening which is why people generally have trouble meditating. Don't get discouraged, just do the homework of squeezing your mental sponge, surrendering your thoughts one by one.

If your life is pretty chill, maybe yoga is good enough. For those who are anesthetized, depressed, or have become numb, I might recommend you to break the walls down by attending some ayahuasca ceremonies. Try crying your ass out, and receive some serious shamanistic healing so that you can quickly move out of the entrapment of those binding frequencies once and for all. Just because we put band aids on our pain does NOT make it go away. The stains remain active in our vibrational frequency until we remove them. The karmic loop will keep repeating. No amount of prescription drugs is going to fix it alone. Those are all band aids. It's very important to practice these techniques if you are taking mental health prescription drugs. In these ways, you can clear the traumas that are causing your mind to break once and for all.

I've developed a way to combine contemplation into a surrender prayer and guided meditation that help you quickly open up to receive all the light our human bodies can hold. The secret is to observe the false programming and old beliefs that no longer serve from the presence of the 'I AM' mindset. From the 'I AM' mind, you realize the thought or emotion is false because it hurts. The thoughts do not feel like the highest truth, the highest joy, or the greatest love. Realizing our mistaken participation in anything that was out of alignment with these highest truths, we take action and move to amend our behaviors and environment.

Knowing the Difference Between the Real You and the False Self of the Ego Mind

This is really basic. God is love. Love never hurts. If it hurts, it is an attachment, and illusion or deviation from the ultimate truth. The root of all suffering is attachment to false beliefs. Attachments are formed from beliefs that cause our energy to feel split. Attachments and false beliefs drain you. These energies leave us thus desiring with a desperation to fill a void. The way to fill the darkness of the void is through surrendering to the light, but a suffering mind has trouble doing that because it is attached to the false belief. In the illusion, the old paradigm, the 3D reality that we are all now shifting out of, external sources of happiness are sought as fuel to fill the darkness. The poorly programmed mind turns to a favorite vise in an attempt to generate pleasure. Yet this is fleeting. The good feeling only lasts so long before the mental crap comes up again subconsciously asking for attention and healing.

In the absence of divine creation these solutions formed from the mind have an unsustainable force which will always need an external pick-me-up. That's what makes them unsustainable. All the power we need can be summoned from the Source available within. We simply must learn to tap into the fountain, listen, and humbly practice being channels for divine creation. In this way, things get easier, abundance flows, and joy prevails. Imagine if there was a 'devil' on one shoulder and an 'angel' on the other shoulder. The 'devil' is fragmented consciousness because the ego thinks IT is God, yet it gets its energy from external sources. Whereas the 'angel' is an infinitely more powerful source of creative joy and freedom to experience pleasure sustainably because it comes from the light within. There is no good or bad, only that which is wanted and that which is unwanted. Ego isn't bad, it's just doing a poor job compared to the renewable sustainable energy of Source.

Understanding Ego

Remember, the first rule of war is isolation. Ego thinks it is protecting you by isolating you from your neighbors, making you think you are special, elite, an individual, unique, gifted, and better than the homeless guy who can't seem to get his shit together.

Ego thinks it is superior. Of course you are awesome. Some of us just let it shine more than others. This doesn't make others any less valuable or their pain any less relevant than your pain. We experience what we perceive to be flaws. We're all 'flawsome'. We all experience the amnesia of forgetting our awesomeness. Ego tries to help us remember our awesomeness and strive for greatness. It just can't do as good a job as certain celestial helpers with higher vibrations, magnetism, finesse, and pure intentions. The crutch of ego is to be in control. The crux of enlightenment is to surrender that control to the highest intelligence. So, I decide to switch teams every time I recognize my ego taking over. I stop and pray into that higher space. I feel distinct shifts in my energy, immediately, when this happens.

In ego, we get attached to the sense of identity, the wardrobe, the titles, the degrees and certifications, the hip zip code, the cool places in which we often dine, status symbols, and recognition from others. We get caught up identifying with the external materialism of the matrix. Ego says you can't change the past, so just deal with it. Ego is, generally, disempowering, arguing for beliefs to which it is attached. Ego uses force. Ultimate human consciousness can heal the present in a way that washes clean the past and the future like a big delicious blanket. But to access it, we have to surrender the ego. Enlightened love is usually attained as a survival mechanism in the face of great loss and requires dedication. Let go or die crying. The egotistical mind cries and feels anxious, depressed, blameful, or ashamed. The enlightened mind lets go, flows, and leaves to Source what is only in Source's capacity to manage. That level of mind generally ranges in the 800s. Nirvana, from the Buddhist tradition, ranges at 850, a vast space where you're tapped into the jet stream between 3D mind and higher realms. It feels like cruise control. It's a thoughtless, traveling, flowing feeling beyond peace and beyond joy. It's a level where you can generally just smile compassionately without needing to react or respond to anything you're observing.

Deciding To Be Happy

To get from one end of the consciousness spectrum to the other starts with a basic decision to always strive for the best feeling feeling. That feels pretty natural unless our senses have been severely interrupted by environmental factors which cause us to settle for less. If that's the case, start by turning off the TV. The good news is, we'll all eventually heal. Even the people who have no inclination for meditation, the 'G' word, or those who feed off drama, because wellness is the natural evolution of all things. The wellness of nature is simply stronger than the mind of man and its machinations. When we allow ourselves to rest and reflect, the balance of wellness is restored. Enlightenment is a practiced decision over time to trust Source thereby eliminating the suffering created by man's mind.

So basically, if it doesn't feel amazing, it's not real and it's not really you. You are divine. You have the seed of divinity within you. We all do. We're all here trying to achieve one thing – happiness. It's just that most of us are entirely mistaken on how to achieve lasting happiness because our egos aren't willing to surrender control. We're vested in our interests and don't want to take 10 days off work to travel to some distant land to take some strange tea with a medicine man in a Central American jungle. How would we explain it to our children, church group, our parents, our friends and lovers?

Enlightenment seems either inaccessible because of time, cost, life circumstances, or the judgements of others.

All of those excuses are the ego trying to keep its control over you through the use of excuses. Enlightened people know God's love and take responsibility to let that compassion flow through them serving as a compass for right action.

Remember this. Ego limits. Spirit expands.

It all starts with making the decision that you deserve to be happy and healthy. Try that now. Say, 'I deserve to be happy and healthy!' Now, say it again, multiple times, with increased conviction until you are shouting it from the rooftops. Go ahead, I won't make fun of you and neither will Source. In fact, the Law of Attraction dictates that you will, in fact, attract more health and happiness immediately. Try it. What's the worst that could happen, a miracle that proves your ego wrong?

Surrender your small will, the ego's will to be in control, for the expansive feeling of letting God and your highest ascended Self helping you.

Learning to be with our Higher Self will literally save our life in miraculous ways.

Chapter 15:
ENERGETIC HEALING

Metaphysical Medicine

I discovered a great book in Spanish where the psychologist lays out the psychological reasons for physical illnesses of all sorts. It's very complete and eye opening. I showed it to my friend who is a licensed psychologist and Reiki master. It's like her physician's desk reference now. I'm mostly using that book as a backup, to confirm curiosities. I stick more to my intuition. What tends to happen is that my intuition is quickly confirmed by firmly rooted science. Sometimes, Source just puts the answers right in front of my face. I'm always demanding to understand things logically, so higher guidance leads me to the answers. The following is a story of how we (ascended masters channeling through me) cured a woman who had been suffering from fibromyalgia for 12 years.

For example, in this woman's case, I knew to explore the root cause of when the symptoms began with the goal of plucking the emotional discord surrounding that incident and beginning of disease. We conducted a counseling session while she received an ionic detox (66) foot bath. Once we found the source of pain, an illusion created by our dear friend ego, she got onto the massage table, connected with higher powers, connected with her Higher Ascended Self, and allowed all celestial help to remove the illusion from her bio-energetic memory. My hands performed what I call Love Touch Reiki, which is where we visualize that my hands, which are channeling exponential amounts of Source light energy, are like a magnet pulling out darkness infusing in the light. With the help of the Violet Flame, (67) we visualized that, as my hands massaged into the body and directed energy into the nervous system. The light was finding all false beliefs that no longer served and transmuting it up to the light. Then we pulled the discordant frequency out of the hands, feet, and head with deeply penetrating, long, loving strokes from head to toe and back up again. Meanwhile, we pushed it out with a series of breath work. We practiced breathing and visualizations of energy moving through her body. We practiced trust and held space for miracles. Next, we used the reiki to balance the chakras and specifically removed blockages from the vital organs.

The degree to which we can release resistance determines the degree to which we can maintain enlightenment. It is a continual practice to release resistance and accept what is. The physical feeling allowed in is expansion in the face of fear, loving into the pain and darkness rather than getting stuck in it. If we don't own our darkness, the darkness owns us. The more you believe, want to believe, surrender and allow Source to present you opportunities- the more magical life becomes. Trust that, if the opportunity hasn't come along yet, it will as soon as you are open to it and ready to level up in your responsibilities to that greater creation. When we trust in the power of our soul and the power of our heart's true desire, coupled with trusting the divine power within, that's when we're most alive. As you can imagine, a burning desire is necessary. Likewise, as you can imagine, after 12 years of daily suffering, this woman had a burning desire to heal. In fact, that's how she found me. She made a decision that she was ready to stop suffering. Soon after, the day came that we were both walking along the same exercise trail. I noticed her uneven gate and introduced myself as someone who might help.

As it turns out, she was involved in an uncomfortable argument with a pregnant coworker 12 years ago. The woman 'damned' her by saying that all her children would have some kind of birth defect. She didn't know that my client's child has downs syndrome. In my client's compassion, not wanting to project any harm onto the pregnant woman, my client instead internalized her upsetness. The shame of secretly wishing harm on the woman and fear for another bad result was internalized. These unresolved emotions combined with the woman's damning energies and were internalized, causing fibromyalgia. My client turned against herself instead of turning against the pregnant woman. She believed what the woman had said and somehow believed that she deserved this condemnation, that it must be true, that perhaps her son had downs syndrome because she had been bad somehow. She felt like a bad mother and a bad person for being so angry at the woman. A dark cloud came over her, as if she allowed the woman's damning words to take hold. The life force was zapped right out of her body thanks to this painful disempowering belief that she felt she deserved.

I suspect that the story goes deeper into past lives, but it has not yet been necessary to explore that, as my client is now better. She comes back periodically because the reframing of thought, getting the mind to fire and the nervous system to respond differently, are habits that take time to integrate. But she's fine now, and simply appreciates having someone to listen and counsel her while we detox her body using the ionic detox machine. It took about 20 hours of working together over the course of two months to heal her- 4 hours of reiki massage, 4 hours of counseling, 4 hours of detox, 4 hours of guided meditation, and 4 hours of chakra clearing.

The body is a chariot. You are the charioteer. It's the tool our soul chose in order to build our destiny. When we learn to treat the body like a temple, we are really learning to be devout to our Guru Within who seeks harmony and balance in all things. If you want a healthy body able to hold the light required to sustain enlightenment, you have to practice mind-body-spirit balance. Thus, so many people utilize yoga. I didn't, But I like to do things the hard way. Yoga seemed too woo woo for me. But that was just my laziness arguing for its limitations.

In what examples can you remember yourself saying something was too far out there for you? Where are you arguing for your limitations? Maybe you are a little more open to trying them now?

Personally, patience has been the hardest value for me to cultivate- patience with my body and with other people. Actually, the reason I got up to 315 pounds was because my way of dealing with the impatience was to binge. Now that we understand logically that it is always safe, that this is an abundant universe, that things take time to manifest in the 3D, it is a matter of training our understanding into all the energy centers of the body. Through each new situation, we are given another chance to grow in awareness and capability, to practice uprooting those old habits, muscle memories, genetically coded and triggered impulses lodged inside our mind-body-spirit. Of course, it is hard. We are rewiring, and reprogramming how the body acts, reacts, and responds to stress. We are plucking resistance, one by one. As the Indian Guru, Nithyananda says, referencing his 21 day program, each day, or cycle, builds upon the next. If we are diligent, infinitely powerful progress is made. If we slack off and take our time, we lose momentum.

It's a simple law of physics really. An object in motion stays in motion unless acted upon by an equal and opposite force. Darkness can never be as powerful as light unless it has constant practice and momentum in your life. Where there is light there is less darkness. Now, we can understand that, by building up a momentum of light, positive intentions & actions, law of attraction is required to magnify and amplify that intensity, perhaps astronomically beyond our imaginations. Do you allow and make room for miracles and magic beyond your imagination?

I have a mantra. It goes, **"I allow this day to turn out more magical than I can imagine."** It is a surrender to something greater than my mind.

The limiting beliefs of the mind will argue for the comfort and safety of what we already know even if it is painful. The pain is an indication of limitation and misalignment from our truth. Working through these reactions in the body will take consistently applied effort to reflect upon and CLEAN UP our fear-based miscreations. How can we trust? What's the guiding compass?

If it hurts, it's false. Every feeling is valid, just not necessarily based on ultimate truth. For example, when I'm feeling puny, and tell myself that someone doesn't care about me, I feel like I've been punched in the gut. That's my indication that the thought is a lie. The feeling of ultimate truth is pure bliss, passion, joy, and wellbeing. Anything else has room for growth. So immediately, I willingly surrender the thought to God and ask for the light to come in. This is an instantly humbling perspective which makes it very easy to forgive ourselves and any poor treatment of the body-mind-spirit as well as any of her subsequent manifestations of dis-ease. Heal the body by forgiving yourself. If there is disease, you can trust that karma is playing a role to teach you a lesson. Our homework is to question, curiously seeking this ultimate truth. Then, you ask God for help to remove the lie from your bio-energetic memory.

If we don't like something about our body, we can try asking our Higher Self why it chose that particular 'imperfection'. Have the courage to point the finger inward and recognize what you may have done to disrespect the temple in this or past lives. Or, listen to the dis-ease to see what life changes it is telling you to make. Be gentle with yourself. Having been morbidly obese, I know a thing or two about all of the discipline and subconscious work that must go into recovering from so much self-hate and resistance to love. I talk a lot about ways to love yourself in the audio CDs.

Commit to full Self-love even if you feel far far away from that truth right now. Commit to cultivating it. Make it your number one priority. Date yourself. Carve out the time to do this. You will find that the order is Love of God (cultivating your relationship to the Guru Within), respect for the body/ mind/ spirit (the Self), and then service to others. We have to serve ourselves first by learning to let Higher Power serve us. When we let our Higher Power flow through us, we become perfectly tuned instruments in an orchestra of divinely moving parts yielding beautiful peaceful symphonies of love. When we stop flowing, train wrecks happen. It is far more noble to care for oneself completely than to poorly care for several others. Admit that you need help. Ask for help, and trust that it will come. Maybe you already have, and that's why you're finding this book. Surrender to the humility of asking for help and the power gained from allowing yourself to accept higher powers. Relax into it. Allow for expansion.

Please understand that it is fine not knowing the root source of our problems. Cancer can be healed. Diseases can be healed, but if one is complacent towards the patterns that caused the disease, it will return and the suffering will continue. However, we are encouraged to explore the emotions surrounding any particular event in which a dis-ease began so that we can make effective decisions on how to think and do in a less resistant manner moving forward. For less resistance to happen, we must put down our outdated weapons of pride, fear, desire, guilt, shame, or vengeance and surrender to love's super power. We must allow ourselves to deeply feel worthy of great love and abundance. We must listen and obey our intuition when we meet someone special who can help. Perhaps we won't understand all the tools they use, and perhaps to avoid frightening us, the procedure won't be explained. Just trust your heart and remember that everything happens for a reason.

"All events are perfectly designed for me to grow in awareness and capability."
— *Wu Wei, The I-Ching Handbook* (68)

It is safe to trust the omniscient and unrelenting love of our Guru Within.

Our Guru Within holds the key to unlocking all the mysteries of life. Knowing this unconditional safety, as Divine children, helps us accept and surrender ego's fears in favor of our birthright of well-being, which is True Divine Love Essence. Having cultivated our intuition, we'll always be able to find the right key at the right time because our Guru Within has the master key and is always on our side.

An important revelation is to understand that we used to be angels, but have forgotten our divinity. We come to this planet as a playground for resolving traumas and karmas that have split our energy away from the truth of our divinity.

Here's an awesome thought from the book Love It Forward (69) by Jeff Brown. "You ever notice that when someone communicates something pure and poignant, it is often characterized as something they channeled. It may well be that, but it may also be something they earned at the school of heart knocks. That is, sometimes we come to those places of great clarity through hard, hard work. We clear our debris, we learn our lessons, and then the expression gets crystal clear. I wonder if we call it 'divinely channeled' because we have so much shame as humans that we cannot claim our magnificence. Why must humans channel divinity? After all, we are that, too."

Please accept my gift to you, a free psychic Reading.

Discover where you are on The Scale of Consciousness right now.

I will tell you:

Where you are on the map at the time of your reading, exact time included.

What your usual level of consciousness is, as of recently.

Where you were 6 months ago/a year ago or at the time of a

particular trauma.

Donations are nice but not required. Your tax free gift can be made directly through our websites at CarinaCarinosaStore.Guru/donations. (70)

If you fluctuate up and down the scale a lot, you can learn more about that, too. Any major life changes that you need help with, I welcome you to try out an extended reading and counseling session: on-line, by phone, at my place, or if I'm traveling to your area soon, we can meet up. At this level, you are invited to tell me about a specific issue that is bothering you. I can tell you what your consciousness is regarding that situation, consciously and subconsciously. The reading would include professional advice, perhaps a parable from my own life story, motivation, inspiration, and tips from many masters for pivoting out of that situation into a more relaxed level of awareness. It will also include some affirmations or mantras, and a guided surrender prayer.

What information is needed:

Full name
Birth date: place and time — if known, if not it's okay
If concerning a relationship issue, please state the other person's name and birth date, as well, if known.
Photographs help. Current snapshot to show how you are feeling right now, one of your best pictures ever, or a picture of how you used to be.
Skype ID or WhatsApp
Phone number
Good times to speak including time zone

We ask for a $100 donation to do an extended reading.

Regardless of your decision to pursue this path, or take me up on any of the above services now available to you, with all my heart, I wish that you may grow, love, and express kindness in every frequent smile.

Infinite Blessings, Love, Light and GREAT BIG HUGGIES to You and Yours!

:D Carina Cariñosa

(The above rates at 986 on The Scale.) (71)

p.s. Remember that you are welcome to sign up to our free weekly enlightenment newsletter where I'll introduce you to a number of masters via YouTube videos, excerpts and articles by yours truly. Just request to be added on our web-form at www.CarinaCarinosaStore.Guru (72)

Everything is connected

For those linear thinkers who get tired of my mind always running in circles, I'm here to tell you that everything is connected. Consider the sacred geometry board game, HelixileH, (73) HelixileH, (74) HelixileH. (75) It explains The Flower of Life symbol and interconnectedness of all that is. The second link shows a game which is a cross between Twister and the social psychology of releasing self-importance. Try to look beyond the hippie clothes and imagine your school, church or non-profit organization doing this self-aware communal bonding activity. The third link is a direct contact for you to buy the board game. I think this should become a popular couples compatibility test. I also believe this would be a revealing personality test for any Human Resources department. Before I hire an employee or adopt a new lover, HelixileH will certainly reveal a lot about the way a person views the world. It could also be an effective tool for healers to identify areas that need cleansing.

So for the loaners and empaths who feel that solitude is safer, I feel you. We need the space to center and create. I encourage you to work on your 'protection mechanisms' so that you can 'safely' shine and thus your gifts be shared. At the end of the book are a number of prayers, and you're welcome to download one of our guided meditations online.

Solitude does not mean retreating to your cave in fear. It means go within so that you can go beyond. Like a star imploding giving birth to a new galaxy, you are infinite possibilities. Just keep LETTING Source do its job of expanding through you.

Heaven knows the world needs more compassion. That's why we're here. It's our job to bring heaven on to earth. Well, at least I know that's my job. Even if you are at that relaxing powerful trusting stage of Nirvana mind (registers 850 on Hawkins' Scale of Consciousness), where you feel totally grateful for every experience in your life, there is still a higher level to be achieved. In the next level, with that gratitude expanding, we pray for everyone knowing that the power of our prayer-filled intentions IS impacting the world.

Please don't stop the flow of abundance from reaching your own shores.

Have the courage to get out and share your gifts for the simple fact that it makes YOU feel amazing. You see me here, baring my soul to strangers. Telling my story knowing full well there will be persecutors. And yet, the power of knowing that someone will be touched, that someone's life will be saved and enriched, that people are going to reach and understand enlightenment because I had the courage to be my best, that knowingness is why I chose to be born an empath during this very difficult stage in the evolutionary game.

Do you know that you chose your body as a vehicle for the evolution of consciousness? I was so grateful when a friend posted that on Facebook for me as a way of developing compassion for my body. I struggle constantly with loving myself through my body. Today, I'm sad that I keep failing to be a non-smoker. My lower consciousness that doesn't love myself completely struggles with this truth, that my body is my teacher, and I'm an indignant student who keeps failing myself for some hidden sad reason. My body is forcing me to raise my consciousness and how I treat it.

Do you know that you also choose your family circumstances, as well? We chose our family. Such a crazy thought, masochistic in fact. Egos can be pretty masochistic. I give props to anyone who had a good childhood and can really love both their parents in an honoring way. Your karma must be pretty good.

Do you also know that it is within your power to heal your family by healing how you feel about yourself? You've heard the saying, 'If mama ain't happy, ain't nobody happy!' It's true because your hearts are interconnected. Did I tell you I stopped biting my nails at the same time my dad did? I told him, and he said, 'Yeah me too.' I asked why he'd suddenly stopped and he said because he'd finally gotten a license to carry a concealed weapon. So he didn't feel like a criminal anymore.

Can you see how the good and **the bad** have made you stronger thanks to the contrast, support, and lessons? Reflect on that for a minute.

Once you can fathom how the worst of times have been perfectly designed for your evolution **and feel peace about it** that's when you know you've reached enlightenment baby. Now, it may take a few well-guided ayahuasca ceremonies to really get that feeling of peace, but then again, you might just be willing to do your homework sober, make space for yourself to reflect, and dig into some deep self-love work, assuming you can hold space for yourself. Most people get trapped in the illusion, and that's why we need facilitators. They hold the space of higher frequency-unconditional love, peace, enlightenment, nirvana mind, and full Christ consciousness. They stand there to speak to the sad mistaken parts of our fragmented souls, and they help worlds collide bringing those soul pieces back for you.

In the 900s, you can realize that you have created every aspect of what happens to you. This is omniscience and omnipresence. It's as though you wrote the screenplay, are directing, and also acting in the film. You see the coincidences and realize that your Will created them. It means that you are also following your Will, have transcended from little will (which uses force) into your Highest Ascended Will which is easy, graceful, and expansively free flowing. You realize from up above looking down that you are orchestrating every detail in your life's circumstances. It's as though you are in a high-rise building looking down at the street, and paradoxically, you are also standing on the street at the same time. It is truly transcendental consciousness.

That's why I went through a bit of an identity crisis for a while phasing between my old identity as my birth name into this new clearer essence we named Carina. We don't stay in these high states of enlightenment at first. We kiss them for a while, then go back to our 3-dimensional creations and work on cleaning up those realities. One day, it'll all be healed. Just keep on stepping towards the light. I can do an enlightenment integration with you and help you break through within an hour.

That totally omniscient perspective is commonly called 'Christ consciousness' which ranks in the 900s on Dr. Hawkins' Scale. When you can realize how the most 'out of my control' circumstances were actually in fact perfectly designed for your soul's evolution, you see how you attracted the coincidence and built the outcome. That presence is the peak of enlightened consciousness. Now, just add a dash of 'world peace intention' praying that every single person, place, and thing can perceive this level of understanding in their own lives. Imagine if just one thousand common people rose to this level of compassion for their own journeys, and understanding their struggle, wished for the healing of all beings. I know that for the skeptics this sounds a bit Utopian, but that's just the ego trying to protect its vested interests, so let's be scientific about this. Literally, within Christ consciousness you are able to effect from 9-10 billion people with the powerful magnetism of your heartfelt-intention. It's as though everyone's subconscious tunes into your radio station of Oneness, and at the hypnotic level, whatever you broadcast will be felt in the hard drive of each individual's wiring. The volume on your frequency is turned on so high that all else melts into it. That's the kind of shaman you want around or want to become.

You may wonder how the mundane aspects of life are perfect. How is traffic, stubbing my toe, breaking my favorite shades, getting hit in the face, or that speeding ticket perfect? Well, for one, it's part of a cycle of birth and death. It calls us to pay more attention to what we are doing and how we are being. It invites us to take better care, to act more gracefully. If we oblige, the seeming imperfections won't be so drastic as a punch in the face. Only when we do not listen, are not honoring ourselves and others does life slap us so distinctly saying 'HEY GO THE OTHER WAY. DO SOMETHING DIFFERENT. CHANGE YOUR BEHAVIOR (which begins with changing your thoughts).'

Obtaining abundance is a formula of surrender and abiding faith. When we sabotage our endeavors and seem to fail, this is actually an opportunity to set the stage for what is truly wanted. The negative experiences force us to think about what is definitely not wanted. Use this to be specific about exactly what IS wanted. Because

Source only hears your vibrational offering, you can't keep focusing on what is if it is unwanted. You have to let it be what it is (surrender) and then get super specific and full of adrenaline about what IS wanted. Follow the signs like they're magic communication from God.

What got me to change was a process I like to explain like this:

Shit goes down.

This shit stinks.

Get rid of this shit. Surrender it like fertilizer. Trusting nature to provide what is needed.

Absorb the lessons from the great Masters, and allow ourselves to be pollinated so that our abundance can bloom and hearts overflow with bounty.

Chapter 16:

SHAMANISM AND KARMA

MY CONCEPT OF LOVE TOUCH REIKI IS SHAMANISM.

What is a shaman?

To reach our destiny, we journey through Hell (fear) to achieve Heaven (love). A shaman is someone who has been through heaven and hell and lives to guide you through it with greater precision. In my 20's I went from being a concert promoter in Texas to finding codependent love in a drug addict husband, later evolving into a 315-pound abused immigrant housewife/ entrepreneur and international asset protection consultant. Deciding not to surrender to diabetes medication or antidepressants, I set off to discover Panama's natural beauty in a quest to escape abuse and lots of habits that no longer served. I couldn't find a teacher nearby, but Lord how I wanted one! Thankfully, this required me to discover that the guru is within. So basically, I just learned how to heal/ recondition/ and reprogram the mind away from trauma so that I could follow and trust my intuition, or as Abraham-Hicks calls it, our Emotional Guidance System. (78)

Newly separated from my husband, and after breaking my knee for the second time, I traveled to the lush flower-covered rural mountains of Panama to heal and subsequently lose 140 pounds. As if that wasn't enough, just two weeks after launching my Panama relocation business, I was widowed for my 29th birthday. The year before, he robbed me in my sleep on my 28th birthday. I didn't take kindly to that, so I yelled him into a corner, and when I spat at him, he boxed his way out, leaving me with two black eyes for my birthday. What I thought was the final straw, happened two weeks prior, when I found him in a casino, out of his mind on liquid rivotril and beer, with a hooker. I called my best friend back in Texas laughing in the cab saying, 'It's finally over. I'm done.' Later that night, I got a text from a friend saying she saw my husband 'tirado en la calle', passed out drunk on the street. It was a major intersection, too. I said to her, 'Well if that's so, it's because he doesn't have any money to get home. Will you please put him in a cab and send him with $3?' She said, 'Honestly, no. After all he's done to you, I don't care to help him.'

So, I got in a taxi and found him half in the street, half on the sidewalk by the hot dog stand. The woman at the hot dog stand called him my husband, and I was so embarrassed that I lied and said, 'No no. He's not my husband. We just live in the same apartment complex.' When he stood up wobbling and heard this, he started to freak out. I quickly shoved him into a taxi and vowed this was the last time I helped him. Two weeks later, he broke my nose for my birthday. It took another few months to finally leave, which included him stealing my passport and blackmailing me to give him money in order to get it back. For the next year, he continued to come around, even though I'd moved 8 hours away from the city. He'd always steal from me, no matter where I'd hidden the money. But basically, when he no longer had me to steal from, he'd steal from tourists. The final final straw happened about a year later when I received a letter, addressed to every tourism and hostel operator in Central America, from an owner who said he'd just stolen 400 Euro from a backpacker. When I told him I couldn't know him anymore, he overdosed two days later. Then, he haunted my house for a couple months, and remained stuck to my energy for another year until a mentor finally helped me release him back to the light. This is when I knew I had ESP without a doubt. I wouldn't accept that my mind was just broken and crazy. I could tell the difference between what was me, and what was external forces acting upon me. I begged God to guide me out of it.

As you can imagine, it took a while to honor his passing. His family would say it's a dishonor to tell the truth here. These are the same people who lied about his birthday, saying he was a year younger, so that they could hide the pregnancy that occurred out of wedlock. They even went so far as to wait an extra year after his birth to ensure that his birth certificate reflected the 'reality' they wanted to be perceived in. They were always trying to cover up the dirty truths to appear high class and invincible. It was always their living a lie that compelled him to use- pretending things were okay when they weren't- staying mute about the trauma instead of getting help for it. In fact, it was the money his mother gave him that he used to overdose. But I'm the bad guy because I won't cover up these facts. Oh, and he fathered an illegitimate child while we were married, too. But somehow, I was the asshole for not sweeping it under the rug and carrying on with the group denial. They left me widowed and alone in a foreign country with zero support. All I had was God and later, my shaman, Jason Kerr, to help me out of the darkness. I couldn't talk about him without crying for about 2 and a half years. I had nowhere to turn, but the internet and within.

Because I'm so stubborn, my life has been a series of fucking up and having to learn the hard way from my mistakes. It's been constant karma cleansing, consistent praying for miracles, spiritual studies and a commitment to be my best to overcome the bullshit. The first thing I had to do was stop the victim mindset and ask myself, 'How did I bring this upon myself?' I had to take ownership. I had to breathe acceptance into all of those victimized spaces. I'm so thankful to have lived through it. If you are determined not to throw in the towel, then it is my pledge to help guide you to the light. We must learn how to see all of life's challenges as opportunities that are perfectly designed for us to grow in awareness and capability. This is a concept that comes from the I-Ching Handbook by Wu Wei, (79) a book that was basically my Bible for the three years I stayed on the side of that mountain healing.

If we wish to feel peace, we must ask for help from a higher power. Remember that I showed you Dr. Hawkins' Scale of Consciousness? Logic and reasoning stop at 499. Trusting in a greater power and allowing it to orchestrate the show is the type of psychology that enables us to reach feelings of peace and joy in the 600s. There's a distinct disconnect between 499 to 500, going from the mind into the heart. Most people need a huge catharsis to go there. I certainly did. I worked at it for about 2 years before I could finally access feelings of unconditional love. Now, my clients can achieve it within 10-30 minutes because the divine master in me commands that the light penetrates your dark places. You, in turn, surrender to the light, and let it flow to you, through you, as you. That's how you achieve enlightenment.

For those who fear that living in an enlightened state is dull, I can attest to the fact that my life is anything but dull. Now that I am a very powerful manifester, miracles happen constantly. Paradoxically, I usually manage to feel that zoned-out blissful nirvana state that can make it hard for me to articulate using words because thoughts, judgements, and opinions no longer easily arise. In those cases, I just try to project a smiling heart transfer of love, aka meta, and I chose my friends carefully to protect my peace. I still get upset, and munch on angry thoughts occasionally, especially during PMS, but one loses the taste for that energy, the angry juice, the blame juice, the righteous juice. One day, you might even look down to realize you are drinking a tall class of crap, crap of your own making. How silly you feel.

In this case, the best solution is humbly laughing and quickly forgiving your ignorance. We have to get from the place of realizing this is crap to not resisting the crap or making it grow worse by focusing on the crap too intensely. We have to own the fact that WE have contributed to the crap AND are ingesting more of it by focusing our attention on it. Eventually we calm down enough to clean up the crap, and realizing that we have a lot of crap to clean up, we admit to needing help. Until we allow the help to flow through, we bottleneck spirit from assisting us.

We then take the necessary actions to manifest a new situation, a healthier type of future. We visualize what is wanted. If we stink up the new future situation with attention focused on crap by expecting more crap, even slightly believing in the probability of more crap, or remembering that crap that happened last time, then this 'reality' combines with other negative vibrations to create Murphy's Law. (80) Murphy's Law says that if something bad can happen at the most inopportune time, it will. It is the impatience of the observer combining with his attempt to fill in the grid by himself, without respect for divine timing, failing to respect that there is a gestation period required for things to bloom into fruition. Murphy's Law is what happens when our impatience and negative expectation collapse into the physical dimension. It would be better never to have heard of Murphy's Law. The expectation of a bad result is created by the observer and his unconscious creations or his karma.

When something unwanted happens, I immediately ask God 'WHY? And How is that perfectly designed for me to grow in awareness and capability?' I ask God immediately for guidance, and I try to listen intently to what comes up without doubting or rejecting the answer. There will be times that you don't like the answer. Keep listening and asking for the light to remind you of God's peace. I can think of no better team than this group called the Ascended Masters. The Ascended Masters are always available and able to manifest into the physical through other beings. My point is to stop getting your juice from unsustainable sources like anger, blame, pride, focusing on other people's faults, or the juice from righteousness. We must surrender all that crap and constantly remember to get our juice from that grade A+ sustainable Source known as Universal Life Force.

What's that got to do with shamanism?

When I asked God why all of this was happening to me, I was faced with pointing the finger inward.

I had to look at my own impurity. My husband, my dad, my brother- none of them were around for me to point the finger at anymore. I found my own corruption instead of his. I found my own addictive nature instead of his. And later, God began to show me the past lives that I'd been corrupt, which helped explain why I had such bad karma. I wouldn't have come upon those revelations without a willingness to point the finger inward, because it SEEMED much easier to play the victim, but that was a lie. To explain why I'd been stolen from, I found that I'd stolen from others in a past life as an accountant. To explain why our relationship was so violent, I needed only to look at my childhood. To explain why I took so much responsibility for healing others, I found the guilt and atonement for having been a Nazi. To explain why I have such trouble sleeping, I could see the trauma of my grandfather's abuse against my Dad while he was sleeping. Things start to make a lot of sense once we realize that we've been on this planet more than once. Karma starts to make sense when we realize that we can carry the trauma of our families, just like we can carry their propensity for certain genetically predispositioned dis-eases. If we choose to hate, play victim, point the finger outward, we'll never resolve the root pain or reclaim the power of or WHOLE sentient Self.

The shaman practices temperance. He has demonstrated discipline applied over time throughout his life experiences. The shaman is trusted by the masters to access and hold a big set of keys that unlock various doors to mind/ body/ spirit dimensions so that we can quickly, safely, intentionally work through karma with precision and grace. It's cathartic. What I've found from working with clients is that my dedication to relieve others of suffering, born in me from deep compassion based on my own suffering, enables me to remove blockages for my patients with surprising grace and speed.

Just remember that, while working through your karma, we don't ever 'deserve' pain. We simply use it for contrast to learn. It's the pressure that catapults us forward like a bow and arrow. This is where the Christian concept of atonement becomes convoluted because of the false belief in sin. Again, sin is just a basic misalignment where you trespass against yourself or others. When they say Jesus died for all of our sins, he wasn't merely asking God to forgive us of our sins. He was allowing the God Life Force to flow through him, which IS forgiveness. We, humans, have been taught to choose pain as a tool for learning, usually by guilting or blaming ourselves for our misaligned thoughts or deeds, calling ourselves sinners. Once we decide to stop blaming, guilting, or shaming ourselves, the contrasting feeling serves to catapult us into what is wanted with greater passion. We get a deep feeling of what is not right, and have an opportunity to become more clear about what IS wanted. The mistaken mind chooses guilt, blame, shame, fear, and desire to create contrast and strengthen the catalyst for surrender to God. But it's not necessary for us to cause so much suffering upon ourselves. The power of pure desire, coming from a place of love, is a product of Source wisdom infinitely more powerful than the suffering we bring upon ourselves. We must surrender to letting that flow in. In this way, we are now able to access more gain with less pain. We can infuse the light into dark spaces without having to relive the traumas. We can cancel and erase the karma in this way. I worked on this for three years straight, healing myself with tools found on the internet. As life continues to challenge me, I keep falling back on these same principles.

For a karmic stain to be cleaned, it must be cleared through the 7-chakra system of the body. Let's take for example, I used to have a very strong anger problem. It stems from deep feelings of betrayal. Anger isn't a bad thing; it actually helps us not to feel depressed or self-blaming. Anger resides on Dr. Hawkins' Scale of Consciousness with 100 points, in the color orange, which coincides with the body's second chakra. The chakras correlate with a set of thoughts, feelings, and emotions which all correlate to the Scale of Human Consciousness and the Emotional Guidance System. Anger resides in the second chakra, with our liver and kidneys, along with our feelings about family, our childhood, our sexual orientations, and how we feel about masculine or feminine influences. People have trouble grasping that we are not defined by our mistakes. We like to box people into a label in our mind and let it fester there. However, we are, in fact, infallible perfect beings. Everything is working out. Everything is teaching us. The question is, are you listening and following your highest bliss? We have trouble seeing this from our limited perspectives while we focus on unloving thoughts perpetuated by the ignorance of others or our own limiting beliefs. We are experiencing a sort of misguided amnesia as we reside in this dense dimension. Our souls are trying to create heaven on earth, but we keep focusing on what is or what was rather than feeling the good feelings of what is wanted like conscious co-creators. Life is paradoxical. There are two sides to every circumstance, the positive or the negative. Decide now to feed the positive.

The good news is that the season for trading in our old inefficient models of acting are now upon us. Beings from all over the galaxy, from higher dimensions of consciousness, are breaking through the veil to assist us at this point in our evolution. That is why we chose to be in this soul group, to evolve quickly under all this pressure. We can now be grateful to have reached a time where a majority of people are desiring greatly enough to stop miscreating so that we are receiving extra celestial contact. In fact, without the pain, we wouldn't have desired enough, surrendered enough, opened ourselves up enough to receive divine intervention. So let us forgive ourselves quickly and move on swiftly toward accepting help from The Masters. Let us allow them to support us rather than wallowing in a festering set of emotions and thoughts that brings greater resistance. Finally, let us relax and play. This is how we will usher in a utopia of heaven on earth. The Masters are able to incarnate through us, through 1 or 1 million people simultaneously. Your job, my job, is to just to keep surrendering, keep being the light by allowing the light to flow through, keep deciding to serve, keep choosing to follow our burning passions in search of ultimate truth, joy, and bliss.

Here is a quote from GuideSpeak.com (81) about Karma: (82)

"Karmic Law" is the result of choices we make, consciously or unconsciously and the cause and effect of the consequent actions that result. By unconscious choice, most times reactions, consequences result. By conscious choice, most times thought provoked responses, consequences result. The Law of Integrity, whether obeyed or not obeyed, sets up the consequences of action both 'good' and 'bad' as a ripple effect, which turns into a wave and ultimately a tidal wave. Obeyed laws create 'positive' consequences and disobeyed laws create 'negative' consequences. Ultimately, all consequences are 'positive'. However, by first going the 'negative' route to end up as 'positive' could entail hardships, pain, healing, growth and evolvement in many lifetimes.

The Law of Karma says no debt in the Universe ever goes unpaid. Become a conscious choice-maker, seeking happiness for you and for all of mankind, generate actions that evolve your Soul through 'positive' healing and growth. Once again, it's your choice, this time your conscious choice, at all times your conscious choice."

What I did to heal my karma and pay my debt, was to commit to being of service. For me, this life is about atonement, until I can finally eliminate my shame, and surrender into my divinity once and for all. I've repented. I've accepted responsibility for my miscreations. I took an oath to strive for positive creations. I decided to allow The Masters and Angels to flow through me to create miraculously effective transformation in others. I asked to download super powers serving the highest truth, love, light, and joy. And I committed that my healing would serve more than just myself, that my suffering wouldn't be in vain, that my commitment to clearing the pain would be for all of humanity and not just myself. That's how I became a shaman. I asked for it, and committed to the responsibility. Then, the powers were given to me as I kept repeating this rededication process on a daily basis.

That commitment, to be a healer, came from a slew of past lives as a healer, which I later found out during an Akashic Record reading by Theresa Martinez. The oath, to be of the highest service to others, was what caused me to achieve enlightenment because it was a profound surrender to the multidimensional truth of my being.

LET THAT SHIT GO.

OPEN YOUR HANDS, ARMS, HEART, MIND, BODY, SOUL, SPIRIT

&

ALLOW YOURSELF TO RECEIVE.

Holding and reclaiming power

"Dear God, if whatever I'm experiencing is not mine, I release it and return it back to Source for healing. Heaven help them. Heaven help me. Bless us. Bless us. Bless us."

Whenever I feel the pain of a loved one, in particular, it affects me. My family has suffered a lot. Though they live miles away, as a telempathic person, it can be very hard to stay focused and present. Thank God my current boyfriend is super stable and non-invasive because I'll have the tendency to feel their pain, or get into my head trying to repair something that is not mine. Then I have to curb check my narcissism about trying to fix things that aren't my place to resolve. The answer is full surrender. "Give it to God " as they say. Often, the empathy creates the opportunity for me to work out on my own emotions, but sometimes we have things to do, a life to live, the day to get on with. Learning how to, as Ram Dass says, 'Be Here Now' is tough when you're experiencing pain, especially if it's someone else's.

Out of compassion for myself, primarily, I will empathetically, for myself, repeat this prayer over and over again. In a short time, I become like a doll, hollow inside, and just invite Source to fill me up with light. I surrender my will and allow Higher Will to protect me, absorbing it like a sponge.

"Dear God, if whatever I'm experiencing is not mine, I release it and return it back to Source for healing. Heaven help them. Heaven help me. Bless us. Bless us. Bless us."

It can be really hard sometimes to get to this place of self-respect. Ego likes to take ownership of everything, including other people's problems. So learning to circumnavigate directly into surrender has been a valuable practice for my sanity. My Twin Flame actually taught me how to do this. Or rather, I developed it as a coping mechanism to deal with his lack of compassion, an element that used to be so resonant in my personality. I figure, to heal him of it, I just have to stay firm in my own self-compassion first and let God do what It Wills. That's why we're not together now. He had too much to work out on, and I was too sensitive to be around for the dirty work. My path of healing was a different road than his.

Non-resistance. Acceptance of What Is

Ascended Master Orin's wisdom on transparency is key to empaths since we feel what others feel, or since the contrasting situation raises previously hidden resistances into consciousness for healing. Writer Byron Katie speaks clearly on the importance of accepting what is. The reality of the situation may not be comfortable, and it will remain so, until **we choose to see** the higher benefit of it. As Abraham-Hicks would say, we must pivot our point of attraction to that of less and less resistance.

For example, each time I am forced to be patient, I generally resist. I was NOT raised by a patient person, so I'm like an adult child practicing this virtue. I get the most practice while driving! My control drama, according to the Celestine Prophecy, is the role of interrogator. My ego personality looks for what's wrong and tries to fix it. The equal opposite drama it attracts for learning is the aloof. That's my Twin Flame. He holds his power in silence. Sometimes, it's really hot. Other times, totally not. When I don't find it attractive, this is an opportunity for me to practice abiding faith, patience, acceptance of the reality of what is, and to focus my energy back inward. He serves as an example for me to see how I must reflect my attention back inward onto my own business, rather than trying to (as Byron Katie says) 'handle someone else's business.' You could easily imagine various scenarios where these two personality types could get into control dramas with each other. I wasn't willing to live in drama, so my heart de-manifested him after about 6 months. One reason we were attracted at a soul level is because we both had a lot of anger in our households. We could relate with that brokenness. He de-manifested because he wasn't willing to surrender his ego to forgive his dad, and God swiftly sent him home to Florida to be with them. As you know, I got sent home shortly after to forgive my mom. Turns out, a couple years later, his dad manifested cancer from all the anger and unforgiveness.

As an empath, because we feel so deeply, can't turn it off, and obviously are compelled to fix things, relinquishing the need to 'handle other people's business' is an imperative survival mechanism. It requires surrender to higher power. Otherwise, you just create a massive energy leak, like a faucet that gets left turned on, zapping your life force. When this letting go is achieved, our bodies open up, Higher Guidance flows through, and circumstances unfold effortlessly. Effortlessly, when we allow them. The problem is that with most surrender comes the Universe swooping in to change circumstances to fit the new vibrational offering or to teach the lesson. **So learning to breathe through and surrender to the flow of changes is a key coping mechanism. If you make this a primary practice, used daily and often, I promise you'll achieve and sustain enlightenment like a Zen Master.**

Reclaiming Divine Goddess Power

Traditional society taught us that it is bad to be selfish, especially if you're a woman. I disagree. Selfishness and self-centeredness are two different things. The key to unlocking the confusion is compassion. Empaths know plenty about compassion for others, but often sacrificing of ourselves first. Remember here that the ultimate goal of every human is full 100% self-love. You just can't love someone wholly if you're not respecting your own soul's boundaries for fulfillment. So I say choose your sacrifices very carefully. Abraham-Hicks tells us that, 'Yes, in fact, the world does revolve around you. It revolves around your vibrational offering.' And then, when we forget to tend to our own vibrational offerings, we fall out of the vortex of easy delicious co-creation. As Byron Katie would paraphrase, we stop handling our own business and thus start trying to handle other people's business, or even God's business. **The new definition of selfishness is, tending to my own business with abiding faith that God will take care of God's business. I also trust others' Emotional Guidance Systems to know how best to take care of their own business.** All

I have to do is allow, accept, and absorb this as my truth. Through the abiding faith, no confiscatory energy is offered into my creation, thus, power is restored. Subsequently, attractiveness and creative energy is restored, and the divine feminine (or masculine) power is once again deliciously readily available like juicy ripe fruit.

I'd argue that a primary reason for such high divorce rates is that people evolve so much more quickly now than before. Our world isn't as simple. We have billions of options at the touch of our fingers. Yet we don't know how to surrender the ego. We need to change the vows from death do us part to 'till vibrational circumstances guide us elsewhere.' Then, we need teachers to help us defuse the control dramas case by case, couple by couple. Unfortunately, that would traditionally be done by a minister, but our society is so sickened by the infiltrated church that so many have forsaken God and Its teachings into their daily lives.

By the way, you know God is an IT right? It is gender neutral, yet has both the divine feminine and divine masculine energy in it. It's like the Yin Yang symbol, completely.

The problem in relationships becomes that we stop taking care of our own business- the business of maintaining our own happiness. We fall into the Matrix' trap of survival rather than thrival, societal norms rather than freedom to express yourself, corporate marketing rather than understanding nature's ways, and the overall feeling of not enoughness that advertisers perpetuate to sell you products.

Nature is abundant. Since abundance gives liberally, we needn't worry about our fruits being picked. We just have to arrive at a place of trust- trusting Source to provide a way where we don't see one. On Doctor Hawkins' Scale of Consciousness, that trust equates to peace (600s) and is the gate to enlightenment. In this space of trusting Source to settle the score, we have confidence that all will work itself out for the greatest benefit. When you know this, and emit this frequency, those closest to you will sense it too. Your presence and abiding faith can literally change the climate in a room.

Osho says, 'If you love a flower, don't pick it up. Because if you pick it up it dies and it ceases to be what you love. So if you love a flower, let it be. Love is not about possession. Love is about appreciation.' In relationships, we can tend to get caught up trying to control situations outside our control, we inadvertently pick the flower of our loved ones, influencing them to take less care of their vibrational offerings, and suddenly we're stuck with a cluster fuck of attack and defend. To further exacerbate the problem, the ego, with its lack of forgiveness, is not quick to apologize or find fault in its own miscreation. Ego is not humble. **Humility is the number one quality to overcoming the dramas because it is willing to say, 'You know what, I fucked up. I made mistakes. I'm sorry. Please forgive me. Thank** you. I love you.'

How many marriages could be saved with that simple perspective of humility, giving an inch first?

Abundance in nature (and Buddhist philosophy) shows us that everything has a cycle of birth, becoming, blooming, and death. Because source is abundance, if we can embrace non-attachment, and appreciate the situation or object fully while we are present with it, then joy is experienced. Thus, we've brought heaven on to earth. Women are like flowers. We birth, bloom, and die every month with our periods. We could be so much more powerful if we learned to surrender quicker. Then, maybe, we could teach the men to embrace this tactic so that they can humble themselves easier in society without fear of seeming weak. In the evolutionary game, we've had so many valuable role reversals thanks to women's liberation that are now becoming coded into our DNA allowing us to play both traditionally male and female roles. In terms of evolution, the days of Man bringing home the money and wife cleans, cooks, and cares for the kids are becoming fewer. And thank Heaven for that! Because it invites more Yin into the Yang, and more Yang into the Yin. A coalescence of masculine and feminine energies is part of our evolutionary process. It also can confuse the playing field as to what role each person takes on.

I want you to realize some key wisdom.

1: **Know that the Universe always supports expansion.** If you feel tied down, restricted, or held back in any way through your relationship or any other circumstance, it simply is not sustainable. I recommend not getting over invested.

2: Follow your Bliss- Seriously. The Universe will support your bliss. I mean, look at how I told an angel, 'I want more sex and money', then became a very successful escort. Following my bliss is the reason why I sing. It brings me back to the present, fills me with joy, and helps the time pass by. Same for writing. **I ask you, what are your 5 favorite things? Seriously, take time right now to think about your favorite things. Do those all the time and be open for opportunities to monetize them.**

3: Tend to your business first and foremost. If you feel passionate about it, if it nags at you to do it, it's your calling, and the Universe will support you on it. In this, you can trust infinitely. Add action to trust and watch what miraculous manifestations come up. Then, just remember to give thanks for that. **Cultivating gratitude as a primary state of being will make every relationship grow better because you're open to the flow.**

4: Ask for what is wanted. Most people expend too much energy thinking about what is unwanted. How is Law of Attraction supposed to deliver your dreams if you're constantly ordering dissatisfaction with your vibrational offering? That's the secret. **You must ask for what is wanted**. Focus your attention away from the negative onto what is wanted. During your meditations, work on giving thanks and rejoice the same way you would as if it had already materialized. In this way, you become a vibrational match to what is wanted instead of the law of attraction working to give you more of what is unwanted. Drop whatever you've been told about it being bad to be selfish and demanding. Ask and it is given. Get what you want out of this life. The divine master in me commands joy, satisfaction and self-actualization. As a divine human angel, I deserve pure bliss. I am infinitely worthy of feeling the bliss of God's co-creative powers within me. Communicate clearly with everyone about what you want rather than focusing all that angry energy on what is unwanted.

6: If you don't trust yourself to prevent from sabotaging, just realize that every event is perfectly designed for us to grow in awareness and capability. **Choose to find a positive lesson.** Focus on internalizing how you can benefit from the 'imperfection' so that you can turn it into 'perfection' rather than a lost opportunity. Practice seeing it as a positive instead of a negative so that you can release resistance, grow and correct course quickly.

7: Remember that wisdom is usually what we get just after we needed it. Hindsight is 20/20. Always reach out. Seek refuge in good books or loving people for comfort and higher perspective. It is because of this hindsight forming wisdom that we need to be more liberal with our sincere apologies and ask for help.

"Our father who art in heaven.... And forgive us our trespasses as we forgive those who trespass against us...." Learning to forgive ourselves is so paramount. You can't forgive others if you can't forgive yourself.

8: Drop the righteousness or victimhood and realize that it takes two to tango. Stop to reflect upon how you co created this situation. Ask yourself, "How am I the trespasser in this situation? How can I do better moving forward?" Remember, every time you point the finger outward, there are always three pointing back at you.

9: **The right person for you will support your dreams**. Maybe they don't share your interest or always want to hear about it. That's cool, it makes room for you to practice selfishness, go get some friends and build a network of like-minded thinkers, aka a Mastermind Group who can hold space for your heart's desires, and vice versa. For example, I found a family of people who go do ayahuasca ceremonies together, and it's grand fun to know these special warrior people. I now have a network of support for my most vulnerable, intimate, and personal illusions. The interesting irony is that I didn't find my current boyfriend through one of these support groups. I told Source I wanted a solid relationship, not a project. So he doesn't share my interest for ayahuasca or other psychedelics because he's already got his shit together. He doesn't feel he needs what I need to experience connection. However, he isn't judging me while I go through my process or say my prayers. I also don't need his approval. I don't let his opinions on the situation prevent me from seeking out that support. This is a really key point because ego isolates. For example, say you have self-love issues. You're critical of yourself. Or like me, I didn't believe people when they said they loved me. That place inside that feels separate, and subsequently hurts, it's an illusion, and we need help seeing that. We need the support of others to hold a space of love and acceptance for us.

10: In a high vibrational relationship, the right person for you takes care of themselves first, AND with compassion lets you be free to do the same.

Now notice, the key here is basically compassionate selfishness and a surrender of control to Higher Will. The drama in this 3D reality seems to be the opposing forces of compassion with selfishness because of a lack of surrender. I'm telling you to merge the three. I ask you, how many super-nirvana-fully-realized-couples do you know? I'm in one right now. We are on the leading edge, my friends. You see, the old paradigms are falling away. Divorce rates are rising because people are changing their vibrational offerings so quickly, and it's hard to impossible to keep up. We all have to stop and work on ourselves because the new paradigm calls for whole people walking parallel with whole people.

The paradigm of scarcity/supply/ and demand has shifted into a new age of abundance. In the old paradigm, one person had to go gather resources while the other took care of the herd. In the new age of abundance, money can be made easily, and a team of supporters easily gathered socially, even if only virtually, because distance is just mental. I can get on a plane and be with you physically tomorrow, you see. Yet, the breakdown of that old paradigm, still has many of us trapped and confused because we have become so invested into the outdated systems that we've created. It'll take a miracle to get us through the birthing canal. SO PRAY FOR ONE. Pray for dozens of miracles, especially if you find yourself trapped in an unwanted co-creation. Allow for the unfolding, the blossoming of a new reality for yourself. Realize that the flower blooms and dies. Trust source to bloom a new bouquet into your life every time. Claim that abundance as your birthright. After all, we all come from the same star dust. We are little stars descendant from the big stars. What's ours is God's and what's God's is ours. With respect, and compassion, claim joy as your birthright, and free yourself from the attachment and suffering. Enjoy now.

As Eckhart Tolle advised a depressed woman who said she just wants to die,

'Then surrender to that truth. Practice dying in your mind.' Let go, so that the cycle can continue to flow and new flowers bloom. Available on iTunes are some beautiful guided meditations designed to help us remember nature's cycle of death and rebirth. Contemplate watching the grass grow, the lawn mowed, and so on. Upon recognizing the metaphor for your own life, you should have no doubt about reincarnation and your personal power to reinvent yourself. I would only ask that you graciously extend this same courtesy of faith to every other being. Stop doubting people's capacity to miraculously grow with or without your intervention. God bless them. Meaning, as the divine master in you commands, so shall they be blessed. Notice how compassion is required. Compassion is the seed. God is the Miracle Grow. We all have it within. Focus on fertilizing your own lawn in these ways, and your grass will be green.

It is safe to make space for the fulfillment of your highest calling. Again, if you don't know what that is yet, just imagine your top 10 interests. The top 10 things that make you feel good, that let the time pass by, that's what you should be doing. In the new age of abundance, your most joy-filled contributions are what our species needs for survival and thrival. Just remember, you don't have to figure out the details of how you're going to get from point A to point Z. What do you really want most?! Resolve to have it, and let Source fill in your grid. Let God handle the how. You can take it a step further and say, 'This or better, as God wishes.'

Perhaps you're a Zen Master and say to me, 'But Carina, I don't want for anything.' Cool, those are Nirvana thoughts. On Dr. Hawkins' Scale of Consciousness, you're at 850 out of a human potential of 1000. Going from 85% to 100% requires the further realization of how you are co-creating your reality. It's like being able to step up from the daily timeline, which can cause confusion and blindness, where one is able to see the perfection of life's unfoldment from a first-person perspective. Self-reflection is required. The more interactions you have with others, the more experiences and revelations or catharsis can happen. If one remains observant over a longer period of time, he can see how his desires or intentions were created. He can see how his force field of will attracted the perfect situations and people in order to make those puzzle pieces come together. That's how the 900s feel.

For example, I realized that my Twin Flame's silent treatment was beneficial because it helped me grow in patience and groundedness. I needed to focus my attention back onto handling my own business, giving me the energy and space needed to do the things that bring me joy (like writing).

I met David knowing it was a blessing to help both of us move through a tough transition. It was also a lesson. The Indigo child in me needed the contrast of my twin to stir up some shit. This gives space for those aspects of our personality to reveal themselves- the monstrous parts that need the healing. Only with distance, time to reflect, and space for healing could the cake be baked.

Meditate on a mental picture of the highest ascended most awesome version of you. Super You!

Utilize your 5 senses.

Let your higher power be the 6th sense that incubates this new reality.

Do that now.

Breathe this new truth into your new reality.

Exhale the violence that your misidentified labels have caused.

Choose peace for you.

Choose to allow yourself to follow your highest path.

Choose the same for your loved ones.

Wash it clean.

Find a healthy distraction that feels great.

Ho'oponopono

I'm sorry. Please forgive me. Thank you. I love you.

Ho'oponopono (ho-o-pono-pono) is a Hawaiian (83) practice of reconciliation (84) and forgiveness. (85) The Hawaiian word translates into English simply as correction, with the synonyms manage or supervise, and the antonym careless.[Similar forgiveness practices are performed on islands throughout the South Pacific, (86) including Hawaii (87) Samoa, (88) Tahiti (89) and New Zealand. (90) Traditional Ho'oponopono is practiced by Indigenous Hawaiian (91) healers, often within the extended family by a family member. There is also a New Age (92) practice that goes by the same name. Source Wikipedia (93)

Whenever you're in any kind of relationship or experiencing a blockage, try Ho'oponoponoing it. From deep in your heart, apologize for your trespasses. Apologize to yourself for trespassing against yourself. Thank yourself knowing that the higher self has received your repentance. Then throw a love bomb on it and watch the situation defuse. Don't let this just be words you repeat mindlessly like something else you've memorized. Use your emotions. I like to call upon the highest ascended self of the person with whom I have beef, and I imagine myself before them, the them I have beef with and the them that is the highest version. I visualize myself apologizing with full sincerity. Thanking them for whatever lessons this may show me, and thanking them for their forgiveness. This detangles all the chords that are likely tangled. Think string theory here. Saying I love you can go both ways too. Say 'I love you' to them, and yourself. This unity consciousness is a salv that lets the situation smooth out.

Remember, "You are God, but you just can't deflate your ego enough to embody that." – *Anonymous.*

Apologizing, humbling yourself, is the deflation necessary for true healing.

Imagine you are like Neo from The Matrix. His operator, or higher self, gives him a download. Suddenly, Keanu Reeves proclaims, "I know kung fu!" (94) He has unzipped the download for higher consciousness and actionable wisdom. Then his guide, Morpheus, challenges him to prove it. All of this happens in preparation for the real battle- an intergalactic fight for dominion over earth. Neo's purpose is to boldly overthrow the life-sucking matrix. It's the story of our times. It's the mission for all indigo children. (95)The Matrix plot, and character of Neo is how I feel when I'm coming off a good psychedelic high. The masters have told me that I'm here to be a reporter and healer, to ground the knowledge into the 3D physical awakening for the first, second and third waves of enlightened beings. Remember that extremely strong acid trip I told you about in the Introduction? I recorded a part of the voyage as Source began speaking through me. In humbly overwhelmed exasperation, I cried, "Who the fuck am I to be given this enormous task?!" To which It responded, 'You are my child.' Let that sink in for a minute. The same is true for you.

I hate the idea of 'We're only human.' It's so disempowering. No baby, you are a DIVINE HUMAN ANGEL raised in a world that forgot its innate power. You see yourself make mistakes and you guilt, blame, or shame yourself. You act like your mistakes are 'sins' for which you were taught to judge and label as unacceptable. Then, you were taught by the church to ask forgiveness of your sins, as if God is judging you. It's all wrong. It's all backwards. It's all part of the matrix designed to hold you down and snuff out your light. You deserve to feel empowered. You deserve to know God's infinite love and compassion. You deserve to forgive yourself for your mistaken beliefs and actions. God's already forgiven us; it's up to us to allow that truth in so that we can stop holding onto self-perpetuating resistance which keeps us from shining our most divine light.

Please believe, I understand if you feel overwhelmed and not particularly trying to radically change your entire life. I get that. But maybe that's exactly what you need. Enlightenment will change you, your interests, where and with whom you want to hang out. Probably, your diet will change too. But you needn't worry about whether it is safe to boldly go where your mind has never gone before. It is always safe to expand. The Universe WILL support your quest for enlightenment and self-actualization. The more willing you are to step into your awesomeness, and allow Source to flow through you, the more protection you receive from your guides. The more willing you are to show up for life, the more amazing and easy it gets. Life is not about suffering. **The matrix is about suffering.**

My life is always full of shit that needs overcoming. I chose a particularly difficult path this time around. I made a decision to repent in my most recent past life. I showed real remorse and earnestness to do my best to overcome all shortcomings of character, an oath to clean up my past for the sake of my future. Now mind you, I didn't become aware of it until, what, like 32 years into this life. It took the better half of my young adult life to clean up all the angst and karma from my childhood and past lives. As soon as one area had been cleared, another came up for healing. Maybe you can relate. Maybe there are people in your life holding you down with their expectations and identifications of who they think you are or should be. Parents are really good at that. Take heart.

Because others cannot vibrate in your experience, they cannot affect the outcome of your experience. They can hold their opinions, but unless their opinion affects your opinion, their opinion matters not at all. A million people could be pushing against you and it would not negatively affect you unless you push back. That million people pushing against you are affecting their millions of vibrations. They are affecting what happens in their experience. They are affecting their point of attraction, but it does not affect you unless you push against them.' -Abraham — *Hicks* (96)

So, the lesson here is, stop giving a shit what others think about you. Don't let their thoughts of who you are or who they think you're supposed to be hold you back from becoming the most amazing version of yourself. And, waste no time defending. There's a saying from A Course In Miracles that says, 'If I defend, then I am attacked.' Don't waste any time defending yourself or your ideas to the naysayers of the world. How great could you be if you could truly give zero fucks about being ridiculed for living your truth? How great could you be if you stopped judging your misaligned thoughts and actions as sin? How much suffering could you silence by accepting your mistakes, reclaiming your power, and deciding to move on and upwards? How much more difficult would it be for the matrix to control if we all committed to forgiving ourselves and our neighbors? If you watch the movie of your life with the conviction to become a Neo, in your own right, you will raise your consciousness above the real matrix (our currently corrupt political and monetary systems perpetuated by the corruption that resides within each of us). In your spare time, ask the highest ascended masters from the greatest and highest good of all to give you downloads,

DNA activations, and programs for higher consciousness. You'll become very adept at jumping out of the 3rd dimension level of suffering where ridicule and judgement reside. I thought the Matrix was just a movie until I started using psychedelics. Psychedelics not only help me realize the inferiority of our self-created matrix, but also gift me unrelenting inspiration by reminding me of our intergalactic connection. Every time I come down from a trip, I feel like a refreshed soldier ready for duty.

A Dear SiStar saw me one day in May 2013 two days after coming off of the most incredibly orgasmic high of my life. I'd taken MDMA, 2CB and acid. I was smiling from ear to ear, took off my shades, and gazed into her eyes. She gasped in awe saying, 'Carina, your eyes look so clear. It's amazing!' As our souls connected, I could see the galaxy dancing in her eyes as our pupils literally dilated and pulsated to an inaudible music. It's as if I was transferring a download to her... as if the totality of my being were saying to her, 'It is time. Arise and seize the day. You're going to win this one. Go get 'em tiger!' She and I have always shared a telepathic connection that never ceases to amaze us both.

On September 11, 2001 as I watched the second tower fall on TV, I knew it was time to get the fuck out of dodge. Oh, how my 280 pound wounded warrior body did not want to live through another battle! At this time, the only psychic gifts I had unlocked were telepathic. The patriot in me decided it was time to vote with my feet and retreat away from the political cross-fires. In the four months leading up to my wedding and move, I stress ate and gained an additional 40 pounds thanks to packaged processed garbage readily available at my Mom's house. I didn't know it yet, but I was gluten intolerant and desperately trying to wrap my mind around this incomprehensible move I was about to make. The fear was eminent. I knew we were about to leave the U.S.A. Matrix, but I couldn't imagine how my life was going to change. All I knew is that I had to do it. In this case, I couldn't compare it to anything; I had no frame of reference. I moved to Panama with 5 heavy suitcases, sight unseen with my Gringo-Panamanian husband as my guide.

Now I call upon stronger angels for support and let them manifest through strangers, friends, and coincidences. I believe in the revolution that starts from within. I call upon my guides for protection, and I act upon my intuition.

You are infinite multidimensional beings. However, in your amnesia, a consequence of manifesting into the 3D physical, you forget this fact. An inferiority complex is likely to develop when the matrix, who stands to profit, sells you their idea of perfection that you should aspire to become. It invites you to upgrade your image to a more advanced ideal self whom they influence you to become. They appeal to your innate desire to self-actualize, but carefully make you feel like you're not enough while doing it. They play off your ego's desire for greatness. Millions are made by helping you produce desire from a place of lack, and now you do not accept yourself or value the real you. Cha ching! Your feelings of lack are very lucrative to the matrix. Just please realize that your feelings of separateness, lack, racism, etc. are manufactured to control and hold you subserviently within the matrix. Take an oath to break free!

The big problem comes with believing that you ARE the lack, which makes you feel unworthy, not enough. Heaven help you if you were raised with a religion that prays like, 'Oh God I'm not worthy of your forgiveness and miracles. Please forgive me if this request is greedy...' Fuck that noise Jack! God is abundant and wants you to receive abundance! God doesn't need to forgive you; YOU need to forgive yourself! You are God's child. OF COURSE God wants to work miracles in your life! Shiiiit! Have no doubt about this PLEASE! You observe the current reality of not-havingness and believe it to be true. You focus too much on the reality of what is in the matrix rather than focusing on your heart's dreams and aspirations. Why is it that in an age of abundance, where we have access to more than ever, people are feeling more lack than ever before? Answer: We give away our power through misperception, misjudgment and misidentification thinking that we are what we have around us, what people say about us, what negativity we say about ourselves, and our past story. That's all ego bullshit. How can you tell? Because if it hurts, it's out of alignment with the Truth of all that is.

We have forgotten our inherent worth. It can be fixed. The way to do so is to relax and allow nature to repair itself. Of course, that is easier said than done because we are constantly circumventing nature's higher Will and operating bodies that are short circuiting from the disconnection to Source while surviving within the matrix. It can be hard to trust ourselves sometimes, much less others. The mind plays tricks and is much louder than the heart. However, your heart knows the truth. So spend more time trying to tap into that, instead. If we can just relax, nature will give us the upgrades we need. That's what I do with people in sessions- help them relax into their inheritance of well being with focused intention.

Case in point: The SiStar received two chakra balancings and did one surrender ceremony with me over the course of about 6 months. In that time, she met her birth father, left a disempowering co-dependent relationship, got off meat, and was practicing celibacy (which cleared her mind from lustful desire). She was reading my book, and making empowering decisions from her higher consciousness. The SiStar also reported astral traveling back to the moment she had wanted to commit suicide in which she whispered to herself 'It'll be alright.', thus saving her own life. When she told me this, sure enough, she tested 920 on the Scale of Consciousness out of a possible 1000. That's Christ consciousness; the level in which you remember your Divine Human nature and harness your innate power with a bird's-eye omniscience likened to Jesus. The power of your creator can be harnessed in new and innovative ways. Just like the birth-death- and rebirth cycles of plants. Just like how we must sleep in order to recharge our bodies, we also must allow nature to provide new types of energetic upgrades on a regular basis, tapping into the heart of our planet and galaxy for guidance.

Enlightenment is our natural state of being. The only reason we don't feel this way all of the time is mistakenness. You are here to evolve and experience the expansive unfoldment of life on a unique planet where anything is possible. You need only to believe in your power to download the major life hacks inherent within Source, inherent within you. "God eternal within the body." —*Terence McKenna*

Resistance to this truth will only cause you more suffering. "What we resist will not only persist but will grow in size."- Carl Jung. (97)

Here's a lesson from A Course in Miracles. These daily emails have gotten me through some dark times and serve as a good reminder.

Lesson 248 ~ Whatever suffers is not part of me. (98)

I have disowned the truth. Now let me be as faithful in disowning falsity. Whatever suffers is not part of me. What grieves is not myself. What is in pain is but illusion in my mind. What dies was never living in reality, and did but mock the truth about myself. Now I disown self-concepts and deceits and lies about the holy Son of God. Now am I ready to accept him back as God created him, and as he is.

Father, my ancient love for You returns, and lets me love Your Son again as well. Father, I am as You created me. Now is Your Love remembered, and my own. Now do I understand that they are one.

Spend some time considering the above from different angles. It's really profound when you think about it.

Visualization:

Take some deep breaths. Do that now.

Imagine saying to yourself:

I am a baby tree in a forest of pine trees.

I might perceive that I will grow to be like them. However, as I develop, I notice that I am not like the pine trees. This doesn't make me any less valuable.

Time passes and it becomes apparent that I make red flowers, whereas the pines grow tall, thick, and erect.

People seem to value the pines because of their many uses, but I am not trying to be a pine tree, I am trying to be as Creator made me.

As I mature and blossom, my unique diversity is recognized as beauty and has value in its own right. People refer to the forest now as the one with the beautiful red tree. My persistence and presence raises the total value of the whole forest. I am necessary. I am a valuable part of the whole.

I take care that my previous feelings of inferiority, now dissolved by my higher understanding, are not replaced with vain superiority complexes. I am balanced. I realize the emptiness of superiority. I realize the emptiness of inferiority. I am now returned to the wholeness of Source, repaired and full in my heart and perceptions. I now breathe in the wholeness of unity consciousness as my truth.

I accept myself as one brilliant unique tree in the forest, part of a whole.

Smile and breath. Feel how the energy changes when you smile.

I add value as much as the others.

They may fail to recognize this value, as I once did.

I continue to hold my power and realize that I will bloom. They will too.

My flowers will fall. Their needles will fall.

My beauty and perceived relevance will come and go.

Yet, I am what I am.

I let go and allow nature to recycle me.

Different Levels of Power for Healing and Miracles

"There are three ways" in which healing flows forth from the Spiritual World, all involving the Holy Spirit, of course. One is through the human spirit. The second is through the work of angels and ministering spirits. And the third is through the direct work of God in Christ. Although all healing flows forth from God and needs the instrument of the human spirit, in terms of spiritual "work classification" there are three ways for it to flow. Thus all humans with a spirit that is strong have a measure of healing power.

Some human individuals have developed their spirits more than others and seem to possess this healing ability (Proverbs 18:14; Romans 1:9; 1 Corinthians 5:4; James 2:26). The healing that flows forth from the second category is stronger and more powerful because it involves both the human spirit at work plus the spiritual presence of angels and ministering spirits who specialize in these works (Exodus

3:2; 14:19; 23:20, 23; 32:34; 33:2; 2 Kings 1:3, 15; 6:17; Acts 5:19-20; 8:26). From time to time, the manifestation of the healing Christ comes upon a gathering, group or community and the most powerful healings take place (Acts 5:12-16).

Of the second category, angels and spirits from the higher spiritual spheres are commissioned and sent by God to link up with humans whose spirits are open to God. To human eyes, it seems that the physical humans are able to manifest great authority and power in healing but to those whose spiritual eyes are opened, the work of these angels and spirits can be seen behind the human vessels. There are rare occasions when humans have walked closely with God Himself in such a manner that the Lord Himself directly channels His healing power through the human vessel. These healing events are extremely powerful and are closely watched by all in the Spiritual World as they also have an impact on the Spiritual World."

— *The Spiritual World (Peter Tan)* (99)

I tell people, my hand is like a vacuum. It senses the darkness, discordant traumas, or lack of light/ energy and pulls it out. Then, light comes in to infuse all of the cells with nourishment. I was so pleased to see Cameron Day's explanation and pointers.

"The Galactic Vacuum"

This is a tool that I use on a daily basis in removing limiting energies, defending my Sovereign energy boundaries, as well as helping clients to do the same. **Any thought-form, etheric implant or soulless being put into the vacuum is taken to the Galactic Core to be transmuted back into pure energy. Any beings with a soul sent to the Galactic Core are either transmuted, cleansed of their darkness and rehabilitated or dissolved back into basic energy (destroyed).**

Either outcome is fine with me, although I am always rooting for them to emerge as healed, sane beings who can become productive members of the universe once again. **Whether or not a being is healed and restored or it is destroyed is between them and Source.** I do not make that decision, I am simply serving as a galactic conduit to send that being to look in the Galactic Mirror, take responsibility for its actions and hopefully heal and regain sanity.

I do warn these beings one time that they are NOT permitted to infringe on my Sovereign energy and that they need to back off or I will use defensive force in order to send them to the Galactic core. Most of them will make a show of standing down, but will try to send in an energetic probe or "feeler" later in order to continue their agenda. When I sense this, I go to the source of the incursion along with multiple Galactic vacuums and "clean house."

About half of these parasitic, demiurgic beings can be redeemed and transmuted back into sane, productive members of the free Universe. That is actually a pretty good ratio, considering how far into fear, insanity, control, enslavement, abuse, manipulation, destruction and hierarchy these beings have gone." 100)

Chapter 17:

LOVE YOURSELF BY LOVING OTHERS

It's late summer 2014, and I am in tears, overwhelmingly grateful for the kindness that other people have shown me. I just got home from a two-week trip in Florida and have decided to leave Panama for a while. I've been here 8 years, and Source is calling me to move on. I'm not sure when I'll be back, what Source has in store for me, and try as I might to really feel into remembering how much Source loves me, loves us, I'm just a mess of tears. (It was as though my intuition knew an era was over and the ride ahead would be paved with sorrowful challenges. A huge chapter was closing, and crying is just how I tend to process energy. I was about to fumble considerably over the next three years trying to truly level up and step into all of my power as a healer. My 8-year vacation in Panama was over, and it was time to face reality in America. The tears are a combination of relief from the sometimes overwhelming pressure of being a single woman plus feeling baffled at how easily life can unfold when we just let it. It's an emotional clinging onto what, I know intellectually, is impermanent. Ah yes, there's that attachment shit causing suffering again!

Knowing something intellectually is often different than knowing something emotionally. Then there's shame surfacing for all the times when I didn't trust- pushed- made it happen. The tears combine with the overwhelming love that comes from knowing that these earthly people really do appreciate me without any obligation to do so. They are simply reflecting back the love I've shown them, the love we all inherently deserve, the love we are, the love I needed but didn't get during childhood. After all, family is obligated to love you unconditionally, right? Instinctively, I never believed my mother or brother's unconditional love for me because they had none for others, and I knew that we are all one, though I couldn't articulate it. These people aren't obligated to love me, they just do. In the sanctity of my bedroom inside my broken home, perfect love was something you only read about, not a tangible 3D experience. So learning to be and receive unconditional love is a real challenge for me, especially when the person I want it from most is my mother. Trying to accept my worthiness is causing a huge energetic release of old anguish.

Breathe it in. Breathe it in. Patience, forgiveness, acceptance, silence, presence, peace, focus, expansion, downloads, upgrades, on to the next test.

Their love is not based on my effort, not what I do for them, but who I am. They use my words and say, 'thank you for being', 'thank you, thank you thank you' and 'blessings'. It blows me away to imagine that people could love me as deeply as I love them. Part of me knows that I love them so much because I have felt such a separate contrast, and I don't want for people to suffer as I have. It baffles me to imagine that we have all suffered so deeply on some relatable level, yet we push away healing and ignore good advice.

You can't make people love you the way you need to be loved, but you can trust Source to find a way to show it, if you will let it.

So part of me feels dumb for all the suffering I've caused myself.... For all of the times I've wanted so desperately to feel and receive love, yet I couldn't or wouldn't let it in. I'll get in my head remembering a kind act that someone has done for me, breathe into the depth of that love, and start crying out all of the shame for having ever been greedy or taken advantage of another's acts of kindness. I'll find myself grateful, and in tears because I just wish they could know how appreciative I am. The tears are actually because I'm afraid I won't show enough gratitude, because I know, in the past, I haven't, and I'm afraid that I haven't changed. A decision needs to be made. It's as though, if I didn't create the pain of the fear, I wouldn't build the resolve to love more and show more appreciation. So, every time I catch myself crying in shame, I catch myself and decide to reaffirm my commitment to being better. I accept the responsibility and the tears dry up.

Ease and grace. Ease and grace.

It makes me wonder about people who don't show their emotions. It makes me wonder if they feel as deeply as I do. Maybe they are just better adjusted. Is there something wrong with me? Are my chakras imbalanced? Maybe I should be more grounded. Logically, I can hear a friend reminding me of Eckhart Tolle saying, 'Remember the power of now.' So I start typing, releasing, confessing, and knowing that I should take my own good advice. When I write, I'm present. When I breathe, I'm present.

What brings you to the present? What can you do that causes you to lose track of time?

Presence=present.

It's this contrast that leads me to appreciate ego. Of course, without the extremes, I wouldn't feel so intensely. If it's the ego that is creating the fear, contrast, illusion of separateness- then finding balance must be the healing of ego. Presence heals ego. So do tears. I'm a cry baby, and I'm okay with that. It's a way of cleansing the water that holds resistant memories. Now, with a higher consciousness, I must infuse prayer back into the body so as to make strong what was broken.

Everything gets fixed through love.

On some level, I know that this tough life is teaching me to appreciate all that I've taken for granted in pasts lives as a pirate, a thieving accountant, a Nazi German, in my bloodline of preachers (some of them highly mistaken), addicts, and in this life trespassing against my family members. It's the contrast and determination to be better, to shoot for the stars, which keeps me going. In fact, since we are made of stardust, and it is the explosive expansion and collapsing that creates galaxies, I think I'm alright. Additionally, I feel the reassurance of friends, plus knowing that Source is doing most of the work, that lets me relax in bed giving time to heal and find myself.

I just ask you to please tell your family members how much you love and appreciate all they do for you. Show gratitude to the ones with whom you are estranged. It will open the door to healing, which heals the world. Don't wait until they are sick and dying. Write some quick emails or texts now. Send a Facebook message, or if they've already left the physical dimension, allow your heart to connect out to their spirit's dimension.

Care for your estrangement the way you would care for an illness. Illness is an illusion. It's misalignment from the higher truths of your divine nature. You deserve to feel the flow of love compounding within your hearts. Source wants us to embody its expansion and to recognize the alrightness of our inevitable implosion and reemergence. If you could only know how infinitely we are love, how passionately Source wants us to feel amazingly safe and protected, you would pray every day for the wellbeing of each person on this planet. You would try to sit at every meal thanking the food, thanking the elements, thanking the people who bring this abundance to you, blessing them, and blessing everyone they know, living in gratitude. When I start to feel PMS, I take one or two small doses of acid to raise my consciousness right back up to that level.

There are so many children, young and old, walking the face of this magnificent planet who don't know that God loves them. It breaks my heart. It's important to God that you find "him". **IT really wants to help. It says the best way for you to know God is to practice appreciation.** The lost don't know God because most people are lost, and when they seek higher refuge, the people teaching spirituality are often lost too. So, of course, it becomes hard to trust God when you can't trust man to teach you about It. You are divine and sacred, and so are the people who told you otherwise. They just forgot. Forgive their ignorance born from amnesia. Invite their souls to remember as you are also now invited.

Feeling disgust or contempt for anyone is like swallowing poison and expecting the other person to die. This kind of mental and emotional poison causes cancer. Trapped hate and anger cause cancer. It is scientifically proven that people who suppress their emotions, or remain depressed are much more likely to die. It is a reflection of your separation from the Truth of Source manifest into the physical. Chemotherapy isn't going to stop that. Allowing your thoughts to return to the Truth of 100% self-love heals every dis-ease. If the person doesn't make those corrections, then the death serves as their reemergence with Source so that they may be healed and transmuted back toward the light.

Obesity is a separation from Source, usually beginning with poor thoughts and emotions manifesting as a compulsion to seek comfort from outside themselves. The same is true for addictions. Having struggled with addiction much of my adult life, and having lost 100s of pounds, multiple times, I can promise you that disconnection from the truth of God's love is the foundation for all dis-ease.

All the people committing suicide are angry because, buried deep down inside, the seed of their divinity knows they deserve better. Their intuition remembers the sanctity of God's love, and knows that death will return them to that.

Unfortunately, for most "untimely deaths", the consciousness of the person at the time of death was either in a low, or resistant state, or shock, and so the situation causes a split in consciousness known as soul fragmentation. This happens also with near-death experiences or extreme cases of PTSD. So, for example, like in the case of my husband, he died suddenly of an overdose. At first, he couldn't accept that he'd left his body, so as a ghost he would rummage around people's stuff looking for things to steal so he could buy drugs. He didn't know how to forgive himself, so he couldn't imagine God forgiving him. Thus, he remained a ghost until my mentor was able to show him God's love and ascend him on to the other side of the veil. Another example is sudden death in the hospital or a car crash where the soul is shocked out of the body quickly and can't accept the light in order to move on. They feel they are supposed to be there to protect their families. The ego is still in charge instead of surrendering to spirit.

Love them. Pray for them.

Stop giving up on God and humanity the way you give up on yourself, the way someone else gave up on you.

Start giving unconditional love, seeing it come back to you, affirming that we live in a safe, abundant world.

Hug that sad little child inside and out.

Let go of the old paradigms of supply-demand- and scarcity.

Evolve into the new age of abundant ease and grace.

I know it's easier said than done. I mess up all the time. But maybe you'll have the courage to look at how you push against evolution (change), your disbelief in Source as an abundant provider and old habits rooted in the old paradigms of scarcity, lack, and suffering. Decide to risk trusting the infinite power of creation within you.

Changing Self-image

Allow me to quote a great book called Psycho-Cybernetics written by a plastic surgeon. It discusses how transformative our lives can become simply by virtue of changing our self-image. This is a technique I use instinctively during my guided meditations. The objective is to imagine yourself as the ultimate well-adjusted human. In my meditations with clients, I tell patients to imagine you as your highest Ascended Self. It's a meditation technique that comes from Wu Wei's *I-Ching Handbook.* (101)

On page 43-44 of *Psycho-Cybernetics* (102) written by Maxwell Maltz M.D., F.I.C.S. it reads:

> "How can you know the truth about yourself? How can you make a true evaluation? It seems to me that psychology must turn to religion. The Scriptures tell us that God created man "a little lower than the angels" and 'Gave him dominion"; that God created man in his own image. If we really believe in an all-wise, all-powerful, all-loving Creator, then we are in a position to draw some logical conclusions about that which He has created—Man. In the first place such an all-wise and all-powerful Creator would not turn out inferior products, any more than a master painter would paint inferior canvases. Such a Creator would not deliberately engineer his product to fail, any more than a manufacturer would deliberately build failure into an automobile. The Fundamentalists tell us that man's chief purpose and reason for living is to "glorify God," and the Humanists tell us that man's primary purpose is to 'Express himself fully."
>
> However, if we take the premise that God is a loving Creator and has the same interest in his Creation that an earthly father has in his children,

then it seems to me that the Fundamentalists and the Humanists are saying the same thing. What brings more glory, pride, and satisfaction to a father than seeing his offspring do well, succeed and express to the full their abilities and talents? Have you ever sat by the father of a football star during a game? Jesus expressed the same thought when he told us not to hide our light under a bushel, but to let our light shine..." so that your Father may be glorified." I cannot believe that it brings any "glory" to God when his children go around with hang-dog expressions, being miserable, afraid to lift up their heads and 'be somebody."

Healing Others

In your prayers today, send love to all the strangers in far distant lands who are committing genocide, stealing, or terrorizing. That's the best medicine, God's love (flowing through you). Believe in God's love for people and let it flow through you projecting love onto the ones who need it most, beginning with yourself. Send them hugs in your mind and allow yourself to receive comfort from everywhere. Open your heart to receive. Tell Source exactly what you are open to receiving more of. Drive through a 'bad neighborhood' and try humbly sending love to all of those people. If traffic is backed up because of an accident, send them love. Practice being like your Self being God-like. The power of Source flowing through you will heal and protect everyone you focus attention upon.

One of the last things we do in a meditation, after we are really open and reconnected, is to imagine our energy radiating out beyond the room, beyond the building, beyond the neighborhood, the city, the state, the country, the continent, the planet, until you can see the planet with your light emanating all around it. Now you are praying/being at similar levels as the ascended masters. Many of them radiate their energy all over the planet just like this. So what happens when you allow your heart to connect with theirs, is that you puncture through the veil, like punching a hole through paper. Now their energies flood through your being trying to ground that energy into the planet. Your job, is simply to continue practicing opening up that channel and grounding the frequency. This is done by breathing through your body, channeling the energy down into the ground, either through your body, as if you have roots buried deep into the core of earth, or by opening a portal of energy in front of you where you command the energy down. You point the energy to a specific location with your mind's eye, pointing it down into the ground (or someone else's body) as if everything you touch is instantly transmuted back up to the highest truth, love, light and joy.

I was living homeless in Panama City, and had been given a room to stay in a rough neighborhood. The gangs (which were always youth under 18) were just normal kids, misguided and looking for connection. When I showed up to the neighborhood, neighbors had the tourism police there in a flash. The youth were playing with water balloons trying to beat the heat and listening to music on loud speakers. They weren't trying to be gang members, they were like independent YMCA's without proper leadership. I wasn't intimidated in the least.

In a short time, 10 tourism police showed up. I knew the adult onlookers behind closed doors were protecting me.

After about a month, one day, the owner and I suddenly got into a conflict and I was asked to leave immediately. I was leaving the building dragging heavy suitcases with me, walking to the street. Simultaneously, police were raiding the building, a cameraman for the news filming, and just as I drove off in a cab, gunfire was exchanged. I knew the angels were protecting me. Remember, you simply can't die before your time. In the meantime, I find that investing in faith and gratitude serve as a far superior insurance policy. By this time, I had gotten very adept at surrendering, connecting, reaffirming my desire to be of service, and humbly asking my guides to lead as I'd promise to obey the call. It became clear to me that this time homeless was meant for me to see what poverty is like so that I could position myself with people of influence in order to make a difference in the world

There's an old Panamanian man with a fiddle always seated in his chair as I hurry by on my way to deal with the cell phone provider. In the past, I've looked at him with loving compassion, or been too busy to stop and throw him some change. Spare change; that's all this man is worth now? But on this day, I was grateful to have received kindness, so I stopped and gave him $5. He wasn't playing. In fact, he looked too tired to play. Now he looked relieved, if only for a little while. I can't say that I've ever heard him play. I don't remember him doing a stirring rendition of anything.

Please understand, I didn't give out of pity, because he needed it, or out of direct appreciation for his efforts. I gave because he was worthy, and I wanted to remind him of that by showing him appreciation. Beggars need to be shown appreciation or compassion for the humanity of our shared suffering. I gave to him out of appreciation for our collective humanity, for his willingness to show up to work, even when he was probably too hungry to perform. At that moment, I remembered how much it sucks not to receive appreciation, so I decided to show some. In hindsight, I should have given him a hug, as well. Yesterday, I was given so much appreciation. It's a mixture of Source's love and compassion, the Law of Attraction, our willingness to show up, to ask for what is wanted, and to recycle those energies into the collective. I asked my client for what was wanted (money), and then I shared a piece of the pie. You do the same thing when you're happy to spend and share your money.

My point to you is that, in order to receive appreciation, we have to show up for it and allow ourselves to receive it. My mom used to say that the first 50% of character is just showing up. I would submit that the same applies to receiving love. Showing up is half the battle. Tell Source today, 'I allow myself to receive love.' Then, get ready for it, knowing that this is so. Put the statement on your fridge. That's probably what you're really hungry for anyway.

Ram Dass explains in a very interesting way: Suffering as Grace. (103)

Integration Exercise: Activating the Portal of "Christ Consciousness" Within

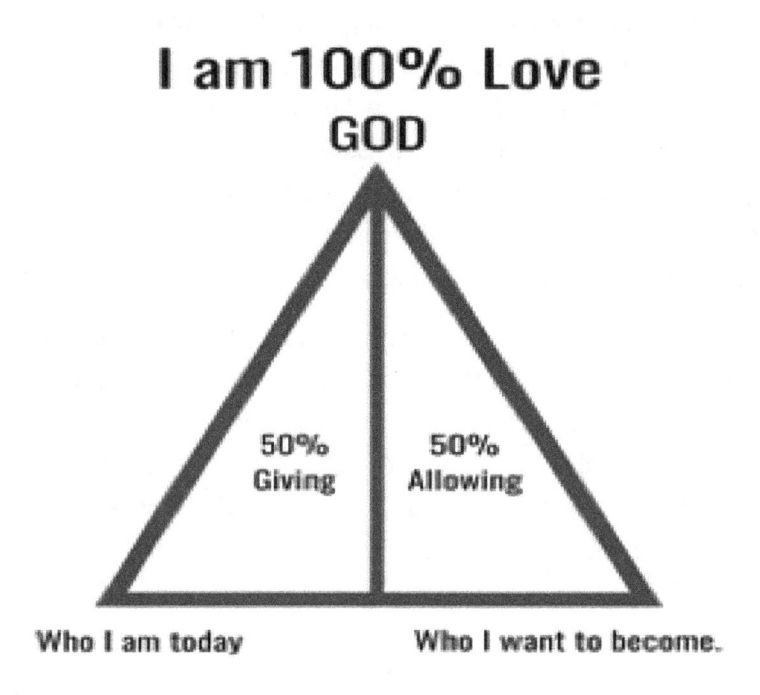

I am 100% Love
GOD

50% Giving | 50% Allowing

Who I am today | Who I want to become.

At the top of the page write: I AM 100% Love

Draw a big Triangle on the page.

Draw a line down the middle, making two even triangles.

On the bottom left, write: Who I am today.

On the bottom right, write: Who I want to become.

— Reflect on who you think you are right now. On the left of the page, write down at least 10 adjectives you use to describe who you currently think you are.

— Reflect on who you want to become. What qualities do you want to embrace more. What character and values do you want to develop. Mind you, these are all affirmative statements. Write down those words on the right.

—Inside the left triangle, write: 50% Giving

Shade in the entire triangle with color up to the percentage that you think you are giving in life.

— On the right, write: 50% Allowing.

Using a different color or just by shading darker, fill in the percentage that you think you are allowing yourself to receive in life.

— At the top of the triangle write: God

Now, using a different shading technique, shade in any empty space between the two triangles.

— Imagine that you are allowing God's love and light to bridge the gap between how much you give and how much you allow yourself to receive love.

Take several deep breaths. Breathe in the light of God, and direct that energy into those dark resistant spaces that need more allowing and more giving.

— Exhale the tight resistance as you breathe in God again and open up more and more.

— You will see that, very soon, like magic, more love will begin to come to you and flow through you, as you. This is you activating the portal of "Christ Consciousness" within.

Breathing exercise:

Repeat several times. (This exercise is precisely how you should be working with any powerful energetic medicine like ayahuasca, ibogaine, acid, mushrooms, bufo, DMT, sapo, peyote etc. It's also extremely effective while sober.)

Go to a sad place that needs more unconditional love. The deep traumas. The profound resistance, where it hurts the most. Give yourself permission to emote. Catch yourself suffering. REMEMBER that it hurts because the thought is out of alignment with the Truth. Breathe the truth of unconditional love into those tight resistant suffering places. This black and brown wormhole of darkness can seem infinite at times, and can take so many multiple attempts. Become aware of how you block the flow and let the Divine Master Within You declare and allow the release and opening of the darkness in your heart (or specific area for healing.)

Ask your highest power to transmute the misalignment back into the truth.

Visualize the violet flame of God's infinite perfection transmuting it. Invite all ascended masters and benevolent assistants. Call upon all your guides. Heck, you can even call upon my guides and the guides of everyone my colleagues work with. Stay with the breathing until you feel a shift.

Breathe in the peace and unconditional love.

Exhale shame and guilt.

Notice if there are places of suffering in your body. Channel the energy, as you breathe, into those spaces. Try laying your hands on that space to help direct your focus. Let the energy move through you, through your hands, into the suffering. See the energy penetrating through your hands, through your mind, through all of the cells, down past the skin, past the blood, past the fat and muscle tissue, etc.

For me, this process can look very violent. If I'm expelling a curse or terrible karma, attachment, addiction, soul fracture, or extreme trauma. The energy will be black or brown. It can transmute to red, which is usually a very resistant frequency, or it could be that your root chakra opens and you can channel energy down to the Mother Earth or suck up nurturing healing from her.

Breathe in unconditional love.

Exhale gratitude.

Direct the gratitude into all suffering spaces. SMILE. Notice how the energy changes when you smile. Let the smile be the miracle salve.

Breathe in unconditional love.

Exhale unconditional love.

Repeat several times.

Tell yourself some positive affirmations that reprogram the old resistant feeling or belief into the highest, lease resistant truths.

Project Unconditional love to all things in your room.

Expand it throughout your house and neighborhood.

Project unconditional love to everyone you know. Expand the love onto everyone they know.

Focus your attention onto those people or institutions you hate.

Practice forgiveness through the Ho'oponopono (104) technique of: I'm sorry. Please forgive me. Thank you. I love you.

Keep practicing this technique until resistance is released and love can be expressed.

Exhale the unconditional love out through your town, your district, your country, your continent, the planet, the galaxy.

Repeat to yourself. "I am unconditional love. We are all unconditionally loved. I allow myself to love everyone and everything. It is always safe to love. It is easy to love. I feel so relaxed knowing that I am loved."

Do that now and have a glorious healing day.

Chapter 18:
THE MAGIC OF CRYSTAL INTUITION

As I began the journey of asking myself, "Why did I allow myself to get so big? What positive purpose did that serve?" I realized that, if I'd not been fat, I'd definitely not have studied as hard, would have played even harder, and would most certainly have a bunch of kids with multiple baby-daddies. This most certainly would have prevented me from achieving enlightenment. I'd have gotten bored and felt really trapped and depressed. I've had to heal from all kinds of karma related to sex, kids, and abusive relationships. I understand abuse, addiction, obesity, adoptions, abortions, separation, divorce, and death of a spouse all from personal experience so I cannot judge anyone for their choices. Desire is one of the hardest sensations to deal within this human existence. For this reason, most spiritual leaders were required to sacrifice the sexual aspect of their lives. I feel like I already did this in another life in the Himalayas a long time before my days on the plantation trading sex for status in a past life.

Our whole circuitry works differently when we abstain from sex. In Hinduism, the Guru Nithyananda says that, to fully integrate into the other circuitry, a woman must abstain for 3 months. The men must abstain for 6 months. Because of childhood traumas, I didn't trust myself to be a good mother. Because I had always felt my mother's resentment of not being able to go out and fully self-actualize, I did not want to put my daughter through that, so I gave her up for adoption. Because my husband and I were literally between homes the two times he was on drugs and got me pregnant, I did not want to have babies with him. Yet, later on, I felt compelled to 'practice', let's say. That is how the idea of the Foundation came about, as sort of an incubator for learning to be a good mother. If I succeed, then I've benefited more than just my own bloodline.

During my first Akashic Record reading with dear friend Teresa Martinez, I asked about relationships. My guides said to think of things more in terms of connections. They said to keep from getting carried away by desires, to do a grounding meditation where I visualize my roots wrapped around a giant crystal inside the Mother Earth. Likewise, imagine roots coming from the heart into the earth.

Interestingly enough, when I asked about sex, if I had to give up sex there was an emphatic 'NO' YAAAAYYYY!! So I asked if I was supposed to have children, and they did not answer. Sometimes, it isn't in our soul's highest good to know everything. Teresa said she saw me in a long blue skirt with several different colors. I imagined the dress based on her description. Later on, when I did the grounding meditation, the crystal I wrapped my roots around also looked like this skirt. I'd never seen this kind of stone before. Coincidentally, a couple weeks later, I was cruising Pinterest and saw the stone. I was seeing a black stone opal whose benefits read:

"Opal, in particular black opal, has historically been thought of as an incredibly lucky stone. It wards off the evil eye and protects those who travel to faraway lands, much as the Middle Eastern 'Hamsa' amulet does. It also blocks bad dreams from your psyche, and works to focus your mental capacities and provide motivation and energy.

"Its psychological benefits also include increased confidence on a deep level, confidence that is independent of external factors and completely based on understanding your core being. It helps you to realize all the externally anchored beliefs and behaviors you have adopted, and to cast them off in favor of your core self. Black opal helps reduce the impact of reproductive disorders.... All forms of opal are useful during childbirth to reduce the severity of pain."

Ok – time out. Part of my hermit mentality is fear of evil-eye because I am sensitive to psychic attack. Confidence on a deep level from within is imperative because it can get a little confusing to my ego to have (or not have) a cheerleading section, which seems almost necessary to prop me up emotionally or from a marketing perspective. I had horrible back labor, which I knew would happen, and have always suspected I might have a child with Down's syndrome. (I had a cyst on my left ovary until one day Mujin Choi (105) healed it in a 30 minute psychic healing session from 5,000 miles apart.) And you're telling me a stone could help fix all this, AND that my intuition knew which stone to ground to? You better believe I got on eBay immediately to look for the stone. Or, I can imagine this stone, now that I understand more about it, and just connect to its benefits mentally.

"Mystical Properties": Opal is a stone of inspiration which enhances the imagination and creativity as well. It helps one release inhibitions and enhances the memory.

Opal is also said to be a very spiritual stone, and can help one be 'invisible' in situations where they don't care to be noticed. It has been known to bring happy dreams, and to ease the process of change.

Opal is a silicate, containing water, correlating with our emotions. Opal clarifies by amplifying and mirroring feelings, buried emotions and desires (including love and passion). With this comes less inhibition, more spontaneity, free visualization, clearer imagination, and more vivid dreams.

"Black": Is known to enhance sexual attractiveness, as well as leading one to a higher spiritual experience. One of the strongest good luck stones. It is told to transform the fears that hold us back from action into optimism and an eagerness to get on with our lives...."

Alright cool, because heaven knows I need all of the above to feel more balanced.

"Healing Properties": Opals are known to strengthen the will to live. They're linked to the heart and told to stimulate the glands and regulate the metabolism. Opal has a beneficial effect on the human psyche, pouring a warm healing energy on broken hearts and restoring harmony ...."

Perfect. When I used to suffer from depression, I was lacking the will to live. With the pre-diabetes, this will help offset that problem. Most definitely, some of my past life reoccurring dreams are of a broken heart where people were stealing my abundance behind my back, as I desired this man too much. Cool beans! You mean a stone is going to help me with all of that? Nice one!

"Black-Brown-Gray": Particularly useful for releasing sexual tension that arises from an emotional cause, as well as for processing and integrating newly found or released emotions. Black opals will absorb pain and/or illness, replacing it with a healing rainbow of light. It may ease chronic bone problems or weaknesses and any disease deep within the body tissue. Use it to counter side effects from modern x-ray or laser treatments as well as to reduce the toxicity of necessary chemical treatments ...."

Hahaha. That's so funny. I used to get x-rayed so much as a kid that my mom would joke that I glowed in the dark! I can believe that the final hardest part of repairing and replacing my DNA is within the bones. Certainly, having a tool to help pull it out with ease and grace would be lovely.

"Magical Properties:
  Energy: Projective, Receptive
  Element: All Elements
  Deity: Cupid
  Powers: Astral projection, psychism, beauty, money, luck and power

The opal contains all of the colors as well as all of the qualities of all other stones. And as such, an opal may be "programmed" or charged with virtually every type of energy used in all spells involving all magical needs.

"Opals are worn during trips of astral projection to facilitate the process but also for protection. Opals are used to recall past incarnations, and are favored by many to develop psychic powers. Jewelry is the best for this aspect, especially earrings. Opals are worn to bring inner beauty to the surface, and one should carry or use an opal to dedicated oneself to improving outward appearance ...."

Ok, great. I've always sort of felt under-dressed, and I was totally thinking earrings and a necklace would be good. I asked Goddess Bridget what she was going to do for me and she said something about helping me understand the underworld. I am now certain that I'll be needing this stone for protection and to help facilitate the successful travels into the past. Boy, my Guru Within sure is far more interesting than I could have ever imagined!

"Black opals" are prized by magicians and Wiccans as strong power stones. More recently in Wiccan rituals used as God stone (white opal being the Goddess stone). Black opal amplifies power magically and an amulet of black opal attracts good fortune.

"All opals are considered luck-bringing stones."

"A **warning**...opals are extremely sensitive to the energies and vibrations of the wearer, projecting the exact same vibrations as the bearer of the stone. Which on one hand makes an opal a wonderful manifestation stone. If one truly believes in an idea strong enough, the stone will beam those positive vibrations out, thus attracting just what you hold possible in your mind."

Good thing I've purified most of my thoughts, eh!

"However, on the other hand, your negative vibrations will also be broadcast with the same amount of power. Do not use opal if you are feeling down, pessimistic or negative in any way, you will only compound the issue.... [It is the] modern Birthstone for the month of October...." which is my birth month.

"Black-Brown-Grey": resonates with the 2nd, or Sacral/Navel Chakra as well as the reproductive organs. Use with fluorite to clean the aura and prevent cording. (106)

Chapter 19:

HEALING THE PROSTITUTE LIVES

From a Course in Miracles
Lesson 268 ~ Let all things be exactly as they are. (107)
Let me not be Your critic, Lord, today, and judge against You. Let me not attempt to interfere with Your creation, and distort it into sickly forms. Let me be willing to withdraw my wishes from its unity, and thus to let it be as You created it. For thus will I be able, too, to recognize my Self as You created me. In love was I created, and in love will I remain forever. What can frighten me, when I let all things be exactly as they are?

Let not our sight be blasphemous today, nor let our ears attend to lying tongues. Only reality is free of pain. Only reality is free of loss. Only reality is wholly safe. And it is only this we seek today."

I struggle with recognizing when it's best to just let people be, since I'll feel telepathically and vibrationally bombarded by the environment. It can be really hard to distinguish if I'm genuinely trying to be helpful or if narcissistic willful arrogance and righteousness has infiltrated my intention while ego pushes against the matrix and the ultimate reality. I find that I prefer to be alone, stewing in my own vibrations, high or low, rather than mixing energies. Teal Swan would say the isolation, born of enmeshment, is inauthentic. (108) As an empath, I still find it difficult not to 'beatmatch' with other people's vibrations, and then from a lower vibration, try to righteously tell people to enlighten the fuck up. On the one hand, I'm speaking through a lens they can hear, on the other, I've just completely lost my peace by focusing on how their shit stinks instead of quietly sitting in Reality. How flawesome indeed. That's why I think it's just better to give people hugs and carry on.

Sometime, in June of 2012, my good Goddess girlfriend Vanessa and I were in Florida giving free hugs at the local Ft. Pierce farmer's market. It was so great to break the ice with people by opening our arms, rebutting resistance, and inviting them to receive a loving hug regardless. It was sad to see how many lonely married men wouldn't take a hug saying, 'My wife wouldn't like that too much.' Vanessa and I just instantly prayed for them to receive more joy in ways they could accept. Most people resisted saying, 'You don't want to hug me. I'm all sweaty.' To which we would reply, 'Of course I want to hug you. You're perfect.'

There was Dr. Pickle, the independent pickle entrepreneur dressed in green doctors' scrubs with a green rotary phone. After about 4 seconds into the embrace, I could perceive his tears surfacing. He had to break away to make a joke and be a showman for the potential clients saying, "Call the doctor to get your pickle fix!" The farmer's market wasn't the place for a good cry. He kept saying that what we were doing was one of the most important things, that we should be going to the old-folks homes too. "If only more people did this, our problems would be solved." He generously gifted us delicious pickles to take home. It feels good to help people restore their faith in humanity.

We shimmied down and visited the woman selling flowers at the market. Vanessa and I referred to her as "The Flower Lady". The vendor's little girl asked for many hugs, and we were happy to oblige. There was another little girl at the market, about 10, standing close by with such an expression, completely distanced, with a deep longing as though her heart was completely closed down. It seemed her youth was being stolen from her. She seemed unable to fathom that she could ever feel that level of intimacy and acceptance. She couldn't accept that joy as part of her reality. It was as though she had accepted defeat. I couldn't help but think she had been molested. I hate seeing kids who don't know how to play. I offered her hugs on a couple separate occasions. Eventually, she accepted. She gave me this pat on the sides like a 'there there.. there there.. let's not bother with real sentimentality.' Again, Vanessa and I instantly said prayers for the little girl, sending her love and light. You can too, even without knowing her. Right now, at this moment, we can pray for that little girl, and all the children and adults like her. We can ask the masters to come in and shine loving acceptance into all of our hearts because you are a divinely powerful human.

Offer love to strangers and people who can do nothing for you in return. Everywhere and every hour is the time and place to project kindness, to give and to receive it, ESPECIALLY when you don't feel like giving or receiving. Lean into it. That's when it's time to check yourself and flip the script on your assholitry.

It's so interesting how, on the one hand, to share a powerful message in today's society, you have to be beautiful and sexually attractive. Yet, on the flip side, if it's going to resonate at the core level, you've got to be vulnerable and let people see the relatable fucked up unfiltered Photoshop-free truth. You would accept a hug from me, a pretty girl, but not offer or give one to a smelly, poor, or fat person. Remember, when people are hardest to love, that's when they need it the most. In a perverted matrix, where is the balance between drawing you in, capturing your attention, and then transmuting the impurity?

In October 2013, I decided to do a photoshoot. I got one of the best photographers in Panama, with lots of music connections as he's in one of the most popular Panamanian bands, and he's politically connected. A hot girlfriend asked him to do the favor. The guy's use of lighting is awesome. A highly intuitive girlfriend assisted with the wardrobe changes. What was most interesting to us was that when we walked into his office, we could feel the 'bad juju vibes'. This is where he edits and photoshops. It was a dark, sexually charged atmosphere. In the studio as well, there was a heavy energy that she and I could both feel. Her super powers are very strong, as well, coming from a long line of mystics. Turns out she is a channel for Goddess Isis, but that's a different story.

When we began, the photographer was trying to pose me in 'sexy & alluring' positions, and I was like 'cut cut. This is Carina Cariñosa, sweet and loving, not give-you-a-boner time.' It was really nice to have creative control over my whole session. I wondered how on earth I'd manage getting picked up by a big label. Essentially, I'd like to capture Marilyn Monroe's essence when she was just a rookie, before the industry spoiled her soul. Did you know her IQ was an astonishing 168? "Imperfection is beauty, madness is genius and it's better to be absolutely ridiculous than absolutely boring." -Marilyn Monroe (109) It's little wonder JFK kept her close. What if we let beautiful women also be respected for their brains?

Shortly after our session, the photographer's band got signed by a big label. Soon after, his pictures began introducing the usual suspect NWO symbols with triangles, one eye, and just generally getting more sadistically sexy and dark. I texted him and asked if he was a Mason now because if not, he should stop using those symbols lest he upset someone of higher rank. He unfriended me the next day. Shortly after, I also witnessed a young aspiring Colombian actor, friends of one of the most influential Panamanians, start using the same symbols. It was as though some Illuminati rep had visited for harvesting talents (and souls).

There's two kinds of desire. There's the enlightened, happy, delicious, passionate, feels-amazing and natural desire. Then there's the wanting, lacking, gotta-have-it, don't deserve it, 'I'm a bad person so definitely can't admit it', gotta hide it, voraciously hungry, fiending like an addict kind of desire which definitely comes from the more resistant levels of consciousness. One feels amazing, no need for outside stimulants; the other is an epidemic in society where people get taken advantage of by giving their consent to external and short-lived happiness. 'Girl, I'm crazy for you' is the suffering kind of desire because you don't feel peace. One makes your heart warm and expanding; the other makes you lust restlessly like a caged monkey masturbating so that even when you get it you can't fully enjoy it. One is whole while the other is a black hole. The status quo increases and markets to your black hole. MSM sells you the solution in the form of a shiny new product to quail the polarity it just created within you. Just look at how we fall for it. 'What's your political party?' The enlightened answer is, I can't label it all into one boxed or fixed term because everything is fluid. All extremism is a tool to rob us of our peace. This makes our 1st, 2nd, and 3rd chakras weak and destabilizes us to create fear, separation of sacred sexuality, and uproots us.

I was certainly not immune to the external stimuli. The impurity was born within me karmically ('sins of the father', soul-fragmentation, deeply ingrained behavior traits through eons of social programming). Turns out, I had been a prostitute in several past lives. As a woman, I'd gotten my security through the man's strengths while patriarchy continued to deny my rightful seat at the table. Conversely, I'd also been a dominating male, and carried this epigenetic energy. Therein, resides the truth to this notion of 'original sin'. We ARE born with 'wanted and unwanted' karma dramas. We do come through with unresolved shit. This is the 'truth' to the notion that earth is a school. Our souls do intend to heal what is broken, and when we experience serious traumas in past lives, our souls become fragmented. Our souls stay among the earthly realm or dimension of density until we figure out how to ascend & heal it through surrender, forgiveness, acceptance, and deciding to keep the lessons and leave the rest.

Come to find out, in several past lives, I chose to maintain independence, support myself and have my fun by selling my sexiness. In this life, and in part, my weight problems have been a manifestation of current and past-life greed issues, starvation issues, some of which were also epigenetic from several generations back. I don't mean standard physical genetics like nose shape; I mean emotional imprints- carrying the scars (samskaras) and karma of your lineage.

The interesting part of it is that of all the ghost removals and exalting of demonic oppressions, the ghost or entity of that prostitute energy was one of the last to heal. Not surprisingly, sex is likely our greatest attachment and our greatest misuse of power. The sex orgasm chemicals are addicting. The fulfillment of intimacy is addicting. It's the closest most of us will ever come to knowing completion.

I'll never forget when my ex-husband once said, 'People do stupid things for love.' It's because we are literally high on oxytocin, serotonin and dopamine, and like addicts, we crave more from a deep void whose origin we can't comprehend so we ignore and band aid with crutches like porn, sex work, withholding sex, shaming it, and other coping mechanism. The fragmented parts of our souls, from this or past lives, craves into-me-see, loving acceptance, and desires to feel whole again. Sex, in its divine form, intends to resolve that. And of course, sex, in its matrix form, is designed to play off our feelings of lack and our desire for connection so it can sell you something outside your inner gnowing. I'll go into greater detail about this in another book which will be dedicated to understanding and healing the sexual wounding for all humans.

In my purest form, I want to make love to everything, sharing my deep internal bliss, to be intimate and authentic with people in a profoundly cathartic and instantly connected kind of way. That's what escorting allowed me to do. I mean seriously, I can view people's emotional profiles in seconds. Once, I cured a woman's sciatica with a hug. I can run my hands across a person's body and scan where their blockages are, and often recalibrate their entire chi, self-image, and outlook on life in under 4 hours. Calibrating people to joy, peace, bliss, and dissolving resistance is what I was put on this earth to do.

Heaven knows there are millions of men on this planet desperately isolated from intimacy. We hear about women's desires for intimacy all the time because society allows us to be emotionally boisterous. However, men have not been historically engineered or allowed to be emotionally vulnerable unless MAYBE it's with the woman he's shtooping. Men usually don't know how to be seen vulnerably, unless it involves sex, and even then we require them to be strong with a big hard dick that can last and last, or else his 'weak' ass probably died in a war somewhere along the way. Fortunately, we are beginning to see a revolution in this area. So for any gentlemen who want a safe person to open up with about their sexual stuff, I get it.

One safe outlet for men to recharge their feelings of separation is within the industry of prostitution. Modern women need to come to grips with this. The way it is described in the futuristic book 2150 A.D., (110) orgies and multiple partners are accepted as 'that's just a need he/she felt called to fulfill', and once you are able to become a vibrational match to your twin flame, then you will never desire any other. But a lot of people don't even marry their soulmates. We MIGHT marry for love, but often we're high, coerced by society, & don't share the same vision and plan of actions for individual and mutual self-actualization.

Society is still very much full of men and women who married for the security they weren't willing or able to create from being whole within themselves first. So, that's from where the jealousy really stems, our codependence. It's a subconscious fear of a lack of resources and subsequent vampirism. It's also punitive anger that s/he lied, didn't trust you, betrayed your trust. Well, if we gave the spouse space to trust our emotional intelligence, and give ourselves space to grow in emotional intelligence, maybe we could stop compromising our integrity and develop the communication skills we wish we had.

Polyamory exists all across nature. 'Uncivilized heathen' societies didn't even have this problem of lies, cheating, infidelity et cetera until conquistadors forced the natives to proclaim the LORD Jesus as their external savior by threatening the lives of all they'd ever love. The ones who didn't comply were raped, pillaged, had their wealth stolen, and have no progeny left to remind you of this fact. If you weren't taught multiple languages in school, this is why- to keep you isolated from intercultural exchange of wisdom. Before 'whitey' stole their abundance, their women didn't need to fear or compete for resources. They raised the family with the whole village in cooperation.

It's that punitive wilful arrogance that makes it even harder to find a lover who could forgive you if you came clean after having compromised your integrity through dishonesty and its disrespect. We'll get into the whole legal arbitrage aspect later. So very many men, and women alike, have had their sexual desires suppressed by the willful arrogance of the leadership enslaving us through disempowering ignorance. When we finally decide to seek liberation from the Church's controlling notion of one spouse till death do us part, we find that people are really either grief stricken, starving for intimacy & connection, or they've come to accept themselves in spite of the social stigma and are forced to hide or be crucified. I say, fuck all that shit. It's time to flip that script.

Allow me to point out that nearly every movie I see these days makes reference to or shows a prostitute because it is literally the oldest game in the book, bartering for connection, offspring and resources. One of the problems is that women haven't yet taken back their power fully over the value they provide in society by offering intimate liberation because of deeply ingrained trauma and misogynistic stigma.

Another problem is that men are also traumatized. I mean seriously... circumcision?... that shit is inhumane. I know it hurts, but I'm glad this whole bomb has been dropped on sexual impropriety. Liberating children from sex trafficking is giving room for women to liberate themselves and step into full power. It's also creating safe space for all of those affected by the religious infiltrations and dehumanizations. Sexual trauma fundamentally corrupts our seeds, our capacity for divine, sacred, balanced male and female connection through the Godhead, and that's what it was designed for. Mother Nature didn't make any accidents. It's okay to talk about the mutilated genitals of young African women, but it's very hush hush to discuss the trauma of male genital mutilation from the church. It's almost as controlling and limiting as the dogmas that don't allow birth control. We have apps to track fertilization now, people. Ionic nano colloidal silver will cure full blown AIDS, cancer, syphilis, gonorrhea, you name it. It's a magic bullet, and Big Pharma has known this. We don't have to remain ignorant and isolated by our inauthentic relating habits any longer.

I'm just sad there isn't as successful a platform for women to find male escorts. That's probably because most women can find a free dick somewhere and naturally tend to be less slutty the more children they have to care for. But, the more children, the greater our likelihood to kowtow to authority or commit crimes or 'sin' outside the bounds of morality to feed those mouths. I just hate that there's so much social stigma still attached to this whole war for resources. Let's get back to nature. Do you have a yard? PLANT SOMETHING. So much of the 'institution of marriage', in itself, was prostitution. Only this time, the arrangements were made between the suitor (buyer) and her father (owner) through a woman's dowry.

The prostitute ghost operating within me subconsciously had a very fragmented soul. On the one hand, I had lived through a very destructive marriage and vowed never to go there again, yet still needed to get laid, hugged and cuddled. On the other hand, this prostitute ghost had a fundamental doubt that she would be protected, believed men would always let her down, beaten & battered countless times, and created that reality through her expectation of a bad result. Her ideal reality resided in the bedroom where she could control the outcome and secure her future in their hearts- labido- assets without the tiresome and thankless labor of children.

Once I realized this underlying doubt within me and prayed for help to feel more abiding faith, the faith in relationships began to unfold. Eventually, I was able to convince this thing within me, literally a ghost, a fragmented part of my soul, that she too could trust in God's love and perfect plan for her. Please notice that at the fundamental level, I was remembering that I am a divine and pure being. I wasn't buying into this false notion of separation from God because I'm a sinner or come from sinners. I also wasn't buying into the twisted notion that salvation was unobtainable because I'm bad, undeserving, not enough, or any of the other lies 'Satan & His Minions' would prefer we believe while they feed off us like vultures. This thing inside me was needing healing through love and acceptance, and I needed money. Rejecting her hadn't worked so I tried the opposite- acceptance of my shadow and practicing self-compassion.

So, for 5 years, my practice grew from rock star massage and energy work, to happy endings, to sex, to becoming quite the proctologist & kundalini awakening specialist, to exploring switching sexual roles into quite a glorious "Love Doctor from the Future" character. I was able to approach all of it from a genuine place of love and acceptance of others while searching for the same self-compassion.

One thing the escorting never grew into was a belief or tolerance that I'm a 'bad girl, dirty girl, filthy slut, hoe, cock sucker' or any of the other deviant control words. Through the escorting, I was empowered to accept my body and believe that I'm truly beautiful. Once I was able to accept, over time, that I'm hot, valuable, desired, loved, lusted after, accepted, seen, a boss entrepreneur & marketer, able to sell myself & profit myself, and all while still weighing 265 pounds, that gave my inner child more permission and perspective to let go of the false beliefs that 'I must be bad'. "I'm a bad girl" was a deeply hidden story my 4 year old brain told for 30 years to justify the pain of my parents' divorce. Insert any rationalization from any trauma because it all lies and says we're not enough through isolation. It took knowing that a quarter million men wanted my essence for me to raise my standards of self love. It took seeing that I could make a ton of money to prove my internal value. I needed to see that I could have a healthy relationship with money and power as a woman. And it took all of that to finally realize my own vampiric nature against using men for security. Hopefully, you can learn the easier way, and if not, I understand.

I needed to witness my humanity and soul corruption in action, watching myself chase the money because the novelty wasn't satisfying anymore as I grew tired of letting unideal characters into my energetic and intimate spaces. Part of this lie that 'money is the root of all evil' is predicated on the somewhat false belief we can't be trusted with great wealth and power. I pretty much believed that I could trust myself. I always used that cash to build towards love, but as my heart became willing to bond with another person, allowing myself to be seen and healed, I stopped accepting half the clientele.

Mind you, I never accepted the assholes who couldn't call because they were texting right next to their woman or at work. I never took the ones who were too busy driving and staring at half-naked pictures to read my profile. I stuck to respectable monogamous daytime professional types, and after a handful of late night mishaps with intoxication, I quit that shit too.

I remember the day a woman from a Christian ministry called and asked if she could pray over me. I'd come to Houston expecting to make about $6,000 that week from appointments. When I pulled less than $2,400 and had to seriously hustle, I decided to visit Joel Olsteen's church that Sunday. I wanted God to take the shame and help me rise above the sexual exploitation. I was ready to rise above it, but it absolutely took a willingness to receive celestial and human assistance from the cookie cutter isolation of yet another hotel room. During a portion of the service, they invited anyone to come forward and be prayed over. They directed me to a woman who put her hands on my shoulders while I cried hard trying to allow the possibility for a miracle to come through. I was literally scared to death of this change.

As I got back into alignment with my sanctification, that clientele number got chopped in half yet again and again until finally my magic unicorn pussy was reserved only for people with whom I share a legit mutual attraction. Spiritually, I view it as a war against the power of Twin Flame energy in which reptilian and other darkies use and corrupt our whole reproductive mechanisms. And I believe that, for a long time, I allowed myself to be used subconsciously through my cross addictive, borderline personality dis-eases while still rejecting the total trinity of mind, body, spirit alchemy.

It's paradoxical. On the one hand, I accepted this fragmented spirit as me (self acceptance), deciding to love her forgivingly (forgiving myself). On the other hand, I knew I was better than this (desire for self actualization), deserving to break free of the suffering this 'thing inside me' (shadow self) was causing. I wanted to serve at a much higher level than just a few people a day. I do not identify the real ME, the truth of who I AM, with the disempowering concept of original sin. Instead, I know I have the power to heal all of that when I let God flow through me. When it became more about chasing the money than service, when the money couldn't satisfy the emptiness, when I stopped feeling peace, when there was something better waiting loyally and patiently for me at home, that's when I just had to turn it back over to God.

To find that ideal mate, I did the Manifest Your Ideal Relationship Workbook. When it came time to level up again, I gave myself permission to redo the workbook in spite of the fear that I might have to demanifest this lover. Fortunately, he continues to surprise me.

My technique is always, 'I'm sorry you feel so badly. Beloved Ascended Masters, please heal us and help us to forgive others as we forgive ourselves (taking a notable page from the Christian Lord's Prayer). (111) Thank you. I completely love and accept you/myself/this situation [taking a notable page from the Polynesian Ho'oponopono. (112)] I know I'm going to get past this. (Not letting doubt steal energy.) I allow love to flow to me, through me, as me. I feel better already. Thank you thank you thank you [Gratitude is a high vibrational magnet for more of what is wanted, taking a note from the Law of Attraction. (113)]' I've used the same technique to heal reptile invasion, demonic invasion, angry ghosts from past lives, and my own karma from this and past lives. We need to understand God's infinite compassion and forgiveness by inviting it into our hearts. I never ask God or Jesus for forgiveness. I always ask for help showing me the infinite forgiveness and compassion so that I can let it reside deep within my heart. And then, some unhealthy admirer mired in self-rejection will try to crucify me, and it literally takes calling forward the forgiveness of Jesus not to energetically castrate those very sad people. The game is so deep and old.

Now, you could do this from an agnostic or atheistic approach, but the common denominator in those approaches seems to be the vibrational offering of doubt or aloneness. Doubt and isolation are not as strong as the openness of faith in a higher power which is readily accessible and wanting to help us out. If I'm doubting in my own power, at least I can count on and call upon my creator for assistance. In this way, you see, I am trusting 'our father in heaven' to provide for me 'his child.'

Flashback to the introduction of this book. Remember how I told you that I'd come home to my mom's house and finished producing the 6 CD's, the new website, the app, and now I was left broke and horny?

I tried Tinder, and OKCupid, but being the rock star that I am, I was bombarded by basically every dude in the region trying to hook up by texting me 'Hi.......' God, how I roll my eyes at that shit. I settled on a local guy whom I'd shared feelings with, but from a distance, never had the opportunity to fulfill. Unfortunately, he refused to tap into his childhood sexual trauma, and with his self-induced erectile dysfunction, I went into a hormonal rage one day and kicked him out of bed. We'd been dating for 6 weeks, and though he was a great kisser and full of heart, I needed to be fucked properly by a man with enough money to pay for the pedicure his foot fetish demanded. A limp dick did NOT sit well with my ego, still doesn't. I took it personally. Also, I needed my lovers not to be broke. So here I am looking at all these broke guys who wanted my attention on OKCupid and Tinder, literally up to 34 new prospects per day, none of them making the cut, and in my desperation I made a call to my porn star girlfriend.

We'd met at my favorite club on drum and bass night. She was wearing a skin tight fuzzy pink outfit that hugged all her delicious voluptuous curves with a big fake flower in her hair. She's what we call in the industry a BBW (Big Beautiful Woman). Weighing in at 205-260 lbs, that was my classification too. It was one of the rare times I was truly attracted to a girl. We made conversation, and she told me about her escorting and porn star work. I thought, 'Maaaan, can I pick 'em or can I pick 'em!?! What were the odds??'

I called and asked for help getting into the escorting business. In my consciousness, I tried to bring light and healing into a dark segment of the population. I tried to share my unconditionally loving and accepting nature in exchange for having my needs met via cash. I sold the energy of my womb's magical healing powers to the top buyers who seemed like decent enough temporary vibrational matches. Subconsciously, I was healing this prostitute life and or acting out her proclivities. Another theory is that dark forces will stop at nothing to distract us, and getting me to trade life force (orgasms) to meet basic needs off course was a deliberate diversionary tactic from Satan, or my shadow self. Or maybe, it's exactly what I needed to stop starving for intimacy. It certainly is a lot easier to sell pussy and naked pictures than it is to save souls. But I needed to experience and heal this underbelly in order to step into my next magic trick where I'm able to heal others on the deepest sexual levels.

The unhealed capitalist in me was a very astute businesswoman, and I took my practice very seriously. This made me one of the most successful professional escorts in Texas. You could literally find me through the first link of a Google search without scrolling down. Over time, because I was dealing with mostly unconscious clients while isolating myself from community, it became much more about making the money and the demand for perfect 10 beauty wasn't satisfying my inner child's real need to be seen and accepted.

At some point, I fucked up and got jaded. It was probably the THOUSANDS of half-assed drunk and lude texts, or the HUNDREDS of no-call-no-shows or starting my day thinking I've got a plan only to read lousy one liner text cancellations worth $300 each. It was the HUNDREDS of emotionally inept men who would handle rejection through verbal abuse and character assassination attempts. It was the insane threatening to harm me or the one insanely jealous woman who hunted me down even though I didn't have a clue who her man was and hadn't even had a text exchange with him. And then it was the dozens of lavish false promises trying to hold me on a pedestal promising my heart's desires in idolatry only to experience the opposite extreme pull-backs when I wouldn't fulfill their fairytale cocksucking scripts, insisted that I was not allowed to wash my vagina or when I wouldn't allow myself to be sodomized all day every day.

I stopped focusing on self improvement as the outer resentment began to reflect my inner resentment. I was so impressed with how much money I could make though, and all the things I could accomplish with the money that I got greedy for more. I made money my idol, and took my focus off 'doing God's work.' Healing was still taking place for sure. I was developing my holistic craft across genres with all the free time the industry afforded for me to focus on self-improvement and self-care. Significant sums of money were being donated to worthy people and causes too, but since 95% of my clientele were not coming for the enlightened reason, it became too much like your average prostitute. That space is empty.

We need to give sex workers, women, men, trans, and the sexually abused permission to come out of the shadows for healing. It needs regulation, protections, not repression of shadow. Until they shut down Backpage, all the divine Goddess SiStars in the industry weren't being forced to step more fully into their power. Until the #metoo movement, and outing of priests, there wasn't enough will for us to break through this oppression. Now there is, and I'm ready to minister to it. No matter what they say, no matter what they do, no matter how hard they'll try to crucify me and may succeed, I have to show you this so you'll know that you're not alone and salvation can be yours.

Eventually, I, and my shadow, grew in self-respect. I decided I wanted to let only the most energetically worthy men experience my hugs and heavenly kisses. Over time, and through the loyalty & consistent discipline of the one man in half a million applicants, my heart began to heal to the place that now I can give free hugs again instead of charging $300 an hour for them. I became able to let real love and into-me-see again. But OH how the women in the various tribes resent me, my honesty and willingness to stop ghosting how we use and abuse each other through economic resources. I became less judgmental about sex and men's sexual performance.

My soul kept demanding that I follow my soul contract, keep healing, and keep expanding. I grew in confidence to the point that the compliments I initially craved became old hat and superfluous. I grew in self love and self respect to the point that I became unwilling to manipulate people with my good looks. I became so comfortable that now I can show up in front of a camera and don't have to look perfect. I grew weary of fornication as my heart became filled by my primary lover. I proved to myself that I could overcome the personal and social stigma of being fat. I grew to not only know my divinely powerful sexual healing powers, but also to respect and preserve them. The reckless emotionally void glutinous single adult and ghost opened her heart to allow herself to be truly loved and respected on a new level as I finally was able to make peace with myself through God's help and my divine willingness to listen and follow a middle path full of self-respect, integrity, and authenticity.

I didn't realize it until the lesson was complete, but God brought me back to the states to heal my childhood and sexual traumas so that I could deliver this message of hope and redemption to everyone. Now that I'm convinced, I was ready to move onward and upwards.

Healing the Poverty Conscious Gypsy

The biggest subconscious reason I went into escorting was not my insatiable libido, or the possibility of reptilian invasion, but my enormous fear and rejection to becoming like one of my many broke hippy healer friends. I'd been an African King in a past life. I was accustomed to a certain standard of living. Having pulled myself out of the trenches in this life, and on so many levels, I refused to downgrade my standard of living of abundant freedom. Plus, so many healers are plagued by a seriously fucked up epidemic of criminally ingrained poverty consciousness throughout the ages. So if it wasn't capitalist greed ultra-spiritually masked as 'abundant living', it was the bi-polar opposite promise of becoming a broke dirty hippy. I couldn't resolve a middle path emotionally and subconsciously.

Allow me to address the poverty consciousness real quick. You see, back in the day, when healers were found to represent a threat to the social and economic interests of the matrix, the church came around and twisted the story about the love of money being the root of all evil. It is the love of money before God that leads to 'sinful' and out of alignment behavior. The church taught people to reject money making it sound like a pious oath of poverty was the only way to be righteous. They convinced slaves to remain enslaved and labeled it righteous while distorting the law of reciprocity. They, themselves were corruptible as they twisted the truth about tithing taking money from their believers to feed their own vices. This extended beyond the West into Eastern cultures, as well. The Guru Nithyananda says that Indians were exceptionally rich, and not until the British came did they begin to experience poverty and disdain believing money corrupts. Remember, absolute power corrupts absolutely. For example, those learning reiki were told not to accept money in exchange for their healing gifts. What a cunning way to chop us off at the knees. I myself, in a gypsy past life, had been subjected to the same poverty consciousness training.

I want you to know that from everything I follow from people claiming to channel celestial beings, the masters have heard our desires for physical sense pleasures and agreed to provide more energy to us in that regard. Spend a day listening to Patricia Cota Robles, (114) and you'll understand how this is true. Please understand, divine celestial beings don't live anywhere near our society's current level of lack and disparity of wealth distribution. Their economic systems have been transmuted and balanced back into oneness consciousness where it's free to learn and free to share info and energy. So while it is true that benevolent energies want us to share our gifts without the limitation of whether someone can pay or not, healers today aren't funded by churches or other major investors. They don't enjoy the social approval that medical doctors receive and the profits generated by the tightly controlled health scare industry. The majority of non-spiritually-minded people aren't tithing. Plus, in order for it to be a tax deductible donation, a healer has to become exceedingly organized and financially structured as I have. Plus, so many healers and naturopaths were labeled witches or quacks and crucified physically and socially.

In the month of June 2017, I took ayahuasca three times, kambo twice, microdosed mushrooms a couple of times, and had two powerful psychic healings from world renowned medium, Rachel Kirkland. (115) What prompted this extreme cleanse was the hollowness of prostitution, and just basically, the ayahuasca offering a subtle level of healing support to where my soul became ready to shine brighter, to step up, to go ahead and allow myself to achieve the next level of greatness even though it felt like certain death. I got off the psych medication, stopped smoking weed, and the mushrooms just quietly removed my resistance to finishing this book.

I rededicated myself to allowing Source to really flow through me, to humbling my will for the greater Will of God, and like magic a miracle unfolded.

Somehow I don't recall, my ayahuasca buddy in Houston sent a recording of her session with Rachel Kirkland. Rachel channeled my friend's recently deceased best friend and helped the departed to communicate his message from the great beyond. The impulse arose to immediately contact Rachel; I followed and acted without delay. Likewise, my ayahuasca buddy said that their usual shaman would be arriving into town the next day to meet up with the local church group who do ceremonies. In my quest for healing, and my disdain for big group ayahuasca ceremonies, I jumped at the chance to have a private ceremony in my house. The Taita, a Colombian facilitator of the ayahuasca medicine, was happy to oblige. So the next day, I had a powerful psychic session and then a private aya ceremony.

In that psychic session, I told Rachel that I've been escorting, and wanted to move out of it, yet I was scared to death of being a broke hippy. Rachel revealed that in a past life I had been a powerful gypsy healer. She saw me resurrecting a child as if from the dead and said that later on I had been strung up to a tree with my tongue cut out and my throat slit. As she said it, I could see it unfold just like a movie. She saw that I would refuse accepting money in exchange for my gifts and services believing that would take away my powers. I would argue with my children about them working for money. It was a constant source of strife.

This gypsy life needed to be healed. Like the prostitute life, it had been acting within me on a subtle unconscious level for 20 years. I thought, 'If it isn't one thing, it's another.' I knew this story to be true because I had lived like a gypsy ever since my mother's stroke at age 17. Again, this caused a kind of psychotic break which lead to drug use, or seeking solace outside myself because I couldn't understand how God could let this kind of pain happen to me. Part of her stroke involved the corruption of the church, so it was that split from God that began my search for truth through Buddhism et al.

With Rachel, I had just seen with my own physical senses how the love of money had taken away many of my extrasensory, or psychic perceptions because I'd shifted focus and closed down my third eye. And I knew that my throat chakra was weak. It had been since the stroke when I stopped immersing myself in singing, saxophone, musical theatre et cetera and started using tobacco and weed as the therapist. Actually, the first time I ever became curious about strengthening the throat chakra, an article came up about the persecution of female healers, in particular. That blog post about throat and neck problems (116) resonated so much that I asked Wolfgang to become my mentor in 2010. Funny how he also practiced celibacy in an ashram for 12 years, but I wasn't ready to access those super powers until December 21st, 2018 during the winter solstice stargate where I and two other sex workers renounced the usery and reclaimed our powers. It made sense that I'd been persecuted. It made sense that I was afraid to be persecuted again in this life. Every time I'd think about really letting my light shine, the thought would become overshadowed by a fear of persecution. It made sense that my throat was weak because of a decapitation.

So, armed with an 'authentic Andies facilitator', I set my intentions for the ayahuasca ceremony and proceeded to experience the most severe case of diarrhea of my life, which included shitting my pants even though the toilet was mere steps away. Unfortunately, this facilitator wasn't strong enough to really help heal the gypsy. He did, however, help me accept and forgive all the trespasses committed against me by my family as a teenager. During the psychic session, Rachel said she could see about 20 knots, or traumas, in my stomach. Two weeks later, I went to her house in San Antonio for a one-on-one shamanic healing session. Now, she only saw 5 knots. Apparently, I had shit the rest out.

Some of the most important things that Rachel told me were that my guides were very adamant that I should finish this book by the end of 2017. (Well, here it is January 2019, and I can see why.) In both sessions, they expressed the importance of my voice, of sharing my story, of writing this book for the sake of humanity. They assured me that so many more people would be able to relate to me because of the truth and transparency. They proclaimed that it would touch a segment of the population where lots of darkness is otherwise, and that I needn't worry. They giggled and approved of the book's title. They admired my bravery, and I was assured that when I finish this life, they will be applauding the work I've accomplished and attempted.

She also said that they showed me sitting with my legs open, and a big halo of white light shooting out of my vajayjay. She said that there was approval and acceptance for my escorting work. This was reassuring. She said to just remember that intention of healing and it will be done.

Then, she started drumming. She got out a big round drum, a rattle, a small wooden pipe and some holy water- typical shamanic gear. The drumming seemed to open my energy, as if I was suddenly traversing the timeline dropping into the gypsy life. She could see that my throat chakra was very stubbornly closed and clogged. I began to dry heave into her trash can. This went on for an extended period of time. Then, she pulled out a pipe and used it to suck out more of the bad juju.

From late June until the end of December, I have felt much more grounded and willing to stay put. I have become way more confident about my ability to make a good living by adding greater value to society as a healer. I've stabilized my healer career into an IRS approved 501c3 Non-profit organization. I've finished this book, and have published my next body of work called Cure Cancer At Home (117) which is a digital directory on where to buy all the known cancer cures from around the world. None of those were decisions that came lightly, yet they were all guided by the light.

To truly heal the anti-female wounding really took the unapologetic diva power of Ingrid Arna (118) giving me permission to be wealthy, 'witchy', and wise. The space she holds is potent because she commands it to be so. It's what I needed to really energetically cut ties with subconscious vampirism of giving away my power to men for my sense of security and wealth. When you observe her language, you feel the potency of the container she's holding. Through discovering her story, she was a top marketing executive, at one point dominating in New York, and then she got tired of the bro-culture can't-get-no-justice-as-a-woman disempowering bullshit. So, she reclaimed her power, flipped the script, and now caters specifically to women seeking to do the same with their careers. As one of her sites says, 'Heal and unleash your high priestess power as you manifest limitless, sovereign and financial abundance, liberating yourself forever from vows of poverty and shame. {Minus the chronic hustle, sleaze and drama of the patriarchal money game}'

Chapter 20:

THE EXORCISM

A.K.A. 1ST CRAZIEST THING THAT'S HAPPENED TO ME SO FAR

I had just moved back to the states, so this was October 2014. I landed at a festival in Asheville, North Carolina and met up with some broke hippies who needed a ride to Houston. (I also met up with Wolfgang, in person, for the first time.) I agreed to give them a ride in exchange for $100. Unfortunately, I too ended up being broke, since PayPal didn't release the money they'd frozen on time. So here we are after the festival, driving past Birmingham Alabama, with no money for a place to stay. I looked to her, a follower of Mother Mary, and I said, 'Do you believe? Do you really believe in the power of prayer? Because I'm about to manifest a miracle here.' She said she did, and I commenced a prayer saying that I needed a miracle stat. We needed two rooms with a kitchen, washer, drier, and internet for free. I commanded this be so, and we kept driving. By midnight, we reached her hometown in Louisiana. The two characters were love birds. He was a kitchen extraordinaire, fresh out of jail for a crime I don't know, but he seemed articulate, well educated, and non-violent. On the Scale of Human Consciousness, he rated in the 400s. She, on the other hand, was a mess. I called her afflicted. She thought she was a healer, and I just thought she was going through a healing crisis learning how to heal herself- easy for me to judge and point the finger outward, eh?

Five am rolled around, and I was stuck in my mini-van hot and restless. I commanded again, 'Hey look Source, I told you I needed this miracle now, and I mean NOW!' For those of you unfamiliar with CouchSurfing, it's an online community of super low budget travelers where people open their homes and leave mutual reviews about each other. In this way, you have a history of being cool, so someone will open their home to you. I had been a host for several years in Panama, so I had about 20 badass reviews saying I was a good character. Twenty minutes later, I got the response. There were only 5 CouchSurfing hosts in that town and one answered. He was in France at the time working on an oil rig offshore, but because of my reviews, he told me where the key was and Boooooom, we manifested a two bedroom house with washer, dryer, kitchen, cable, and internet able to stay there for a full week no strings attached. Thank you Source!! (Side note: This guy was actually so high vibe that we were able to have psychic sex together, in which I vomited a ton of intimacy rejection.)

As the week progressed, she'd gotten very upset that I didn't want to let her work on me. Basically, she just wasn't high vibe enough to work on me, and I didn't want to catch her affliction. But after cleaning the house up for our host, and after packing up to head to New Orleans, she convinced me to let her do a thing. By this time, she had confessed that the group they were going to go squat with in Houston practiced the occult dark arts and did shit with pentagrams and dark forces. I definitely was ready to drop them off and get the heck out of dodge.

But first, for whatever reason, I let her do something to me, which I quickly regretted.

By all accounts, what she did was normal. She stared into my eyes, held my hands, and repeated this paragraph that sounded pretty normal, about breaking the bonds between us and lifting any karma, etc. But suddenly this thing jumped inside me and took over my body to where I was shaking uncontrollably.

"MOTHER FUCKER!!! WHAT DID YOU DO???"

She had some lame answer about how it was already there within me. I strongly rejected that notion. After you hear my 2nd most crazy paranormal story, you'll understand why I'm telling you about this one.

All I knew is that NOW I was possessed.

I ran outside, resentfully cussing, got on the ground, and started shooting all my celestial healer bullets at it to no avail. This thing was writhing around inside me all through my body without stopping. I called upon my highest ascended self and asked God almighty to come in and intervene. My high self asked me what its name was. So I asked it to spell its name. I got to R, then A, then freaked out and said. "FUCK THIS! I don't care what its name is!" Then, my High Self said to ask what it wanted. It replied, 'I want you to go to the bayou. Cut off a snake's head, and drink its blood.' To which I freaked the fuck out and said, "HELL NOOOOOO!!! This has to go NOW!!!!!"

I called my new colleague in New Orleans. He said, 'Would you like the number to the exorcist?' I said, 'Most definitely pretty fucking please!'

He gave me the number to Dave Diamond, (119) a chaplain in northern Louisiana. I called and said, 'Mr. Diamond. You don't know me, but I was given your number by a colleague in New Orleans. I'm a healer and something has happened to me. I need an exorcism stat!' He began calling upon Christ Jesus and commanding this thing out. After about 15 minutes on the phone, I finally began to feel this thing subside. It came out of my body through my head, but it lingered in my head for a while. Dave said to call him in a couple of days to check in.

I had to go to New Orleans with these people. We had a schedule to keep. The car was packed, and we headed on our way to the colleague's house to CouchSurf for a few days. The thing tried to leave my head and enter into theirs. I'd had this experience once before when exorcising a demon from a friend's house. It had gotten stuck to me, and while in the car, it tried to go over into my friend. I called out, 'By the power vested in me by the grace of Christ Jesus almighty, I command you may NOT enter into this woman's body. You must leave!' My friend confirmed she would not allow entry. I did the same with these two characters, rolled down the windows, and eventually the thing jumped out of the window into the bayou along the way to New Orleans.

A couple of days later, I called Mr. Dave Diamond. He said that the thing had come through the phone signal and road on his back for a few hours, as well. He said it was a snake. Ah hah! I thought. That's why it wanted me to chop off a snake's head and drink its blood! If you can imagine a snake writhing inside your body, that sure is what it felt like.

Needless to say, I was done being around this woman.

Chapter 21:

FORGIVENESS

Growing up, I had no idea about forgiveness. I bought a book about it once, and never read it. I had learned to be bitter, angry, and hateful. As cliche as it sounds, what I needed was Jesus. I told you it took a loooong while to forgive my mom, 37 years, in fact. I was back in the states, staying at my mom's house, completely triggered and surrounded by shitty vibes, immersed in the traumatized painbody of that 4 year old child. One of my besties called, and said to me, 'You know Carina, I know it sounds cliche, but it makes me think of Jesus on that cross, with his hands nailed up, and how he forgave them for their ignorance.' She asked Jesus to come in. I begged Jesus to come in and show me the light of forgiveness into my heart once and for all. My tears subsided rather quickly, and in seconds, I was healed, if just for a while. Not because my belief in Jesus was so inextricably strong, but because I wanted to let go of this so badly, and Jesus is simply the teacher for forgiveness. So I figured, he was the right man for the job.

At the time of writing, February 2018, it's been almost 3.5 years since my return to the states. My mom has managed to get under my skin time and again, and when she does, I still rage in anger at her. Completely triggered. That same friend called when she read that I'm facing breast cancer. She noted how good I am at radically rejecting what's not right for me, since I'm still dealing with radical self-rejection, not loving my body, eg loving myself, letting love in. And she suggested radical acceptance, of which there is a lot of material available by Psychologist Tara Brach. (120) My healer friend SiStar Theresa Martinez also turned me on to the work of Bethany Webster and her work as it relates to healing the mother wound. (121) In an attempt to finish this book, I'll elaborate on this work another time.

For now, I wanted to share this message from A Course in Miracles, (122) a body of worked channeled from Jesus by Helen Schucman, a woman who was not herself a follower of Jesus' teachings but who was called upon to write these lessons. You can sign up to receive a daily lesson.

Lesson 62

"Forgiveness Is My Function As The Light Of The World.

It is your forgiveness that will bring the world of darkness to the light. It is your forgiveness that lets you recognize the light in which you see. Forgiveness is the demonstration that you are the light of the world. Through your forgiveness does the truth about yourself return to your memory. Therefore, in your forgiveness lies your salvation.

Illusions about yourself and the world are one. That is why all forgiveness is a gift to yourself. Your goal is to find out who you are, having denied your Identity by attacking creation and its Creator. Now you are learning how to remember the truth. For this attack must be replaced by forgiveness, so that thoughts of life may replace thoughts of death. Remember that in every attack you call upon your own weakness, while each time you forgive you call upon the strength of Christ in you. Do you not then begin to understand what forgiveness will do for you? It will remove all sense of weakness, strain and fatigue from your mind. It will take away all fear and guilt and pain. It will restore the invulnerability and power God gave His Son to your awareness.

Let us be glad to begin and end this day by practicing today's idea, and to use it as frequently as possible throughout the day. It will help to make the day as happy for you as God wants you to be. And it will help those around you, as well as those who seem to be far away in space and time, to share this happiness with you.

As often as you can, closing your eyes if possible, say to yourself today:

Forgiveness is my function as the light of the world.

I would fulfill my function that I may be happy.

Then devote a minute or two to considering your function and the happiness and release it will bring you. Let related thoughts come freely, for your heart will recognize these words, and in your mind is the awareness they are true. Should your attention wander, repeat the idea and add:

"I would remember this because I want to be happy." (123)

It's June of 2017, and I've done 3 ayahuasca ceremonies this month plus 2 sits with kambo. I started working on the book again, and in so doing, prayed for more guidance and support. As if by magic, Source answered with great speed, and situations miraculously fell into place. In one day I managed to be given the contact of one of the world's best mediums and secured a private ceremony with a Colombian ayahuasca facilitator at my home. The next day I was in San Antonio to meet Rachel and that night had my ceremony with Hector, who often facilitates in Houston. Rachel Kirkland (124) said that she could see lots of knots in my stomach area, traumas, that needed to be released. That night, towards the end of my ceremony, I had an emotional breakthrough. I started crying about all the trespasses my family committed against me as a teenager. I opened the wounds from my step-dad's tyranny and cried in victimhood. The Colombian man told me to forgive them. I didn't want to. I wanted an apology. He said to ask Jesus for help. In about 10 minutes, I went from not wanting to forgive, to praying for Jesus' help, to acceptance of what is, and letting it go. "I forgive you, and I forgive myself. I accept that this happened, and I let it go. I return it to Source for healing once and for all." The ayahuasca opened up deep wounds while Jesus cleansed them out in short order.

I can't stress to you enough the importance of forgiving, the importance of accepting what is/ was/ will be. For the sake of your health and enlightenment, we must learn to forgive.

Remember, the victim mind does not want to accept. It rejects and looks for someone to blame. Remind yourself that blame does not make you happy. If you desire happiness and peace, you've got to do the work and forgive. I always call upon Jesus for help with forgiveness.

Forgiveness of self is paramount. In my first half dozen ayahuasca ceremonies, forgiving myself was the key theme. It comes up over and over again. I go in with the intention to heal my current self, my past lives, my family timeline, and my future selves. It is ingrained into my being as part of my purpose on earth now. My first ceremony, I was writhing in pain and anguish without really knowing why. I later came to understand, through the help of some of the facilitators that night, that I was reliving a gruesome death experienced during one of my lives as a slave. In my third or fourth ceremony, I cried uncontrollably for hours, relinquishing the guilt from having been a Nazi. Later on, I fell into a meditation in which I was shown that I'd bombed a hospital that struck the birthing ward. I could feel all of the angry souls cursing me. I asked their forgiveness, to put our souls at rest once and for all. I asked God and Jesus and a team of volunteer angels to bless their families, to send miracles and healing to their families past/ present/ and future. In about an hour, they were all blessed up. But in my guilt, and mistakenness, I still haven't fully forgiven myself, so my self-punishment and rejection is my mistaken form of repentance even though logically I know that the real repentance happens with my good deeds. Aaahhh the difference between knowing versus feeling. How long must I suffer before fully giving myself permission to be better?

Well, during an acid trip in December 2014, after having my fun and asking for a spiritual experience, I was shown the hands of a man (me) choking the life out of another person, and could hear their soul cursing all that I'd ever love. It demanded I repent. It demanded a confession. Its spirit stayed with me, plaguing me, until February 2015 when I returned back to Panama for an ayahuasca ceremony. I was on the toilet in agony, begging for help to remove the curse and dark energy attached to me. In came a rattlesnake to protect me, and something — mother aya — Jesus — the snake— something came in and said, 'Why do you provoke them? . . . Stop provoking.' I made a promise to stop provoking people, demons, reptilians, ghosts, etc. It's something I got a lot of juice out of as a child. I later did the Ho'oponopono with my brother, to forgive my trespasses as a kid when I would provoke his hostilities. Like magic, my relationship with my brother changed to one of more peace.

The next night when I took the medicine she told me to respect everyone, and not wanting to accept that responsibility, I cried until my face hurt so bad that I gave in like a tired child. In 2018, I can tell that my lesson is to keep my mouth shut more in order to improve my bedside manor- censoring judgement to avoid attacking others.

Please understand that I don't consider myself a Christian, though Christ's words have always resonated with me as the truth. Jesus himself was not a Christian, he was Jewish. Side note, I'd love to learn from and work more closely with members of the Jewish faith.

There was certainly a time in my life where the mere mention of Jesus would provoke great resistance. It was during my awakening in 2012 that Jesus made his way back into my heart. I was homeless, living in hostels in Casco Viejo, the UNESCO World Heritage Site in Panama's colonial district. I was humbled to poverty suddenly, and began to ask for help from those who seemingly had nothing to give. They would come to me on the street and ask for a quarter. Instead, I would offer a hug. I remembered the immense heart opening experienced when an elderly man offered me food any time I needed it. I remember how humbling it felt to 'be on the same level' as these people, many of whom were black latin. Their love was compassionate and tangible. I walked into the cathedral, turned on a fan, and gave my life to God, thankful for having been shown love in the most unassuming place, thankful for obviously being protected, and thankful for feeling acceptance, thankful for this opportunity to realize our oneness where I had been prejudice. I promised to become the highest version of myself. I promised to be a servant of God's will and work. I said, 'If Jesus is my savior, then show me.' That's when Jose came into my life. Jose prayed over me, in Jesus' name, and things got better. On two occasions in particular, Jose prayed over me, in Jesus' name, and I experienced miraculous shifts. Another time, I had become possessed, and Jesus saved me. So, even though I'd grown up with so many reasons to hate the ones closest to me, to loath being in my body, to not believe in the good things coming, Jesus has consistently shown up for me.

On The Scale of Human Consciousness, 1000 being the most amount of light that the human body can hold, Jesus' consciousness rates at 22,000. Ayahuasca is 2,000, King Solomon is 6-7,000, Goddess Bridgette is 18,000, and the various other Archangels are from 15,000-18,000. Whether you believe in Jesus' power to help you or not, it is my hope that you'll open up to the possibility of letting him work miracles into your life. Just invite him in. I especially encourage that you call upon his help when it comes to matters where you need help forgiving.

Dear God, I allow my heart to connect with your heart today and every day. I allow myself to be shown great miracles. I'm asking for help to receive Jesus' love into my life. I am asking for help to receive Jesus' forgiveness into my life. I am open to receiving blessings and miracles. I am open. Please show me how to help myself. Thank you thank you thank you.

Chapter 22:
PROSPERITY & ABUNDANCE THROUGH GOD'S WILL

"All good things are mine because God intended them for me."

— *A Course in Miracles*

Dirty Money

Money that is earned through control, coming from a place of force, lies, not given willingly, or is known to cause harm it is 'dirty money.' Therefore it is dirty energy. It has a karma which you are powerful to cleanse. An example, actually, is the transmutation of drug money laundering into socially beneficial infrastructure. Tough pill to swallow, but a lot of illegal drug money saved the US economy in 2008. Can you imagine that heroine is actually a sacred sister for those addicted to pharmaceutical opiates? Mind fuck right? My eyes open wide, for example, when a new friend actually said oil was sacred. I'd never thought of plastics, coming from sacred oil before. It's all in how we use, or rather, misuse the energy. And that's why so many people have such incredible hangups with it being the root of all evil. They are afraid to step up and transmute their own tendencies toward the evil misuse of what that much power and responsibility of resources can allow. Stop blaming the money. Start transmuting your own internal corruption.

Because we are so accustomed to being made slaves to our bills, paying into a corrupt system that has no love or appreciation for our efforts, working for similarly unsympathetic corporations in which we are made to feel dispensable, it is very natural to resist paper monopoly money as an adequate energy exchange. After all, it's really a downgraded outdated form of energy exchange. Yet, I still can't pay the electric bill with free hugs, or so I think, and therefore it's true, until I reframe that thought and command the vision that by giving thousands of free hugs, appreciation will grow and abundance will flow and transmute into dollars or free solar panels so that I can actually pay the utilities with free energy. But nothing is free; there's always some cost, some price, some level of responsibility. Ego would much rather we not accept these facts, so we lie to ourselves and say, Well they're the chosen, have an unfair advantage, must be immoral, etc.

I CHALLENGE Source with my ego by saying, 'God, bring me the abundance is such magical ways that there's no way I, the tiny self, could have orchestrated that. Make it be so amazing, that I can only give the credit to you flowing through me, and therefore testify to glorify your name!' And God's like, 'Oh you are ready for more? Here.' and then my ego goes, 'nah. I changed my mind. I don't want to step up and grab that train. I'll take this other one.' and the train comes, and I let that one go too. Source begins showing me so many reflections of how I am a powerful creator, of how I can manifest anything I want, and I just keep dropping the ball, leaving myself with nowhere to point the finger but inward.

Why am I self-rejecting? Why am I rejecting the abundance? Why am I holding myself back?

Ah, because I don't trust myself with the power. I don't want to put in the work necessary to be responsible for my inheritance. I'm the one forgetting that I'm God and therefore not allowing it to flow through.

Sound familiar?

What kind of shit is that? Oh on so many levels it is bad programming; eons of it; so many lives, so much ancestral shit. And God just stares at us like a frustrated parent to a newborn wishing we'd put the damn spoon in our mouths while we cry in Its face about how hungry we are.

At the beginning of my ibogaine experience, little I was begging God, "Please see me... Please please please see me." Until finally It raised it's voice with annoyance and firmly said, "I SEE YOU." like move on with it already.

The relationship to money changes dramatically once you commit to following your purpose. Purpose, on the Scale of Consciousness, calibrates around 813 out of 1000 as Maslow's Hierarchy of Needs (125) affirms.

Money simply becomes part of the machine needed to birth your projects and interests. At this stage of the game, to hold animosity toward money is a disservice to you and the God life force energy that desires expression. So to deny accepting currency's power and ability to flow to you, through you and back to you is like choosing not to breathe air. You might become very adept at holding your breath for long periods of time, but eventually you'll surface desperately gasping for sustenance.

One of the reasons I held off on finishing this book, as described in the introduction, is that I was afraid of becoming a broke hippie. In my first psychic reading from Rachel Kirkland, (126) one of the world's best mediums, she told me that this extreme

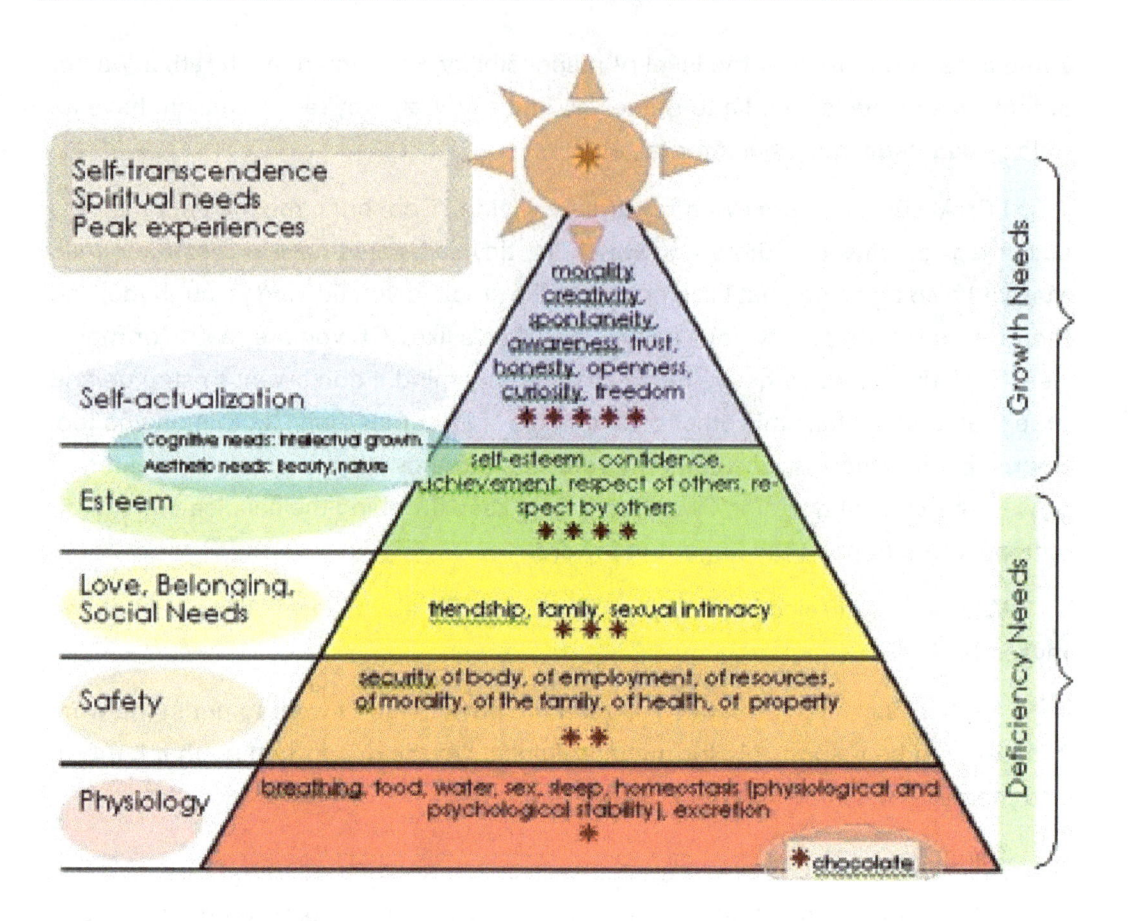

[Maslow's hierarchy of needs pyramid diagram:
- Self-transcendence, Spiritual needs, Peak experiences
- Self-actualization: morality, creativity, spontaneity, awareness, trust, honesty, openness, curiosity, freedom *****
- Cognitive needs: intellectual growth. Aesthetic needs: beauty, nature
- Esteem: self-esteem, confidence, achievement, respect of others, respect by others ****
- Love, Belonging, Social Needs: friendship, family, sexual intimacy ***
- Safety: security of body, of employment, of resources, of morality, of the family, of health, of property **
- Physiology: breathing, food, water, sex, sleep, homeostasis (physiological and psychological stability), excretion *
- *chocolate
- Growth Needs / Deficiency Needs]

fear I had was rooted in a past life where I was a gypsy. I refused to accept money. I believed it would weaken me and strip me of my powers. She and I saw this gypsy basically resurrecting an adolescent. Later, I was later tied to a tree, had my tongue cut out, and throat slit. Two weeks later, I drove to San Antonio to sit in on a personal healing session where we invited Source and Guides to heal the poverty consciousness of that gypsy. Unfortunately, many lightworkers today face a similar poverty consciousness. It's a real hurdle to surmount, especially because we do live in a time where cash is needed to fulfill our dreams. So it's up to the healers to heal themselves of our relationship to this form of currency. It's up to us to finally reject the indoctrination that was taught in past lives of training that we must take vows of poverty.

God, we, give ourselves poverty, because we misunderstand deservingness, don't trust ourselves with power, and because we get far away from God when we do. Unfortunately, it took asking poor people for mercy and spare change on the streets of Panama as a widowed immigrant for me to humble myself enough to connect with God. Sometimes we like to learn the hard way. Then, as I think I mentioned, I came back to the states, and, afraid to become a broke hippie, started doing sex work to make ends meet. And it went great, until I'd finally healed the prostitute ghost and my self confidence and self-esteem. Then, the lesson became seeing myself with money and power, and learning how to balance that, then getting out of alignment and having to come back in on a tighter budget to regain my commitment to God.

So just keep thanking THEM, your guides, the MOTHER elements, and your HIGH self for the abundance, and you should see it keeps flowing as long as you are walking your purpose.

What's your purpose? Fulfill your greatest joys and passions.

Remember, the universe always supports expansion.

Joy and appreciation are money magnets because they are very fast and high vibrating life giving frequencies. When you do something you are passionate about and love doing, Law of Attraction responds by aggregating more like resources, clients and atoms cluster in response to your electronic energy offering. The same happens when you daydream and imagine the havingness of all you desire, in the present tense; it flows to you. The God life force energy flows through you, and the remembrance of the God creator presence says, 'Yippy! We're manifesting!' It's just an important balance that "Yay! I'm God" thinking with recognizing, "This could get excessively egotistical real quick if I forget to appreciate all the outwardly cooperative components that helped me as God created this. You set the intention that everyone who is looking for and in need of your offering WILL find you. Then, continue walking the path removing obstacles along the road and asking help from the Masters for those too-big-for-you challenges.

I don't know if it's ego grandiosity, or acceptance of the God presence, but I would like to be the answer to people's prayers. I would tack on 'as much as possible.' to that wish, but then I'm afraid of being overwhelmed. Since I'm also still a tad afraid of not having enough or plenty to share, I tack on 'Please bring me plenty of high net worth clients so that I have plenty of energy to share with those who can't pay me back now. And thank you thank you thank you for keeping me safe. Please help me to remember more and more that I TRULY AM powerful abundance.' That seems to work, but I have this tendency to only take when I need, having failed yet to develop that consistently disciplined total self-love that just chugs away at the daily grind... you see, I'm expecting it to be hard work... I'm manifesting that it must be a grueling day at the office. What I should be doing, to reframe that, is using the same easy relaxing exhilarating feelings as I get from manifesting money from escorting (Choose whatever situation you can honestly feel into that's easy relaxing and exhilarating.) and apply that to visualizing myself being abundant in my passions as a healer.

And boom, awareness to resistance. There's a limiting belief about abundance feeling hard or unsatisfactory that stops the flow. In my case, I keep going back to that traumatized gypsy's belief that she'll be killed for this. So my ibogaine guide asked me to write a different story, one of triumph and victory where the plot twists in my favor. Meanwhile, I'm working on healing that throat chakra blockage that I willfully shut up through smoking. Just keep swimming, swimming swimming.

Love of Money

There is a lot of drama surrounding money because of the mistaken willful love of money, making money our God. That's the part you were warned not to fall for. I will admit that a piece of me got lost as an escort for the love of money. On one hand, I was practicing allowing money to flow to me easily and with minimal effort. I was using Law of Attraction and really winning at it. On the other hand, I became caught up in acquiring money, forsaking my other hobbies and interests to get it. I hadn't yet healed the gypsy. I began to sell my soul, lose my higher essence by allowing my energy to commingle too much with people who were objectifying me as a pizza instead of a Goddess. As my self-love developed and healed, I grew to accept fewer types of clients, making space for more time to develop my passions, which ultimately made more space for God to flow back in. To an outsider, one of the hundreds of guys whose face I hung up on, I'd actually become seemingly shallow as a result of getting more honest and selective. At first I was curious and willing to try all kinds of new things. After a few years, having tried it all, with government regulations making it harder and harder to express my unique desires, demands, and requirements, it got harder to qualify leads, and that made for more low quality interactions, which made me jaded, less appreciative, and therefore more resistant to receiving abundance through that medium. Ah government intervention fucking up a good thing again. But it IS time for the global collective of sex worker Goddesses to step up, speak up, and vote more loudly with our ballots and our dollars. Heaven knows, we keep the economy running too. No doubt, I have a mentor who uses me as a muse. Balance balance balance. I knew this would be the challenge. After all, it appears as my Sun and Moon signs, along with Scorpio, so watch out injustice! I'ma sting ya!

Seeing which side of the coin you're on, can be challenging. We have to consciously practice observing ourselves. Often, we fail to observe until just after we've reacted harshly, or until the anger subsides, which can take a long time or requires the observations of others to guide us. It's no wonder our heart's desire sometimes is to throw our hands up in frustration at the matrix. Sometimes it truly is easier to play victim and blame the matrix rather than to step up out of it by humbling the matrix within.

The ego kind of surrender implies loss, and that's not surrender to God; that's ego victim manipulation. Surrender to God feels empowering, loving, protected, extremely peaceful and safe. Can you access those feelings while meditating on abundance? It feels like trust that you are doing the right thing. That trust is the gate of enlightenment. On the Map of Human Consciousness, it's in the 600s. Eventually the suffering of not using the money currency will make your hungry belly begin wishing for, willing forward, abundance in any form you would allow yourself to receive. So, repairing our relationship to money and other forms of abundance currency is a cycle of death and rebirth that is happening in our evolution individually and as a collective. When you voluntarily empty this will-filled cup of closed-offness and call upon God to supply, if you are truly willing to allow, accept, surrender, and relax, it will come miraculously. But you HAVE to surrender the fear, so I cover that next in the Surrender Ceremony chapter.

It took about two weeks to manifest Rachel Kirkland into my life. I had become willing to surrender my fears through that microdose of mushrooms summer 2017, and began writing again. I opened my heart to receiving help from anywhere serving the highest truth, love, light and joy. I began to call in the Divine Feminine and Divine Masculine energies again. I began to call in the will of my highest ascended self. No sooner had I expressed to you on paper my fear of being a broke hippy did Source create a miraculous series of circumstances that would bring Rachel into my awareness. She told me of the gypsy. We healed it, although that throat chakra is stubborn to forget her scars, and now that mistaken part of my soul is being set free more and more. The healing I needed was beyond my perception, and yet it came swiftly as soon as I was open.

By the way, if this whole persecution and closed throat chakra thing is really resonating with you, that's how I found my first mentor, Wolfgang by reading this article. (127)

Clean Money Paradigm Shift

To clean up the money, we have to return to a paradigm of character and integrity in which we devolve, if you will, from the big city I don't know you — you don't know me — anything could go wrong so let's sign some papers and use the legal system for protection and make everything a financial transaction. We've gotten away from that neighborly love from our agrarian days. Nature is requiring us to return to the archaic to the times where a person's word was their bond, before ego fragmented the value of words with its fast talking city-slickin' salesmen. Returning to the archaic doesn't have to mean we only exchange services in a barter-type scenario or using precious metals as currency. In modern global society, this does not support expansion. Believe me, I've tried it. The above lacks appreciation for compounding, automation, and passive residual income which you deserve.

Enter cryptocurrency! If you're curious and just getting started with crypto as a form of freedom, just like all things, there's corruption there too, so I've put together a beginner's guide to help you get along. Find it here: https://carinacarinosastore.guru/bitcoinbeginners/ (128)

Typically, we would barter for 'in kind' like value. However, in an emerging society of people self-actualizing, the Will to offer more than what could ever be returned arises as a driving force. Some folks, at this level of mind, think you shouldn't charge for your gifts, because they feel so full, but if they aren't experiencing plenty, then this is a trick of ego limitation and outdated resistant beliefs. You may be willing to 'give until it hurts' or give to an individual beyond what they could ever repay you knowing that you'll be taken care of. That's a pure feeling. How do we put a price tag on the value of sharing a healing hug? It's like me asking how much your soul is worth to you. The best things in life are 'free' because they are so priceless, implying emotional value which is hard for the human mind to quantify. I try to think of it as good karma points or abundance points. But the fact is, you have to cash in your points. You deserve it, so you have to ASK for what is wanted, and allow it to come through. By not getting clear on that asking, you're playing small in the world, and that's actually very selfish, to pretend to be humble, giving it poverty consciousness, and using that as our excuse not to show up in the world. Kimberly Maska, (129) a coach for the spiritual coaches, agrees that if you're not making 6 figures in your spiritual business, you're being selfish by playing small because you can't serve at your highest level without the currencies we use to make the world go round.

We can quantify value utilizing a higher more omniscient perspective which respects the totality of our soul's karmic timeline, if we practice connecting with and opening that portal. I like to think of it like sowing seeds. Say I set the intention today toward sewing a row of Deservingness, planting those seeds of inspiration in 10 people today. I expect and allow other natural phenomenon like sun (education) and rain (experience) to compact the ground (karma or samskara) in which the wind (time) and temperature (depth of awareness) will encourage the seed (you) to grow with each passing day (measure of progress). Did you catch that? It's turtle medicine. It's connection to the Mother earth's elements. It is understood that the intention of deservingness will abundantly bear more deservingness fruit or other magical gifts to society beyond imagination.

Let's say your improved self-concept is like a perennial bush that continuously bears fruit season after season. (Remember, that bushes have to be trimmed back in order to be stressed to branch out, grow, and bloom more.) My gift of properly nurturing you as a seedling is going to compound into a smorgasbord of abundance in which I deserve residual fruit, literally or figuratively. So I'm open to collecting residual interest, and that's how spiritual leaders should be able to justify the business model currently being pitched where we build a product that automates and leverages our capacity to share.

Unfortunately, people still need to be seen and heard. We want the custom contextualized give-me-now guidance. Thus, I keep my practice focused on helping individuals as much as possible, which is 'harder' work than selling an automated system. So it's easier for me to justify a high price tag, and the delicate balance of 'getting a big head' has to be leveled from time to time. Volunteering helps that, it's also a tax write off, by the way. In your natural appreciation, you'll share a percentage of that abundance back with me. Unless I have issues with deservingness or a false sense of humility, I am obliged to receive your gift. We are children of God, and God wills for his children great abundance, but just like disobedient out-of-line children, karma takes away what we don't 'deserve', aka not willing to be responsible for.

So practice visualizing yourself being a kind, abundant, and balanced wealthy person, easily and dutifully showing up to do what you enjoy every day.

Review:

Dirty money stays dirty because the coding of the intention was stained. You have the power to transmute that, if you dare. It starts with forgiveness and radical acceptance of what is which then loves in the miracle in unimagined ways. Clean currency stays clean if the intensity of the coding is intentionally and consistently set to override the force of resistant energies.

"An object in motion stays in motion unless acted upon by an equal or opposite force." —*Isaak Newton*

So we 'good people' have to be mindful of how we intend for our currency to be a positive force that is stronger than the 'bad guys'.

Examples:

I used to be stingy about paying people. Likewise, I would demand to receive payment before doing the work. One day I realized, 'You're going to have to WANT to give your money in order to receive back the desires of others to GIVE you money." This was around the same time I realized that by going completely off the grid, I had closed my pathways to receiving abundance. I was going to have to open bank accounts, and credit cards, and online payment processors, and pay my pound of flesh to some 'evil' system. It reminds me of a particular religious tradition, I forget which country, in which they leave an offering outside on the front door, to pay the 'evil' spirits their pounds of flesh so that they wouldn't come inside and would stay at bay. That opened up my willingness to pay some taxes. In the matrix, but not of the matrix.

I saw how an admirable Panamanian friend would always kiss his currency when a client would pay him in appreciation to God. He'd touch the cross on his neck, kiss, lift it up, and pocket the cash. He owns a barber shop, video game zone, tattoo and piercing studio. So one day, in a very relaxed attuned frame of mind I said, **"Source, I now download a program for more grace in how I invest my money. I allow money to be my friend, ally, and commit to using it more responsibly for the benefit of myself and others. And this is so."** Now, before making a payment, I try to remember to kiss the bills and bless the currency saying (often in front of the person for their own education and awareness programing), **"May your abundance multiply a million fold."** I take communion with the money, the same way I take communion before every meal in remembrance of the sweat equity it took everyone to bring me this opportunity to share abundance. "Thank you god for making me so abundant. Bless everyone who brings this abundance to me. Bless everyone they know. Bless everyone this currency. I WILL benefit."

We've got to consciously use currency, intentionally raise its vibration, and systematically improve our opinions toward how we wish to utilize that energy tool. If you put out good vibes with what you produce, good vibes will come back, as long as you allow them.

Stop rejecting the flow just because you have a lot of old resistant beliefs still in need of releasing. You'll become more and more abundant with each percentage point of surrender. Our time is all about aggregating resources by releasing our stingy primordial scarcity consciousness. Each time you empty your cup of animosity toward the broken monetary system and allow yourself to be filled with new ways of receiving positive abundance, the more fiscal power you will acquire toward the fulfillment of your purpose.

Of course it's tricky, you say. Even if I firmly set the intention to only attract positive financial abundance and associates of high character, how can I really trust? You must rely on your own ability to rise above and to co-create a mutually healthy outcome. This implies that in the toughest of times, you will ask God for guidance, allow the guidance to come through, listen and obey and attempt to accurately interpret the signals, and let God flow through you AS YOU knowing you are God creating. How can you know you're on the right track and not being tricked by ego? Again, if it seems like the highest truth, the highest love, and the highest joy, you can trust the data and it was not forced and does harm to none, then your abundance karma is clean. In a way, drug money laundering is atonement just as much as harmful drug sales are simply our karma for still treating ourselves shitty, and until we stop demanding to learn the hard way with ego throwing money at unsustainable situations, it's just the caduceus eating itself over and over. It is no wonder people who share the same faith or beliefs tend to feel more comfortable doing business together. They are recycling karma.

What you must release is the gripping, closed, life-taking feelings about the energy of money, and settle how you're going to feel letting it flow to you, through you, as you. Knowing vs. Feeling. You have to sit down and do the work of feeling into these spaces with more intense positive belief than the negative doubt or fear energy in which you may have been more practiced. Manifesting abundance takes practice of flowing faith in action. You must give yourself time to do this emotional homework. I can't tell you how many hours of subliminal money abundance audios I've listened to on YouTube. I had to get down with my limiting beliefs on paper, asking myself why I was afraid to be rich. I was afraid of using money as a control mechanism the way my Mom did. I had trouble seeing myself as a moral wealthy person because it had never been modeled to me. So I had to get mentors, and began working closely with awakened wealthy people. These are the kinds of people who give to get. So I had to give it to get. And you will too because they won't be a vibrational match to less. The truly generous give sometimes without charging, just because they are dedicated to service, but I can almost guarantee they don't own their own homes and have trouble paying their bills. Since we're dealing with feelings again, logically, my words on a paper can do only so much. The short of it is that you'll have to allow yourself to practice being in a good feeling place about money, surrounding yourself with abundance-minded energy. You'll have to use forms of abundance currency using your imagination first to generate those positive emotional connections from within.

Do not believe that you must sacrifice your passions in order to inherit the kingdom. At some point in your awakening, your life may destruct materialistically so it can bring you closer to God by giving you fewer distractions. It may be that you are called upon, by misbelieving you deserve tough lessons, to remind people of self-rejection through the appeal or begging of money and resources. Most likely though, that's just the sick poverty consciousness, and it's a trick you're using to learn reliance upon and faith in God's deliverance. How much self-sacrifice you need depends on how stubborn, self-rejecting, unforgiving of self or others you may have internalized and focused upon in ignorance of the laws of attraction. Abundance is your birthright. Period. Full Stop. Our energy is being harvested and farmed by an enemy that's got us so well trained we whip ourselves and beat our own dead horses for them. We must only sacrifice our attachments to false thoughts, forsaking false Gods which no longer serve and reprogram our relationships to material manifestations of abundance. Let go of what you've been told about money being evil. Love of money instead of the love of God is the problem, not money itself.

"Thou shalt have no other Gods before me."
— *Exodus 20:3 (KVJ)*

Affirmation:

I am allowing joyful abundance to flow to me, through me, as me in all forms spiritual, financial, material and physical. Our God is an awesome God and he wants the best for me. I am now willing to receive great abundance. I step into this power humbly grateful before God. Any belief to the contrary of my true worthiness is now transmuted back into the light for healing by the power vested in me by God Almighty. Blaze Blaze Blaze by the violet flame that stinkin' thinkin. I am now releasing, releasing, releasing. I am free. I am divine. I am Pure. I AM worthy. I claim all these truths and abundance as my own. A-ho

Seriously, write that out, by hand once a day for a month and tell me what happens.

Others have said it best, as you read in the quotes below. In my experience, big financial wins always happen after seeking deep refuge with God regarding how best to emerge and fulfill my purpose.

"It's funny when one links job satisfaction to financial compensation alone, they're never paid "enough." Yet, when they see "work" as a way to dance with life, meet new people, and unleash the creative tiger within, they become very rich, indeed.

Every kind of rich.

More gr-r-r-r-r please, The Universe " — TUT

Below is the later half of an article that I agree with, based on personal experience. Source: http://www.greatgenius.com/gods-covenant-of-prosperity-is-what-blesses-you (130)

"Earlier in my walk with God, I had a visionary experience with the Lord where He stood before me with a hot, fresh loaf of bread in one hand and a scepter in the other. He told me to choose one. I knew that the scepter represented power and authority and I wanted to do great things for the Kingdom, so I reached for the scepter. As I did, Jesus pulled back the scepter and extended the fresh bread to me. He said this: "I will not release overcoming kings until I first have consecrated priests." This launched a season of my life where God began to teach me what authentic supernatural Christianity really is and how God sets the priorities in our lives.

As believers, each of us is called to live a priestly lifestyle and a kingly lifestyle. However, in order to live in the authority and power of the kingly lifestyle, we must first learn to live the consecrated priestly lifestyle. The Bible says we are the "royal priesthood" of God (see 1 Pet. 2:9)." (131)

"The first thing God is looking for before He starts granting you higher levels of authority in the kingly lifestyle is that you learn how to be a consecrated priest. Galatians 4:1 tells us that even though you are a child of God and an heir of God, and therefore the master of everything... if you are still a child, it is as if you are a slave. If a king has a son, and the son is the heir, he is the one who will own and administer everything the king possesses. But when he is still a little child, he does not understand those responsibilities, and doesn't yet have any commitment to it. A good king and father would only give more authority, responsibility, and power to His son as he matures and becomes more consecrated to the King and the Kingdom."

"People who live in this way, in the priestly lifestyle, will be the ones who live a supernatural lifestyle, full of the glory of God. They will be the ones who experience deep intimacy with the Lord, and experience His presence in a very real way. These people will be the ones who literally carry and manifest the substance of who God is to the world around them. They will be the ones who operate in the authority and power of the Kingdom as they demonstrate a kingly lifestyle.

So, we see that the first element of authentic supernatural Christianity is living the priestly lifestyle of wholehearted passion and love for God, in a supernatural lifestyle. The second element of supernatural Christianity is the kingly lifestyle. Daniel 11:32 says, "but the people who know their God shall be strong and carry out great exploits." This is the two-fold expression of authentic Christianity: the priestly lifestyle of truly and intimately "knowing our God" and the kingly lifestyle of "being strong and doing great exploits."   — *School of the Supernatural (Ryan Watt)* (132)

"Most Law of Attraction and Positive Thinking practices overlook one important factor about reality, and that is physical dimension (at least on planet Earth) is cursed with a curse. "By the sweat of your brow you shall eat". (133) Creation is cursed. There are evil influences that suppress full creative and life experience. People are hindering our manifestation efforts with their fallen human characteristics. "The wages of sin is death". (134)

That is why incomplete thinking does not work to help us live sanely in this sphere of existence. There is a need to acknowledge the fallen state of existence. In other dimensions (like Heaven), it is true that the default state is one of pure positive, but not here. The default state on Earth is death and evil. Everyone needs to work for their sustenance, people need to protect themselves against accidents, thieves, scams, incompetent people, etc.

Law of Attraction practices try to pretend that there is no curse, creation is perfect, humanity is good. That is why there is always something missing, and people just can't put their finger on it. The world is not perfect. We are in a fragmented hologram. The dream is broken. "The whole creation groans and travails in pain together until now... waiting for the adoption, to witness, the redemption of our body." (135)

The Way that truly works is to depend on God for redemption. We need to rely on grace, mercy, provision, protection, assistance, favor, blessing, good fortune and victory from Heaven and Angels. We need to rely on the forces of Light to overcome the forces of Evil. That is why God sent his Son, a superhero, savior from another world (that is perfect) to be the Way, the truth and the life.

"Blessed is the man that walks not in the counsel of the ungodly, nor stands in the way of sinners, nor sits in the seat of the scornful. But his delight is in the law of the LORD; and in his law doth he meditate day and night. And he shall be like a tree planted by the rivers of water, that brings forth his fruit in his season; his leaf also shall not wither; and whatsoever he does shall prosper."   — *Psalms 1:1-3* (136)

"It is not just the Law of Attraction that we need to meditate upon, but also the Law of the LORD."   — *Enoch Mind Reality* (137)

"What is the most important meal of the day? It is not breakfast. It is the Lord's Supper. Take this meal and your whole day will be blessed. You can take it any time of the day and as many times a day as you want."   — *Enoch Mind Reality* (138)

"You can use cranberry juice. It is red and grows on vines. Grape juice would do too. Wine is made from grapes. Jesus is the Vine and the color red represents his blood."   — *Enoch Mind Reality (139)*

"Taking Holy Communion is the only thing that Jesus said to please do as often as you can in remembrance of Him. In this one act is all the elements of power. There is prayer, there is declaration of faith, there is speaking of the Word, there is faith in the Name, the Blood and the Finished Work of Jesus on the Cross. When you take in Holy Communion, you are meditating upon Him. This is the most powerful magical ritual there is. You are doing something beyond the ordinary. You are doing physical actions that accompany your faith. All you do is to eat and drink, and believe and confess your salvation in every area of your life. There is peace, prosperity, wholeness, health and love from this one act of receiving God's blessings.

Taking Holy Communion activates the Covenant of God's Blessings upon your life. Taking Holy Communion is not just a ritual but it is a Relationship with God. You are talking to Him, fellowshipping with Him and partaking of Him. That is why it is called the Lord's Supper. It is a good practice to do it at least once a day. That is why it is called the daily bread. In it is provision for all manner of blessings and heavenly assistance in your life. Taking Holy Communion is a physical and spiritual act combined as one, and it releases spiritual and physical blessings into your life." — *Enoch Mind Reality* (140)

"When you take Holy Communion, it is not about going through the actions. It is about connecting with God. It is about coming to God and drawing from him. It is about a relationship with Him. When you speak the Word of God, it is not a mantra that you are repeating over and over again to make something happen. It is about revelation. It is the revelation of God's love towards you and His grace and blessing towards you." — *Enoch Mind Reality* (141)

Conclusion

By now you realize that your Will to change is an inextricable part of the equation toward releasing your impoverished ever-improving relationship with money and abundance in all its forms. Likewise, you now realize that perceiving yourself as having 'bad luck' with money is mostly due to your mistreatment of it in the past, aka 'bad karma.' or your constant affirmations of bad luck manifesting into reality. You can also see how your unwillingness to obey God's path of receiving and giving abundance responsibly has kept you from the keys to the castle. But since karma isn't God wanting you to be punished, it is simply a phenomena of physics, you are in full power of your money domain. As soon as you have a proper heart-to-heart with Source on this subject, surrendering to God's will (which is the same as saying Your Higher Will), then I guarantee you miracles will occur and more abundance will flow to you. You are reminded to tithe in some way to remain flowing.

The first thing I recommend is to remember grounding.

The Remember Grounding CD, and other productions are available at https://carinacarinosastore.guru/product/remember-grounding/ (142) and everywhere else digital materials are mass distributed like iTunes, Amazon, and Spotify. Visit the site if you're curious to access the massive benefits of a good grounding meditation. From this place, we access all wisdom and supportive energy needed to evolve.

You can also sample this CD and others by downloading the Carina Carinosa App by clicking on the iTunes tab. **And I have an exclusive special discount just for you because I'm so proud that you've made it through the whole book! By downloading the app, you can click on the "Exclusive Discount' tab to get all 6 of my CDs plus a distance healing session for a deep deep discount!**

Source gifted me a sincere person, a conscious connector, who suggested the path for how I found the perfect production team. On two magically aligned occasions God has brought me some amazingly affordable talent to create these healing sounds all designed to help raise consciousness and improve the quality of your manifestations.

People experience our work together and say it is truly impressive. At the very least, I hope you are inspired to not mess up as hard as I have, inspired to learn from my lessons with greater ease and grace. And if you are being called to have some really hard awakening, I hope this book helps you find comfort that you are not alone. Remember, Eckhart Tolle had to basically live homeless on a park bench for three years before he got it all together. We don't know much about Jesus from 18-33. Ghandi was racist, and the historians who make it into the history books usually were puppets to a hidden or even covert agendas. So again, take what resonates, "God forgive us our trespasses as we forgive others, and lead us not into temptation, for thine is the Kingdom and the Power and the Glory forever and ever. AWOMAN!'

I used to be very resistant to using the banking system. In fact, I created a whole career based upon the concept of private asset protection strategies, often termed 'hiding money offshore.' It went well, but not amazingly well because I resisted rooting myself in ways to receive payment, aka abundance.

In fact, this whole book content was revamped and can be credited to Anne Gordon's psychic dolphin reading. In that reading, Anne channeled that the dolphins said, "We are so pleased that you've chosen to connect with us. We've been waiting for this moment for a long time. We wish for you to understand how we operate so that you may choose if and how you would like to work with us. We heal using sonar technology. For example, when a pregnant woman is in the water, we can see inside and may choose to swim with her encouraging and stimulating both the baby and the mother. Because of this technology, we want you to know that we operate in full transparency. Are you willing to operate in full transparency? You can trust that we will be supporting and connecting with you if you Will it."

I thought, "Holy shit, this means I have to become open to telling people my birth name, paying taxes to a corrupt government I disagree with on my worldwide income, and also be willing to let people know the real me, warts and all. FUCK what a daunting commitment! Heaven help!" And they did, they do.

This manuscript was originally 38 pages; it'll finish somewhere near 236. The amount of value that is being added by my willingness to share the deepest pieces of me combined with my intention for it to help you heal, ensures that I'll have plenty to cover basic needs and also to further self-actualize.

The finances to produce the album came from a benevolent stream of intention. Remember I told you the formula for my first surrender ceremony? It's coming up next. I was homeless squatting in an apartment with no electricity with a handful of small crystals and salt water singing Do, Re, Me, Fa, So, La, Ti, Do. I pleaded for God to help me, and decided that the money would be used to further my purpose and passion. Within three days, I'd closed a $12,000 sale and had half of it in hand. A week before, I'd been taking handouts from other poor people. I repeated this process a year later. Soon after, that same miracle client referred me to a second miracle client and within a couple of weeks I'd negotiated a $40,000 sale.

The intention for that money was to help people clean up their act so that we can build upon and further God's divine and loving will for our lives. Now that I'm legitimately coming full circle with having experienced myself being greedy and then coming back to God, it's finally all coming together and able to reach you. So please, let's build together. We'll build a better world for ourselves, our neighbors, our children and the future for all sentient beings. Your contributions to The Carina Cariñosa Foundation reflect your commitment to the evolution of consciousness within yourself. The proceeds of that intention will spread to seed the consciousnesses of countless other sufferings.

Our federally recognized non-profit organization is committed to supporting smaller groups who are making a difference but who may lack official incorporation. Of course, generous and publicly visible donations will be given to life changing organizations such as those committed to bringing clean water, housing, education, free energy, and protection from abuse to the vulnerable. Together, may the abundance of our positive intention multiply fruit for generations to come. Check out our original website, https://carinacarinosa.com (143) to find out more about how the foundation is involved with the community. Don't see something of interest? Chances are it's a bespoke service so shoot me a message and get properly screened.

Abundance Prayer For Those Not Quite There

Dear God, please fill my thoughts with the belief that all my needs will be amply provided for. Let me believe, breathe, manifest, and be abundance in all its' positive forms. Help me to allow in prosperity, in all its forms. Come in. Come in. Come into my heart and transmute all poverty consciousness or false beliefs in lack as my reality. Help me to recognize all your gifts. Help me to create a new truth full of favor, abundance and sharing. Thank you for all the abundance and prosperity I am now enjoying and stepping into. May I always remember that you carried me through that threshold, that you gave me the strength. Thank you thank you thank you.

Once you're ready to level up on this prayer and bring it into the presence because it resonates as the current vibrational truth that of which you can feel into, pivot the language into the present by switching 'please' to 'thank you' because you realize it's already done.

Chapter 23:

CHILDREN VS CAREER & GETTING CLEAR

As I surrender my fear from the comfort and solitude of my apartment, I'm begging God to let me know for sure if I want to be with my man. Is he here for a season or for the long haul, and do I want that, because he wants kids, and I'm scared I won't complete my mission. I'm afraid he's not exactly what I want, but maybe I'm just too stubborn to step up to the responsibility required to get everything I truly desire.

This is coming up after our second argument in 3.5 years, but I'm adamant it's so good because we have space to miss each other. We're not in too deep, ya know? Plus, I'm anal about wanting things to be clean around me, and I'm afraid he won't pull his weight. In fact, I already resent it, even though he's trying. I just don't want to become a nag. I can so imagine myself nagging about other people's mess, even though I allow my own mess. It's easier for me to bark like a drill sergeant when secretly, I want servants. That's the ego side. The balanced side just wants harmony at home, and I have that now in a way that I've never had living with others. Solitude is easier than being a good person all the time. I've just gotten accustomed to a high standard of living, and now I'm resenting that he wants to raise the kids in the states, where I can't afford a maid and nanny like in Panama. The town I want to live in has high property taxes, and I already feel priced out of the market. What I want to custom build in Panama would cost at least half as much. My ego is so cunning at making valid arguments not to trust love.

I begging to help me get clear, and the yawning becomes intense and insane. My mentor, Wolfgang, taught me that the yawning is an indication of something attached to my energy. I must evict it. The divine master in me begins commanding it go. All chords, bonds, hooks, attachments, curses, whatever, just please please God take this from me! What must I do to get clear? What must I learn and obey?

Addiction, The knowingness says.

It came up in my very meticulously chosen tarot cards- the devil and addiction must be released.

"Okay, okay! No more cigarettes!"

Earlier it was stuck in wanting, that anxious thing inside feeling for something external to satisfy. That thing I'd thought I'd conquered back in Panama while healing in solitude on the side of a flower crested mountain. But not really; not when tested. I'd thought about the promise I made to my daughter 16 years earlier while pregnant, deciding to give her away. I promised I'd clean everything up.

I dreamed of her the night or two before. In Panama, searching for her on the beaches and paradise coasts.

"Fine." I cried. "If that's what I must do to get rid of you (the stifling yawn monster), then fine. I give it. Take it! I commit! God, Source, all benevolent beings, TAKE IT!! Have it!!! I'll learn my lesson I swear!!.... but I don't want to..." the internal struggle continued. "I'm tired! I'm so so tired. I want to feel inspired."

"Then let me in." It began.

I muted the Knowingness to Google "Will having children ruin my career?"

IT had already told me during the ibogaine experience that it would ignite my career in a new way and teach me to speak in the simplest of ways so that all ages could understand. IT could work through me to teach and raise a new generation that can continue to turn this shift around.

The articles echoed this.

"But I want to be selfish! I like my space! I need space!"

Knowingness showed me in the expansive backyard that I could simply say to Chris, "I'm taking space." And he'd give it to me.

So I picked up the phone and began to write:

"I'm so afraid to love you to death

Till death do us part

It breaks my broken heart.

To fathom treating you anything less than the best

Because you are a masterpiece

Because I don't forgive easily.

I can imagine so many things going badly.

It haunts me all day and night long

Hormonal imbalance

And a childhood gone wrong."

I stop to check my ovulation app. Yep, entering PMS. And I know, I notice, I listen: I'm unhappy because I missed my chance to procreate again. Fight with all my might, it's still there, waiting for me primitively. The reason I chose a female body.

"I'm waiting for you." She says, a little girl, a woman, and all at once so much more. "He's waiting for you too."

He's farther away, and I'm not trying to listen deep enough.

I continue.

'So much hurt and victim mind

Selfishly demanding

Self serving while serving others

I cant have both. I have to put things on hold.

I appreciate you holding on, but there is so much more that can get out of hand.

And while I'm sure the good times will be good, the bad times will be bad.

So I'm chicken.

Your lazy mindedness or lack of IQ even though you are intelligent, it slows me down and questions my authority. '

IT/ God steps in.

"You'll be fueled by her.

Desperation transmuted into victory out of a refusal to fail or keep yourself down.

See that you can be loved while showing up fully in your career first.

Then submit, commit, get on with it.

Your creativity will not be stifled.

On the contrary, you'll shine like you always do. You are thunder booming, unable to ignore.

She's waiting for you, no worries. She has more patience; Him too. We'll teach this to you.

A little boy learning from strong female influences... soft calm and gentle males.

He's not going to leave.

He's proven he's committed.

That's you. Mirrored.

But his strength is your weakness. We gave you this gift because you chose it.

True, he does not need what you wish to teach, but millions do, and so, yes, you must put the world to the test, and know we will make it turn out for the best. That's what we're here to do. We listen to you.

Symbiosis. Get with it.

Fall in line.

No more escaping.

Profound action, Jackson."

We giggle a little.

"No more crying, just grounding and relying. Willing to listen and follow through."

IT hears my fear of monogamy.

'He'll do. You don't need others. He gives no static to letting you frolic and play around. You won't want to. Your joy and extreme elation for connection with this bundle of excitement will reignite that which you have lost and so desperately seek. The energy. The spark.'

IT hears me question the responsibility.

'You may not wish to accept it, but it was the symbiosis to love and be loved, to be granted permission to explore and grow beyond all you'd ever known. It's the gift you most want to give yet you prevent it within. You may not understand, because you are not meant to until you do.

Oh how you'll surrender day and again. Praying and calling us in. Letting us dance through you in all that you do. Gloria in excelsis Deo!'

I pause to look that up.

I can hear my mom in the choir singing it in group rehearsals. I am quietly letting her, entertaining myself while being entertained. Giving her space.

Wikipedia (144) says,

'Glory be to God on high

And in earth peace, goodwill towards men,

We praise thee, we bless thee,

We worship thee, we glorify thee,

We give thanks to thee, for thy great glory

O Lord God, heavenly King,

God the Father Almighty.

O Lord, the only-begotten Son, Jesu Christ;

O Lord God, Lamb of God, Son of the Father,

That takest away the sins of the world,

Have mercy upon us...'

Update: I've since, had two tarot card readings, and they keep saying to stay, that glory and supreme success are coming. It's the universe telling me to have hope, and turtle medicine saying to give it time. A few weeks later, the devil on my shoulder wanted to sabotage this again. That's when I found Pastor Mike's sermon 'Planted not Buried.' (145)

Say Hello to Munchy

The Spirit of Addiction, Ibogaine & Inner Child's Frustration

I wrote this to Tulsi Gabbard hoping it would find its way to Bernie Sanders' and JFK Junior's desks. I'd REALLY like to shed some light in terms of FIXING the addiction crisis. It's a medicine called Ibogaine.

Ibogaine is a root from a bush that grows in Africa. It reconnects you to the mother earth, the same way a root is connected down into the ground and sucks up her blessings and nourishment.

The 52 different alkaloids work in the brain in so many ways science will never be able to isolate and synthesize it. Thus it will remain illegal by the FDA.

Addiction is about disconnection and anesthetizing yourself because you can't cope with the traumas, pain, and harsh realities, so you must escape your body and this reality.

The ibogaine experience is like bleaching a dirty tile floor. The grout is your trauma, stains, samskaras, skars. It resets the knotted up traumas in the brain that aren't synapsing properly. It calms, satisfies, ionizes, smooths out the neural pathways, bulldozes, reconnects, and paves a superhighway for the energy to break through the traumas and physical addictions just like roots break through the ground, or lava breaks through the mountain of pressure.

The treatment is a serious experience lasting several hours, but, for example, in my case, it gave me the ability to listen to my willpower when it comes to quitting smoking. It gave me that ability to connect deep within to that satisfied knowingness so that I can power through the rest of my detox process, which, aside from eating like an American, drinking like an American, where everything is 'Go big or go home', includes detoxing the anger, resentment, and grudges that I've been carrying, or my propensity to hold a grudge because I'm just angry and resentful at life.

I admire Bernie so much, and as a healer, I understand sacred plants, and am so sad that wanting to prescribe food and nature to heal people is illegal in this country. On the matter of addiction, crime and punishment, we've got it all backwards. The people know something is wrong, but they don't have a clue to properly diagnose and treat it because we act like no one outside the States has value to contribute to our society. Africans have this medicine. It was the South Africans that ended Apartheid. Apart-Hate. Just like Dave Chappelle recommends in his new Netflix series, we need to do like they did. We hold the loving space of forgiveness so that bad guys can confess their crimes, be forgiven, be healed by the forgiveness of their 'enemies', humbled, buried in the ground by their own surrendering of ego, and allow that enlightened space of God renew and birth a newer, more whole society.

The health Scare system is rigged to kill us, and it won't stop until our politicians are exposed to the benefits of the various sacred tribal medicines.

Three weeks post-treatment integration help needed please: I'm detoxing from cigarettes. I want to drink but I know it doesn't serve. I get allergic reactions to it, and people are taking me seriously about watching out for the cross-addiction. I call it munchy mind. The blue monster is my inner child personified. It just wants to munch on anything outside of itself. It's a TV mind controlled consumer. It's my distressed inner child not knowing how to cope with these serious childhood traumas I'm still left with.

First, it was divorce at age 4 where I blamed my mom for breaking my heart and making my dad go away. I am the love of his life and could feel her jealousy on so many levels.

I've been shopping, overspending. It's something I really want, but it's still outside of myself. So I really sat down and got serious with the spirit of addiction and evicted that bastard, but ego shits little stem cells upon exit. You know how a mushroom drops spores. It's bringing out how much I hold grudges and resentment. Now that I'm not rejecting myself I'm aware of all the shit I was subconsciously rejecting. I've been aware of it, I'd just left it by leaving the country and divorcing myself from my dysfunctional family. But I've been back in the country for nearly 4 years and it's time for this shit to come full circle once and for all.

And my mind is freaking out. On the one hand, the little inner child is throwing a fit about not wanting to take on more responsibility. She resents being a good example because they sprung that on me by handing me a younger step-sister after I'd only known the new step-dad for 2 weeks. Suddenly they asked me to be a ring bearer and signed a witness to their wedding, and now I have to set a good example to this stranger little kid I suddenly have to live with. What balls man!

I need a crutch or new coping mechanisms for all the shit I was brushing under the rug.

Ibogaine got me like, "Oh hahahah, you remember how your mom had that stroke when we were 17, and it destroyed our sense of security? And how you played a hand in that by fighting with your stepdad so much? Hahah, yeah I'm still here waiting to be dealt with.."

I need to go destroy some shit, the way my security was destroyed. I need to pound in someone's face the way fear has pounded away and eroded away my safety of free speech. I need to fuck something up now that I'm not fucking up my self. Gotta burn up the anger and resentment energy or else it'll just sit there simmering on the backburner and come out as amped up hostility. It's why I can't commit to having a family or children because I'm afraid I'll resent not having my career and meaningful impact on the world. I thought shooting a gun would be good, but then I'd get good with a gun and increase my chances of committing homicide against my brother. So maybe it's time to try boxing.

I KNOW the answer is shut up and breath into the mother, and give her all my shit, BUT I need a witness who truly loves me to shake me by the shoulders. Like I'm mentally begging myself to please relax and let it go, but I can't let it go because there's too much injustice in the world. I resent hell for forcing me to fight so hard when God intends so much glory and abundance for our lives. People say, 'Oh you're so brave, and you're so strong."The wounded warrior just rolls her eyes, sighs deeply, and resents her scars while the world corvettes and steals the innocence of babes.

The Mother has told me so many times I don't need drugs, or even medicines to arrive me at peace. I just have to become willing to listen to her and intentionally do the work of connecting. Drugs, even psychedelic ones that force you to hear, for me, are just punishment because I'm too stubborn to sit with myself. So here I am asking a group of strangers to please witness my insanity, called to share my story as a messenger, begging people to please stop hurting yourselves and one another because it's so hard to live in this world where we shit on everything. I don't want to be a hero, immortalized, vilified, or revered for having the courage to show how much it hurts for us to destroy ourselves and our loved ones. I am definitely the reluctant hero, forced to risk my life saying what others are too afraid to stand up and die for, afraid to have a family for fear they'll be sacrificed or used against me as leverage to shut me up and allow the system to carry on farming our souls as usual.

I'm really angry at how fucked up everything is on this planet. As in my subconscious/ now front burner awareness is just all, "FUUUCCCKKKK!!!" Everything I am doing is a response to that feeling. It was my first thought when the ibogaine medicine took hold. "Fuuuuuuuccccckkkkk", echoing in my mind; the word my mom and brother say all the time, and I'm just a fucking misprogrammed parrot cursing on autopilot. I am going to go try meditation. Spirit gave me 8 years in paradise, 4 in a veritable ashram, so that I'd have the tools to face this, and finally stop feeling so neglected and traumatized deep inside and just below the surface... because the mother is always there, and I've got to remind that broken child over and over that she's safe now, she's save. We just tune out the mother and ignore like the defiant asshole children we are bread to be.

But yeah, that's what I'm working with right now. This is why the spirit of addiction has us by the balls.

A Brief Word About Exorcism

The resource I have finally come across, after a good 5 years of awareness on this subject, is Bob Larson, a minister and exorcist who has an online training program that takes you from apprentice to master exorcist. I prayed to be shown. I prayed for guidance. Because I am finally humbling myself enough again to be the student, willing to obey, Spirit sees this and delivered me to Bob Larson's work. I had to go through a four year cycle of wading through my old shit before I was finally willing to get serious about it all, and exorcise the Spirit of Addiction.

I remember the day clearly, in the year 2000. I was four months pregnant, drunk, crying in my beer and making the decision, coming to the realization, that I had to give up my child for adoption because of the spirit of addiction. My dad had been forced to give up his family because of this demon. Here I sit, 33 years later, coming full circle with the promise I'd made that sad day sitting in a bar in Tyler, Texas. I promised God that I'd quit everything and get completely clean, no abusing anything. I knew that was what I had to do to deserve being in my child's life. I was always so thankful to my dad for not being there to mess me up with his shit. I keep the hope that she'll have such mercy for me.

Deserve is such a misused word. The elders point the finger at the Millennials 'sense of entitlement' resentfully as if they don't deserve to inherit a kingdom of wellness and abundance. It's part of the fight between conservatives and 'progressive' democrats. Universal health care, free college, debt forgiveness, $15 minimum living wage jobs. Ego blinding itself to the shitshow legacy we have left our children. They have a right to be pissed, and their votes should count more than the elderly since they won't be around to inherit the shitshow 60 years from now. Spirit says it's not a matter of deserving from a place of judgement, the way elders were abused to believe as children. It's a simple matter of earning good things through karma and the effort of being responsible enough to maintain your nice things. Otherwise we destroy them, and thus don't 'deserve' to have them. It's simply the karma of unappreciation and lack of care.

We have to reverse the karma of misusing oil. Fuel, single-use-plastic, electricity, prescription drug deaths, polluted vaccines, water safety, corporations polluting and stealing natural resources and tax dollars paying for war games where both sides are funded by the deep state and military industrial complex. And our addictions. We have to reverse our vices and greed. I didn't 'deserve' the preciousness of the baby, or the right to influence her, because I'd have messed her up, the same way my dad would have messed me up with his infectious dis-ease and afflictions. Here I've been wanting to have a relationship with my daughter, who is now 16, remembering that promise. It's a promise I'm making to my future children too. I refuse to give them life until I've worked this out. So that's my tough love self-punishment and self-denial for failing to innerstand that self-discipline equals self-love.

The whole truth of the story is, it's mid 2018, and I just had to have another abortion; my 3rd. You see the book isn't out yet, and I haven't left the escorting yet, but I'd finally begun to get on board with having kids with my boyfriend. So, the moment after my ibogaine experience, I stop smoking cigarettes, evict the spirit of addiction, and finally become more open about having kids, and boom, I got pregnant, not by him but by a client.

It was an important test and lesson.

Remember to be very careful what you wish for.

After the ibogaine experience, for 6 weeks, I believed I was losing my mind from the onset of perimenopause, detox, and ego trip over this addiction thing. I felt so crazy at one point I had to break down and pray and beg hard for Spirit to show me if I was really supposed to go back on psych meds or start hormone replacement therapy. I pleaded. Spirit came over me. I yawned for a couple of minutes, and the peace washed over.

My intuition knew deep down subconsciously. The boyfriend and I picked names for our kids when I was about 3 weeks old. Finally, I started to notice my boobs hurting all the time at the nipple. One morning, while in lucid state, IT told me, 'You're pregnant.' I got up, got a pregnancy test, and sure enough. At that moment, a deeper kindness washed over me. I couldn't tell if it was shock or Mother Mary, probably both. The feeling was this great big loving kindness that was helping me love into my body, have compassion for my situation, make sense of why I was feeling energetically constipated. Oh, how deep the compassion for how we just weren't ready for this.

I became very gentle with myself. I was in shock for a couple of days. I began doing muscle testing, looking at my ovulation map, and reviewing my schedule to see who was likely the father. I got real still and quiet listening deep inside for guidance. It was silent. This decision was all mine. Unfortunately, all indicators said it wasn't my man's, and I knew he didn't want to raise someone else's baby. Neither did I, nor was this a stable time. Again, it just didn't feel right.

In the half day before telling him, rehearsing how to say this, I got a massage and found myself being extremely kind to people. I contemplated how good it felt to think about the baby being his. It was definitely a beautiful joyous feeling. My mind flashed forward thinking of him coming home over and over again as my belly got bigger. I love that 1950's Leave It To Beaver (146) version of everyone greeting Dad at the door. I remembered the vision of him holding two children at the beach.

He arrived at my apartment, and sat down Googling about remedies for my constipation. I said, 'Yeah... about that... so you know.' Speaking really slowly, "You know how in my line of work there are certain occupational hazards, right?' I raised my eyebrows, opened my eyes real wide and nodded my head poignantly. "Yeah, so...." Giving him time to think about the worst possible scenarios.... "It's not yours."

"You're pregnant?"

"Yup. And all indicators say it isn't yours."

He was really amazing. He took it like a champ, hugged me and started listening. I told him about the clinics and how sad and mixed my feelings were, and that even if it was his, I feel like we're not ready, but looking at my calendar it said no, and my intuition says no, the muscle testing says no. I want to get through my career transition, and he needs to become more cooperative with cleaning and plan accordingly for the financial adjustment, and possible roll reversals. He agreed. (But deep down inside, something died a little in his heart and libido. The seed of doubt was planted.)

I figure it's easier for the guys. Or maybe it's just an obvious 'Hell no" situation. He and my best friend said, just take care of it, learn the lesson, and move forward.

It was hard, but I only had to wait 5 days before the procedure. Man, was I ever sad and grieving. You know, that hard core grieving over the death of a loved one. I elected not to take the anesthesia because I didn't have anyone to drive me home, and they wouldn't release me to an Uber under the influence of a .5 milligram xanax (rolling eyes). Somehow, my brain failed to compute, and I didn't realize anesthesia would have blocked the pain. It did not occur to me that the alternative would hurt like hell. I felt everything. They started with three needles in my vagina. They didn't wait for the painkillers to kick in, and within moments they began to pry open and yank. My pussy is cramping up just thinking about it. Thank goodness it was only about 8 minutes of torture, but I felt like I'd received the 1940's back-door version abortion. (The two I had in Panama were a cake walk compared to this, by the way. Even their humble doctors were gentler than these American-trained professional women.)

In a way, perhaps sick, I feel like I paid my pound of flesh. Abortion = $700 + complete telempathic awareness and mutual agony with the baby. It might be a justification, but in any event the grief and sadness immediately subsided. I prayed a lot for the angels and guides to be with us, as I knew they'd been. I'll keep burning a candle and blessing up the situation until I can think of it all without tears.

I feel relieved. I'm not totally energetically constipated (figuratively and literally). I'd been having serious dizzy spells, I suppose from dehydration. I'm reaching milestones with the foundation and other businesses. I'm turning a corner, and this showed me that yes, I do want to have children with him. I do want to step up and collectively move forward toward that goal. I've spoken to less than a handful of people about this. One being a very enlightened shamanic student. He assured me the spirit doesn't enter the body until later. (The typical belief is that the spirit enters at the 3 month gestation period when it chooses a gender, but I think that timeline is fluid.) I don't know, honestly. I'll be sure to ask that during an entheogenic journey. I'd like to hear more about this topic and hear feedback from mothers who have sat with ayahuasca etc. while pregnant.

In the two years following the abortion, I've been learning to administer the sapo, aka kambo medicine as well as the bufo alvarius medicine and bringing all of our products and services to all, however, I've been led to invite the Holy Spirit into my heart, to let it reside within my heart and entire being. We can search to use any external thing to make us feel better, but the instant healing of the Holy Spirit, it's ability to thwart any evil intent, is an amazing miracle.

After I wrote the above two paragraphs, I began intently looking for my best sapo and bufo medicine providers. I journeyed to hold space at a ceremony and wasn't invited into the circle, which was REALLY strange. Later that night, someone even got paranoid and flushed a quarter ounce of mushrooms I'd donated to a friend. They were having to leave their sacred land. My friend and I could feel the bad vibes. We knew something wasn't right there. After constant 'cock blocking', one day I finally realized, 'This is against my free will. This blocking is not just me. Heck, I'm really really going out of my way here.' It was an 'Ah ha!' moment. So, back to the drawing board to hunt demons.

'The Divine Master in me commands by the power of God almighty, the highest Supreme Creator and by the grace of Christ Jesus, I now command that all energy which is not mine MUST EXIT MY BODY NOW throughout all worlds, times, spaces and dimensions, past/present/future and parallel lives throughout infinity you must leave!'

Then I dry heaved violently and coughed up a reptilian again.

The next day, I went to a very awesome party, a legit rave. I took about 150mg of ecstasy in the form of a pressed pill. Then, a friend gave me a Dutch MDMA capsule and a few bumps of Ketamine. I was in kitty mow mow heaven for about 4 hours. There I sat, nestled in the back corner of the rave, lights glowing and strung up everywhere, tucked inside a kiddy pool tube trippin' balls. It was as though the ecstasy had cracked open my grieving heart and third eye, and now, we were pulling stuff out, activating the divine creatrix, and again I literally had the Midas touch. (147) I literally spent an hour with my forehead and chest mashed into the ground releasing that which no longer serves, begging and thanking Pachamama to take it all while doing tiny healings and activations onto my caregivers. Their doubt and concern, transmuting.

The following week, I worked with LD Porter, an elder healer who uses zero point technique. On our second encounter, at first LD couldn't find me. He was very curious and amazed saying, 'This has never happened to me. I can't find you.' Through a series of coincidence and confirmations, I came to understand that it was the darkies hiding me. I began assisting LD by calling in the light, doing my little activation process and asking Archangel Michael for protection. 'Ahhhh...' LD said. 'THERE you are!'

I came to LD with a big dirty laundry list of things I wanted to work on. Healing the trauma in my womb from the abortion was a top priority. So we focused our attention there, the cysts on my ovaries, and the womb. I could see many colors, but as I earnestly prayed for God and Its helpers to assist, a light blue ray of light came in. It felt good, but it also had specific consciousness, like a being. I asked in my mind, 'Who are you?' It got warmer, very gentle and kind. Then it flashed into subtle form and showed me. Mother Mary.

'Okay Mother Mary. PLEASE PLEASE PLEASE take this from me!'

I felt the warm, gentle, kind, and soft energy reach into my womb. Suddenly, all of my PTSD came up. I began weeping super hard. She said, 'Give it to me.' I opened my will to release and POOF, in an instant, I felt the baby's spirit ascend, and all the pain and anguish began flowing up into 'heaven' through the galactic flush. She showed me the peace of forgiveness and compassion as I prayed for it all to be returned to Source. She spent another 30 seconds or so, comforting me as I searched through my psyche looking for any more trauma. She reassured me, 'It's okay. It's over now. You can relax. Everything is alright.'

And so it is. Aho!

The next day, I saw Master Mujin Choi (148) advertising that he was beginning his Blue Ray technique 'course' on Monday. I jumped, and the next day he did a third eye and pineal gland activation. At first, it felt like the calcification was being cracked open like an egg. I could see the dark implant and asked him to remove it. After pulling it out, the blue ray light began shining through. Then it began vibrating and reverberating until it turned to gold light. But while it was blue, at some point, about 2 minutes in, I began to see images of Shanti Deva, Shiva, Ganesha, and even the living Guru Nithyananda appeared.

"I wonder if the Blue medicine Buddha and all these Hindu Devas are related to the Blue Beings who work through Mujin?" He IS from Korea, after all.... So curious. Does anyone know evidence of this being a true connection? I need David Icke on speed dial! Hahaha

Friends who have been following my story have asked how I'm doing. This week,

I feel like the real me. The truth of who I can be, embodied. I feel like the ME I've been missing for 4 years ever since coming back to the states. The Holy Spirit protecting, opening, and connecting. It feels great to be back in the safety of my own personal Ashram, but this time, with the doors open. Just gotta protect this connection.

I write goals on my bathroom mirror. Complete with a little She Ra magnet above the sink. It's been saying, 'One psychedelic experience per month.' I resisted this for so long, but now I feel very comfortable with the idea of taking a week off for my period. During that week, I feel like I should do total self care complete with mud, getting dirty while creating some kind of art, and perhaps using psychedelics to help process and surrender what's been buggin' me for the past month. However, the guides have been clear, I can give it all to the masters without medicines. I think whatever I do, it's important to just BE during that time.

I really look forward to getting back into my body. Another Goddess sister is providing blacklight yoga complete with DJ and mats on the ground. As she says, 'Your tears don't glow [under the blacklight]. So let it go.'

The boyfriend and I went to Asheville, North Carolina to celebrate our 2 year anniversary among the fall foliage. We ziplined through the trees, with me dressed as a German beer maiden for Oktoberfest. I realized it was another chance to visit with my first Mentor, Master Wolfgang. Then I realized, it's been exactly 4 whole years since I returned to the states. It took a four year cycle to finally release and heal my childhood wounds and deepest fears. Wow man. Just wow. Four whole years- a drop in the bucket of infinity. It's been 20 years, almost to the day, since my mom's stroke, since my super hero died in my mind. I rejected the church, because the administration was part of the problem. I didn't turn my back on God, per se, but I did start looking for answers elsewhere.

In the following two years, now that I'd really rededicated myself, his love helping me become more authentic, back to that place of worship, boundaries, and confidence to live my best life and explore interests, our relationship began to unravel. Subconsciously, I resented him for the abortion, certain and afraid he wouldn't have stayed with me to raise the kid. Perhaps I needed to make him the villain to avoid accepting my punishment for not being more careful and for not living my truth.

You see, I'm still holding space for that feeling from my first ayahuasca experience. In it, the couple working together resounded as the type of marriage I want. But this soulmate wouldn't step into it. When I was doing the Manifest Your Ideal Relationship Workbook, I clearly stated someone who does not use any drugs or medicines or alcohol. That's what I got. It's the healthiest relationship I've ever known. He loves me for whomever, but he holds back, can't transcend his shit. The more I get out of my on way, the more I listen to my heart and work toward my dreams, the more distance grows. He's there to hold space for me, but doesn't have the wingspan for where I'm going and who I'm becoming. He can't keep up.

So after lots more 'spell work' to clear the prostitute lives, getting way more strict about who I let into my space, in dances the new soulmate with his mighty DMT sword just in time for Valentines day 2020, the Foundation's 8 year anniversary. The contentment was so potent it sent me into a bipolar flip as I finished coming to terms with the death of my feelings for the old guy. I'd been so afraid of losing him, yet now I was the one letting go, even though he's still there.

To release one good thing for another even better feeling thing, as a woman of childbearing age, that's still considered culturally very selfish and resented by all the other women who made the sacrifices. Well, rest assured, I remembered that it would have been the baby's 2nd birthday. I cried hard, a friend reaching out to remind me that freedom isn't free, and we all make sacrifices. I felt guilty for how happy I finally am. I cried for wanting my dreams more than that man. I cried for fear that my daughter, about to turn 18 and graduate high school, won't want to have a relationship with me. But as soon as I return to the present and show gratitude for all that is NOW, it's easy to see that God's got my back no matter how deep a hole I may dig for myself. Now, I'm faced with empty nest syndrome. I'm super grateful for a new man who is experienced in holding space with The Spirit Molecule.

An excellent article summed it up to an atrophied heart. This is where we deny ourselves for so long that the expansion of letting ourselves embody all that love and abundance tears like ripping and building new muscle. Without medicine, it's a slow process. With ancestral medicines, it's blast off, 5 years of therapy in one day.

Regardless of whether you choose to work with any of the ancestral medicines, please allow me to save you some time. Invite the Holy Spirit to reside deep within you. My path isn't for everyone. As a girlfriend put it, 'Spirit told me I can't have it all at once because it would be too destabilizing.' Hopefully, my story shows you how very true that statement can be. But don't shy away from deeply knowing your divinity. Just ask God for the quickest, shortest, and easiest path filled with ease and grace. And when the going gets tough, may you reference our work for help and inspiration to return to Source.

AWOMAN! Amen! Aho, and this is so!

The IRS asked me what percentage of our sales we expect to come from goods and services, and who could access our work. I'm hoping this journey is relatable to many people in many different ways. I'm hoping these discoveries and powers will be harnessed to the maximum. I'm hoping we can become like a Federation of Damanhur (149) where everyone just comes and gets the healing.

(Update October 2019: For my 39th birthday, I was called to Hawaii, aka the tip of Lemuria. I was guided to complete my integration at the magically ideal 12 acre Hawaii Nature Retreat, (150) where an 11:11 portal for freedom and ascension had been activated. The medicine bit my bipolarity indecision and helped me complete this 6 year rollercoaster of dealing with my ghosted complex PTSD from childhood. It showed me what a great artist I would become.

The owner offered to let me convey the property. She is an 80 year old woman with no successor. I spoke to her about how to put the property into the jurisdiction of the Carina Cariñosa Foundation. The next week an elder explained that only a church can buy a church. I realized that since we now have more than 25 people gathering per week, that we qualify to raise from Public Charity status to Church status. Another elder then asked me to do the paperwork because there is another 45 acre paradise wasting away, with a 75 year old sickly elder who needs to transfer stewardship. Having been consumed by a hurricane and lava flowing over the road, it was suggested that the transfer might even happen free of charge. [Good, I thought, because the helicopters and drone goggles won't be cheap.] It's where Evlis used to film all of his Hawaii movies.

One could be our healing home for small gatherings, and the other a Global destination. I realized if I can stop dropping the F-Bomb, I could be on Hawaii public radio. For the juicy raw stories, there's Sirius XM Radio where we wish to marry the Aloha Rainbow Bridge with Austin's Live Music scene to encourage global impregnation.

When I returned home, there was an able bodied assistant and alchemist ready to protect our interests. For my birthday, thanks to all of those warm wishes & prayers, Goddess Bridgette gifted me the economic plan. She advised that we invite you to donate $100 per month to the tax-exempt and tax-deductible Public Charity as a membership fee. This will get you an all inclusive trip to the Hawaii Nature Retreat healing center where the volcano will fully support you to let that shit go once and for all. In this way, we don't have to nickel and dime, sell sacraments, or sell beds. If we created a crypto coin, that would also be outside of Babylon's jurisdiction.)

I'm hoping maybe you know, or someone you know, would be willing to help us get the healing into many more people's hands. We need grant writers, and serious interns. I'm hoping we can receive grants and contributions so that scientists can study what's happening to clients and myself during psychic healings or in ceremonies. I want to monitor the changes during the course of a long term treatment for serious diseases treated online and telepathically. Because heaven knows, when we can learn to release, and let divine power flow through, we are transformed in very powerful ways. I also just discovered that PayPal's founder got FDA approval for research using psilocybin to treat depression. (151) We'd love to develop the kind of facility and relationships that could contribute to this kind of work. Hopefully, The Right To Try (152) bill will allow us to do this work in the States (Hawaii). If not, I'm looking for a new home where you'll need a passport.

Shortly after writing that paragraph, a potential colleague decided to attack my qualifications. Facebook heard us say 'bioenergetics' and I was introduced to the brand new bioenergetic diagnostic tool which uses infoceuticals for treatment. The infoceutical is basically programmed water. I can't wait to do a comparative study where we do the following: Client comes in. I do an energy diagnostic and write down what I think is going on. Then, let the machine do a diagnostic, and see what it says. Next, I do an energetic healing. We use the diagnostic machine to see how effective it was or was not, and proceed with the infoceuticals. We'll use Karilian photography (153) to capture the energy signatures and auras of increase. Rinse and repeat as necessary. I'm interested to see how to make the experiences more clinically observable, measurable, scientifically studied. I've developed three stages of plans that go from small center space, such as the Hawaii Nature Retreat, to a lush biodome complete with an alternative 'hospital' and tourist destination. Who will help?

I'm also hoping we can get more funding to finish out the Cure Cancer At Home digital directory. It needs money to market and manage clients.

If you want to have Bob perform your exorcism, you can go to his home base, or visit while he's globe trotting. At the time of writing it costs from $600-800 for an experience. That might seem a little steep, but I've thrown money at a lot of programs that sat unopened and did me no good thanks to those big blockages. The demons won't let you read or watch what would save you.

Should you care for me to remove something for you, I'm currently asking for $300 an hour.

Whether you want to call it demons, or your small self, or the ego, or your primal nature, or attached entities, or evil alien attachments etc: fact is- that shit is real just as much as it is an illusion- a powerful amnesia and vail subverting us from living in the truth of the divine. Bob remembers your divinity; he remembers his own; and frankly; it really works to say to that thing stuck inside, 'The power of Christ compels you. You MAY NOT stay here. YOU MUST go into the light. I am sovereign. You have no other choice. You may not hide. Your seeds are burned. You MUST transmute. I Will not let you escape to infect others. I will not let you go back to where you came for future infection. By the power vested in me and by the hand of Christ and ALL that is holy we command you to be gone. Blaze blaze blazed by the power of the All Mighty."

If entity attachment and vices are a thing for you, as soon as you believe that level of authority exists within you, be CERTAIN that ego doesn't creep back in and trick your resolve. It lays seeds as the gates of heaven are opened, planting seeds of doubt. It shits little spawn in a last-ditch attempt to carry on the species. It blocked me from bringing you my gifts for about 3 years, until I was truly willing to forgive and repent on all levels.

Here are some links to his Ministry resources:

http://internationalschoolofexorcism.org/ (154)

https://www.boblarson.org/webstore/product-category/special-offers/ (155)

Please, work on your sanctification, and don't neglect this aspect; Jesus never did.

I pray your journey and karma are easier than mine.

Maybe the reason this book can finally come out, is because the spirit of addiction is no longer blocking it.... Shine Starlight Shine!

From Windsong Movement, (156) a mantra we sing throughout the Dallas tribe,

"You will be called child.
You will be with me.
Your name is Starlight,
And you are worthy.
Oka hey, Oka hey, Oka hey, Oka hey"

Chapter 24:
THE EXORCISM PART 2
2ND CRAZIEST THING THAT'S HAPPENED TO ME SO FAR

ACTUALLY, I THINK I'll save this story for the sequel. Here's the set up. After becoming more intimately familiar with Mother Mary, aware of the curse against Twin Flame souls reuniting (which we're lifting), Arc Angel Michael put me in the room with a physical human of similar name to take a sacrament and hold space while I had a showdown with the demon of pedophilia.

Why? Because my intention is to evict the bullshit from our world's religions and reunite the tribes in a responsible way. So, I'm being called to step into my power now that I've caught 'the enemy's stench' like a drug dog and am growing in awareness, responsibility, and rapidly shedding lifetimes of programming. I can spot the darkies and lies for what they are. No more hiding. No more doubting or denying. No more chameleon reptilian energies posing as me. No more suicidal ideations, crutches or bandaids. No more holes in my energy for manipulators to hook into. This is full on spiritual warfare. Full completion. Eminent.

The answer is 100% clear thanks to the Rainbow Warriors out there reminding us to smack a rainbow on it and inject the darkness with love and wisdom. Smurf the lies, so they can't hide, and reclaim our individual and collective sovereignty. The Rainbow Warriors of Venezuela's Alchemists send the entities to 'the nothing.' I refuse to exile or condemn any energy. After watching the latest Star Wars movie, Rise of the Skywalker, (157) about the Sith coming from exile stronger than ever, and the two dyads (twin flames) ascending beyond the exiled, I feel confident this decision to always incise them back to Prime Source for full healing and reintegration is a higher truth.

(Side Note: I also soon came to learn why I had to face the demon of pedophilia. Come to find out, my father had been molested by a neighbor repeatedly as a child. I could remember being 8 years old, crying at the ceiling asking why my life was so messed up. The answer was that pedophilia had traumatized my father, causing deep epigenetic trauma which was passed on to me. Then, my parents' divorce was rooted in this sexual trauma and caused their divorce, although my mom didn't know until it was too late. Turns out, this whole time I'd been carrying resentments toward my mother, I was empathing my father whom I identified myself as being, in a subconscious way. This was the truth of my core wound. This was the reason God put me through so much sexual healing work, so that I could defeat the demon of pedophilia and hopefully bring this healing to Hollywood.)

(Side Side Note: I brought this revelation to Rachel as I continued to uncover why I carry such deep rage issues. What sparked this one was that I'd been text canceled on, without apology or remorse, by yet another black man and found my subconscious entertaining a deeply racist thought, picturing the merciless beating of an insubordinate nigger slave. I asked my Daddy to pray for me, and he said, "That's definitely something your great great grandpa would have done." I realized, that the unrepentant reflection from this black man at present was this unrepentant energy from my bloodline. Oh Karma, what a bitch you are! In listening to the accounts of this relative, I suggested to Rachel that maybe he had been one of those pedophile Baptist preachers. She firmly said yes. In the session that followed, I found myself letting go of many deeply trapped feelings, ones I wasn't even sure were mine. But we kept coaching the fragmented psychosis into the light for full healing while Rachel and I commanded that I would no longer hold this for them.)

Back at the ceremony with Michael, it became apparent that the young man had been molested by a priest. I quarantined this demon, who first appeared as OCD, then schizophrenic. Then he went full out psychotic to the point that I understood the need for a padded crazy room and straight jacket. It showed me all of its crazy as it totally abused, sodomized and fought the young man. This boy literally got used by the demon of pedophilia while he relieved his worst childhood trauma refusing to ask God or anyone for help silenced by lies, abuse of power, and nonacceptance. Again, what kind of God would let such a thing happen, he believed? Understandable, right? The whole time he kept running the water and abusing the use of the water. Like the holy water the priests had abused? The demon was wailing and gnashing, inhumane demonic screeching like straight out of the Bible's apocalypse. Meanwhile, Michael was being sexed by that damn serpent thinking he was a lizard.

Remember how I first physically met Wolfgang in Asheville 4 years ago? Wolfgang worked on a circle of friends from Skype on December 21st, 2018 for the solstice stargate portal. We had a fire and renounced the sexual impropriety from our spirits for once and for all. Now, I don't really have an urge for masturbation, much less the voracious sexual appetite. That night, Wolfgang said something about how I'd betrayed a Pharaoh. Meanwhile, a sex worker friend who'd previously been lead to believe she was an intergalactic cat by an Owl Demon named Moloch, (158) reclaimed her divine Egyptian connection. Two weeks later, it was face off time with the demon of pedophilia and the serpent.

A couple days after the solstice, my cell phone gets hacked and it's time to finally get super serious and step up my game as the majority of contacts were erased, even from the encrypted Signal App. (159) I called Dave Diamond again to ask for help.

This damn lizard thing keeps coming up, and whenever I look there, I find King Solomon and that dang serpent in Hollywood trying to hypnotize us. This time, I've got Hollywood's entire blackbook in my back pocket and I'm no longer afraid of the camera or of being blacklisted.

As the possessed young man punched me in the face, and I saw I'm able to surrender with the forgiveness of Christ, I realized that I was able to remain calm because I had health insurance. I decided it's time to get a life insurance policy, write a will, leave strategic instructions with a custodian and have serious disaster preparedness exit plans. Suddenly Facebook shows me a term life insurance policy for vegans. I'm having the examination next week. Meanwhile, I'm realizing that Munchy, my blue imbalanced starving inner child, is the voracious spirit of flesh eating.

So as I'm dealing with this demon, I put out an SOS call for help on Facebook. A Goddess sister was in Egypt and said her boyfriend wanted to do a protection prayer over me. The next day, I paid for the session, the guy is channeling some ancient languages, and when the prayer was finalized, I saw a big rainbow hallow through my opened third eye. Mind you, I was in Texas, he was in Egypt, and my graphic design assistant in the Philippines was working on updating our logo.

Look at what she sent me....the darkness receiving a rainbow halo of love protection.

My friend, a vegetarian who was getting sexed by the serpent thinking he was a lizard, and then staring at me all cute and playful like a cunning cobra, he bit me a couple of times. The next day I saw myself trying to bite my man and munch on his flesh. Maybe for every person that buys this book, we should help serve one more vegan meal. All I know is that Munchy wants that pound of flesh!

I found a good Life Insurance company that doesn't mind about marijuana and will pay out claims on suicide as long as it's over 2 years from the beginning of the policy date. So the clock is ticking to see if the darkies try to take me out like they're doing to these other doctors uncovering the hidden cancer-autism-vaccination agenda. Now if I do die soon, we'll publish the prophecy that empowers a yellow vest revolution of rainbow warriors across the world. The Foundation's gunna get paid to carry on the Mission. (Take that Liers! HAHAHAH!). The vegan policy provides one more clear boundary, tool, and mechanism for me to give up meat again. I say that while my boob pain has resurfaced, so I'm munching on apricot seeds and sipping pomegranate juice with extra garlic in my diet now. I'm doing pretty good at laying down all addictions even though I'm literally having panic attacks trying to allow this book out. The doctors haven't explained a cause for the pains, but I know it's that cancer trying to creep back up demanding I get more plants, less meat, less anger and more peace. Oh, and I've decided to get an internationally accredited Psychotropic Plants certification since Facebook was magically handing them out for 29 Euro. So stay tuned. We're in for another wild ride!

Chapter 25:

SURRENDER CEREMONIES

You remember I told you in the introduction, that I did a big surrender ceremony and manifested a miracle client. Then later on, I did another surrender ceremony and the first miracle client had referred me an even bigger miracle client. Miracles happen to me all the time now. Let me show you how.

Now, there's all kinds of modifications you can do to this. The first time I didn't have little sheets of paper to write on. So, instead, I used an object that represented love and I gave it all my fears, like an offering, letting go of these fears which were holding me back.

It's eye opening, in hindsight, how I've been living with so many fears the past couple years now that I've been back in the states. It's because I stopped doing these surrender ceremonies. A regular bloodletting of your fears is necessary. Ego tries to hold on and do more than what is in its power. In ayahuasca ceremonies, I hear people cry because it's too hard. Whatever they are doing is too hard; trying to love themselves, trying to let go of some kind of pain, or hold onto a painful experience, and they are just begging for mercy. At least I am. The mercy must come from within. We must have mercy with ourselves first before God's light can shine through. The mercy happens when you become willing to let go and let that greater expansive part of where you come from to do the work on your behalf. That's the surrender of the ego. That's where ego says, 'Alright fuck it! I don't know what's going to happen next, but God take the wheel!' and poof, there's a feather bed waiting for you to float onto.

This is true because the greater totality of what we come from, of what we are, what we're made up of, is comprised primarily of compassion and unconditional love.

There's no forgiveness. There's nothing to be forgiven. Spirit and our souls brought us to this place for learning, understanding, repair, repentance, practice forgetting and remembering. Everything is a perfectly evolving co-creative expansion with infinite perfection encoded within. It's OUR jobs to forgive ourselves, not mistakenly plead mercy from some judgemental mistaken construct of what God is. Jesus didn't come to save us. He came to show us how to save ourselves. Only man can be so mistaken as to think that we need God's forgiveness. Karma isn't punishing you. We do that to ourselves. Look baby, what you need is to forgive yourself. What you need is to have mercy upon yourself for all your amnesia and sin. And just what is sin? Sin is when you are being inauthentic with yourself... out of alignment with the totality of your purpose and passions. Sin is misalignment from the Ultimate Truth. So forgive yourself for all the times you trespassed against your body, yourself, your loved ones. That's the key to the kingdom. Self Forgiveness. Releasing the illusion and amnesia. Surmounting the matrix with love bombs.

You can only have self forgiveness through surrender of your ego. So the ego is the part that holds onto the fears and limiting beliefs. The ego is an old survival mechanism which helps your beautiful brain process and calculate. But it's limited in its processing power. It can only draw upon past experiences, your previous story, what it has experienced, and oh how it remembers trauma, guilts blames shames and holds grudges. Forgets but not forgives.

The Source which created the ego is obviously more intelligently designed. The good news is, that surrendering ego can be exceptionally easy once you get some practice with it specifically because it is a derivative of all that is. It's like a program that has always lived inside of you, but which you only ever unpack and utilize in extreme circumstances. It comes from Source, so the encoding to make things simple and effortless is right there. You just gotta unpack the software and do the work.

So here's how I do the surrender ceremonies, which always manifest big miracles and exactly what is wanted.

I make an altar. Personally, my altar has a Tibetan singing bowl which I use to make fire. I put salt and high volume rubbing alcohol into the bowl. Obviously, one should be careful when working with fire. I put various objects of significance, maybe totem animals, or my big healer crystals, flowers, and I have a notepad of small paper with a pen.

I begin writing down all the negative stuff in my brain. Any lack, limitation, ugly things I might tell myself, all my fears. I let that subconscious depressed part of myself that holds me back come to the surface and be heard. I write a new thought for each piece of paper. Sometimes I am very surprised by what comes up. I listen to the depressed inner child. Her sadness, her blame, her self-condemnation, her unforgiveness and lack of acceptance. Once, I saw myself write that I wished my parents were dead. I didn't know that it was floating around in my subconscious so close to the surface. Writing it down gets it out, helps you see it, helps you minister to it as you bear witness to it. Half the time, it just needs to be seen and heard.

So the exercise of writing stuff down can be very revealing. In more esoteric cases, this could be an opportunity for you to discover that there are discarnate entities attached to your energy field. In which case you would want to open a dialogue with these feelings to see if they originate from you, or somewhere else. Is this an external thing or thoughtform posing as me? I recently heard Tony Robbins say that an Indian guru had reminded him to tell everyone that it's THE MIND, not just YOUR mind. The mind is full of junk. The misqualification is our misidentification with THE MIND as the truth of who we are. We are so much more. So for help remembering this, you might ask for a team of volunteer angels to ascend that aspect back to the galactic core for healing and reintegration. But let's just say, for the sake of keeping this example vanilla, that you're only working with mild blockages. Hahahah. They always seem like boulders to me.

Now, I'll be honest, I had serious blockages. There were entities piling up on me trying to keep me down. I always attributed this to my shitty karma for having been a shitty person in several lives, and also for the consequence of having taking an extreme oath to resolve my karma and become a benevolent ascended master as quickly as possible. So it's like I switched from the dark side to the light, and have hell to pay in terms of repentance so I can rest with peace of mind in heaven and continue my work from beyond the veil. Interestingly enough, that repentance doesn't seem to show up so much in the form of service to others, as it does in service to thyself. Just being better to myself seems to void or eliminate the negative karmic loop cycles that have played out for lifetimes. Practicing self love, saving myself, instead of trying to save everyone else.

Back to the surrender ceremony. Once you've exhausted yourself of writing out all these negative illusions, it's time to light the fire! FIRE FIRE FIRE! (Bevis voice) But first, let me explain to you about the Violet Flame. (160) Saint Germain is the gatekeeper of the violet flame. (161) It's like the strongest fire to blaze away and transform, aka transmute energy. You can learn a lot about Saint Germain on Google, and through the vlogs by Patricia Cota Robles, (162) so I'll save you thathomework for later. Basically, what we want to do at this point is to alchemically transmute all these negative thought forms, one by one, and transmute them to the highest possible thought form. This can take some practice, but essentially what I'm asking you to do is to look closely at each negative thought and then turn it to the highest positive thought you can legitimately feel. So for example, 'I wish my parents were dead.' gets burned into the sacred violet flame of transmutation and I think to myself,

'I deeply and profoundly love and accept my parents.'

(By the way, I've been having one hell of a time hyperlinking that owl demon reference and still can't get this pdf document to function normally. Hopefully the editor has better light saber skills than I.)

Clearing Your Chakras During Surrender Ceremony

Another aspect that works really well for manifestation is to clear out and activate the resonant frequencies in your chakras. This is especially powerful if something has gotten stuck to your energy.

In my first surrender ceremony, I'd just gotten a kit of little crystals that coincide with the various chakras. I went to the beach and grabbed a gallon of ocean water (sea salt baths cleanse the crystals). Also, it creates a container of intention, like little pools of divine harmonics and intentions surrounding your portal activation to puncture the veil. It was a full moon, and I put each one of the crystals in its own little container and set it out under the moon. Then I sang Do Re Mi Fa So La Ti Do. I sang Do long and fully, letting my mind resonate with the root chakra, seeing red, feeling the sound of DO resonate throughout my root, and when my voice was able to clearly sing DO nicely, I moved on to Re, and so on. I found I had trouble at La, and so I took a lot longer to sing La until it felt cleared. This is the throat chakra, which we've established I've had lots of trouble with. I did this up and down a few times, until my whole body was resonating from having sang these notes throughout my toroidal field. This helped to clear the fears away. This is how you align and attune your frequency.

Once you are feeling the peace, allowing it to quell all doubts, comforting you with the knowledge that you are being heard and watched over, now it's time to give great thanks and appreciation.

Manifesting What is Wanted

The final most important aspect of doing a surrender ceremony is to ask for what is wanted. Now that your guides, angels, and benevolent beings are directly dialed into your frequency, give them and Source clear instructions to help you manifest pure joy, abundance, peace, nirvana mind, pure Christ consciousness.

All too often, I ask people, 'What are your 5 favorite things?' and they can't answer. You have to know what you want and love in order for Source to give it to you. If you vacillate on what's not wanted all the time, so does the reality you create spin like a broken record. Having cleared the headspace from negativity, and having resonated with the rest of your being, now it's time to get specific with Source about exactly what it is you're wanting to show up in your experience. And as you focus on each thing 17-62 seconds, visualize and physically draw that manifestation down into your being, flowing to you, through you, as you, down into the earth, and back up through your roots. You visualize growing roots, grounding fear, thanking the elements and earth for transmuting all your shit until you realize it's done, faster than the speed of light, and you start slurping up all the abundant fertilizer through your roots, trunk, branches, leaves, flowers, fruits.

Remember, this is not a time to PLAN how your manifestation will come through. This is where you surrender your desires to 'The Manager' and let yourself be carried on that feather bed. It's also the space where you make decisions to take on that greater responsibility and obey your calling and passions. For without this new responsibility, this expanded container for creation, there will be no growth and you'll keep vacillating in the illusion of disempowerment.

Chapter 26:
PRAYERS

I've placed these prayers, hand written, on colored index cards on my refrigerator. I also have a stop sign there. In this way, the anxious 4 year old within who couldn't accept the pain of her parent's divorce and who could only find comfort in the fridge, she stops and the adult becomes consciously able to make decisions. It's been very helpful to distinguish the difference between REAL ME vs. outdated-subconscious-mistaken-who-I-no-longer-am. This is basic stuff: if it hurts, it's outdated.

The first prayer, my dear Goddess girlfriend Vania writes on Facebook the moment I put down my pen from the last chapter.

Dear Universe, Help me restructure my compassion to where I can still be selfless but not poisonous to myself (and my aspirations). Bless me with positive abundance. With love, light and infinite gratitude, Me

My yoga teacher and personal trainer, Amanda Sides, recited this prayer during our first private class just before savasana. It comes from Stephen Cope's book The Wisdom of Yoga: A Seeker's Guide to Extraordinary Living. (163) Placing hand over heart, it resonated with that broken little child inside. The tears began flowing liberally as I surrendered to the physical reconstructive journey. With little girl screaming because she knows it won't be instant, and requires her willing participation, with each repetition of the sentences, I began to love my body into the subconscious core for the first time in 30 years. It's on the fridge, on a pink index card, representing the heart chakra, at eye level. This is known, in the East, as Metta Meditation.

May you be protected and safe.
May you feel contented and pleased.
May your body support you with strength.
May your life unfold with ease.

The next four prayers come from Ernesto Ortiz, author of The Akashic Record: Sacred Wisdom. (164)

References: pg 162-164, Balboa Press. (165) Ernesto is a beloved teacher of my soul sister Teresa Martinez, who guides people on how to access the Akashic Records, aka The Book of Life, which has a reference in all religions, to my knowledge. In his book, I have learned how to heal past and present moving forward with greater ease, grace, and inspiration for the future. It's like my daily spiritual coffee break. Before opening the fridge, I can fill up on this first. It's given me a protocol for daily protection like my spiritual armor. With 'life stuff' happening all around us, which distracts from the focus of being a healer, Ernesto's quick prayers help me to handle tougher healing cases without fear of the potential dangers of dealing with entities, ghosts, and demonic forces which may try to sneak in on a daily basis thanks to 'life stuff'.

Ernesto's book has made it easier for me to vanquish my own demons, release resistant energetic tendencies, and keep from unwittingly attracting them back into my energetic field. Basically these prayers, and the primary Sacred Prayer for opening your Akashic Records help seal up the gaps. If you can imagine your aura or energy field as having holes like Swiss Cheese, for me, these prayers do the trick. You can access a reading from Ernesto directly through the link or from Teresa by downloading the Carina Carinosa App for smartphone. It is because of the powerful reading Teresa gave, which confirmed so many of my deep intuitions, that I was able to access the first printing of Ernesto's book. Ernesto is the definitive author on the subject of the Akashic Records.

What I like most about the following simple prayers, is the extra strength I feel, just by knowing that my intuition sounds like Ernesto's prayers. Maybe you'll experience the same. For me, it's confirmation that I can trust my instincts. It gives me a sense of community to know that Ernesto was the third student to learn and receive these prayers. In other words, the message hasn't gotten lost in translation over the years by institutions and misguided professors. I hope that the prayers will inspire you to write down some of your own affirmations, and place them wherever feels right. What's cool is that if anyone else sees them, they'll instantly connect with your humanity, the humanity within themselves, and that causes thoughtful healing. So there's no reason to feel weird about having index cards all over your house, car, or place of work. By writing up some of your own affirmations, it generates the strength and belief in your own power, so that you can learn to trust yourself and the divine Source within you to the fullest extent.

Ernesto writes:

Forgiveness Prayer

If there is anyone or anything that has hurt me in the past, knowingly or unknowingly, I forgive and release it. If I have hurt anyone or anything in the past, knowingly or unknowingly, I forgive and release it, for the highest good of others and myself.

Prayer for Releasing Outside Influences

If what I am experiencing is not mine, may God have His shield around me and I release whatever it may be to Him.

This prayer can be used at any time one feels a physical sensation (somatic/emotional/mental) that may be empathetically taken from someone else. Empathetic absorption is done in an effort to understand or relieve the burden or pain of someone else. This unconscious action is not a service to God, others, or you. Use this awareness to help that person and yourself release all to God. Therein lies the healing.

Prayer For Loved Ones And Entities

Father/Mother/God, we ask that this entity/ soul be sent on its spiritual evolution for the highest good and mutual benefit of everyone concerned.

Sometimes when we open the Records, we may feel there is a block or interference in connecting to the information available. This prayer releases that energy back to God so the information can flow unobstructed. An entity is an energy form that is attracted to the light. It is not a form trying to enter or possess your body. An entity may be a part of an addiction that comes to take your light using your body as a medium. A ghostly soul is the energy of someone stuck between dimensions out of body that is confused. It may need help so that it may continue on its evolutionary path. I see this a lot in hospitals and places where people have died abruptly. Again, this happened to my ex after he overdosed. This prayer is useful on a personal level to release any energy that interferes with your own personal evolution or advancement.

Prayer For Personal Clearing

I ask God for His shield of Love and Light to illuminate my path. I ask for clarity so I may be able to see with my inner and outer vision and clear all obstructions and obstacles from my life.'

These prayers/meditations I wrote.

Disclaimer: Mine are sometimes less politically cautious, as I anticipate my target audience to have a generally more open sense of discernment. If it doesn't feel true, discard it for now. If it seems poetically difficult to accept/comprehend, try seeing it from a higher perspective. That's my challenge to you. These prayers help me jump up to new levels of consciousness quickly. When worked with from the heart, not the mind, we can unlock new facets of our awesomeness with amazing ease. These are examples of the guided surrender meditation work I do with clients. Take your time and breathe through them. Feel into the words. If you don't physically 'hear' responses, but rather, you feel them or see visions, that's perfect too. YOU have the power to create your own spiritual experience. These activations help me to unlock my psychic gifts and claim a new sense of magical power. When you are thirsty for more, a host of meditations, prayers, and lectures are now available on iTunes, Spotify, and our store just by searching keyword Carina Carinosa.

NOTE: DO NOT REPEAT THIS WITH YOUR MIND. SAY IT FROM YOUR HEART WITH FULL CONVICTION. Call out to source as if you demand to be heard. Then realize, they were always available, you just forgot to connect. We were the ones disconnecting with our free will. They have been waiting to receive permission to connect faster than the speed of light. It works that fast when we remember to allow, accept, and absorb.

Calling All Divine Powers

Dearest Beloved Ascended Masters,

I now allow my heart to connect with your hearts today and every day.... I allow your love to flow to me and through me, as me today and every day. Thank you thank you thank you....

To me as my Highest Ascended Self, I allow you to flow to me, through me, as me, today and every day.

What messages do you offer me? What guidance do you wish for me to listen? How are you here to help? (Pause and practice listening. See what you hear/feel.)

To my divine feminine power, I invite you to now dwell within me. I open my heart to allow you to flow to me, through me, as me. Thank you thank you thank you.

What messages do you offer me? What guidance do you wish for me to listen?

Thank you thank you thank you.

To my divine masculine power, I invite you to dwell within me flowing to me, through me, as me today and every day. Thank you thank you thank you.

What messages do you offer me? What guidance do you wish for me to listen? How are you here to help? (Pause and practice listening. See what you hear/feel.)

To my divine totem animal, please speak to me. Let me see you. What are you doing? How can I learn from your ways? In what ways are you here to support me? I now allow you to reveal how I may utilize your powers as my own. Please show me the way. What more would you have me know?

Thank you thank you thank you.

Reclaim Your Birthright of Abundance

I now claim my inheritance of well being, and God's gift of salvation from the matrix of duality and suffering. Help me to remember the peaceful feeling of silence, your grace, your wisdom, your expansive emptiness. Help me feel your infinite forgiveness and compassion. Source, please deliver me from the suffering of my miscreations and that of others. Thank you thank you thank you.

I now allow the peace of your grace, the truth of who I AM.

I now accept the peace of your grace as my own, returning me to the truth of who I AM.

As I now surrender my little will for your Greater Will.

I absorb, absorb, absorb and activate, activate, activate this new reality and these new codes within me.

It feels so good to relax, relax, relax!

Surrendering Our Will for Higher Will

Dearest Prime Source Creator,

I allow my heart to connect with you, and I surrender my little will for your Greater Will. Right now, I can't see the plan. Please give me eagle eyes as I float above the matrix on the back of angel wings. I trust that my heart's desire, that which brings the greatest joy, is my purpose and Your Divine Will for me, thus my divine birthright. I claim my divine right by surrendering to Your Will in remembrance of my soul's mission and contracts. I allow myself to be delivered into your loving arms and carried down the stream, not needing to understand where I'm going. I trust that you are taking me to the shore of exactly what is wanted. I allow you to keep me on course. When I fall, I thank you in advance for all your help to get back up. It feels so good to be in alignment. Thank you thank you thank you.

Humble Worthiness

In humility, I allow my cup to be emptied, so that you may fill me anew. I allow and accept abundance as my birthright, but first, I dump my righteousness propped up by unworthiness and lacking dignity. As children of God, little stars, descended from the big stars, made up of star stuff, I now remember that I am of God, Source's magical power within me, and therefore always worthy. Help me now remember God's will of abundance, blessings and favor for my journey. The same holds true for my enemies and trespassers. I now recognize and heal the trespasser within me. Let me feed this separation no more. Let us all be returned for healing equally. Let us remember your love and our worthiness. Let us forgive ourselves for all of the ways in which we trespass against ourselves. With these new eyes filled with compassion for myself and others, I can no longer judge the trespasses of others. Knowing I am forgiven, I can no longer judge myself. I can only lift up our souls to your grace and ask for the light to shine to, through, and as us. Please do that now. Help me grow to believe that I am worthy, divine, amazingly powerful, a magnet for blessings, a conduit for love in all it's creations. Thank you thank you thank you. Thank you for bringing peace to our souls, more and more throughout all worlds, times, spaces, and dimensions. For all of the moments that I have forsaken myself or given away my powers, I forgive me and reclaim my authenticity now. What's mine is God's and what's God's is mine. I am worthy because I AM.

Generosity:

Because the truth of who I AM is abundant and gives without prejudice, to remain in alignment with the truth, I now download a program for generosity to become active within me, operating fully as me throughout all worlds, times, spaces and dimensions. Multiverse, please support me to give generously, as I have been given. Through the power of the divine free will, I deliver myself from fears of lack, anxieties for the future, and depression from the past by sowing new seeds now. I attend to my personal garden, sowing row by row with care, calm, and attention focused in the present moment on each segment of manifestation. I sow love. I manifest love. I flow abundantly, gracefully, generously, wholeheartedly. I share what is extra as a means of remaining in the flow. My abundance is recycled and renewed because I dare to trust, and I dare to share. I share equanimity throughout the timeline, an enlightened and abundant thread in the tapestry. I weave. I dare to believe that tomorrow the sun will rise. Perfect opportunities are always finding their way to me. Let generosity become naturally active within my every thought and intention. Let me know that it is always safe, and thus always safe to share. I now remember and breathe in this truth of the great I AM that I AM.

Safety

Beloved Ascended Masters, please help me reprogram my feelings to know that I am always safe, loved, guided, and protected. Show me your peace. Flow it to me through me as me, as I now surrender all doubts for my safety. Help me to attune to this Universal Truth of Safety and let go of any contradictory earthly beliefs. I call upon the divine feminine power and allow her to flow to me, through me, as me. I call upon the divine masculine power and allow him to flow to me, through me, as me. I call upon my highest ascended self and allow him/her to influence my every decision towards the greatest and highest good for all. I now call upon al Christed beings serving the highest truth, love, light, and joy to coach me through all resistant beliefs for transmutation. Thank you thank you thank you.

Discipline

I now download a program for Higher Will and the discipline to carry out the plan set forth by my heart's true desire. Knowing that all elements must come into harmony, I use my divine Free Will to select which elements

of my life require more discipline, and I focus loving attention to those spaces now....... I will not struggle; I allow....... I am open to receiving and listen to the signals; I am listening now....... I have the discipline to try new things with hopeful expectation of a positive result. I have the discipline to begin and to finish. I can control the mind by surrendering it back to Source for requalification and updating. I have the discipline to expand in new ways. I allow myself to grow in awareness and capabilities. I have the discipline to let go and allow new experiences of grace over those vices and seeking externally. I am a magical co-creator. I let Source do Its part while I focus on now. I ground my spiritual practice into all aspects of my daily routine of well being. I am the sage. I allow this truth to unfold as I practice the graceful discipline flowing to me, through me, as me daily.

Flowing In Love

I surrender my will back to You, the truth of who I AM, and give all that I have for the taste of your peace and infinite love. In harmony with the flow of energy, I give what is received, without prejudice or favoritism, as it was given lovingly to me. i take what I need, and project the rest through my heart centeredness. My heart is opened, and it is safe as I now remember to breathe. I AM the peace. I AM unconditional love. Yes I AM. I love myself unconditionally. I'll repeat this until I remember completely.

Perfect Wisdom

I am safe in your eternal wisdom and perfect unfolding. I trust the lessons obscured from my current perceptions. Please give me the eyes to see and the ears to hear as I seek to accept and understand the perfection of all creations. I allow your wisdom to become my own. If I defend, then I am attacked. (166) Please help me never go back. I promise to listen before I react. I allow and breathe in your advice quietly..... speaking to me... from within. I AM "God Eternal Within The Body". (167) I let my life unfold with ease and delightful surprise with you as my ever-wise guide. What is my next best move in this game of life?

Forgiveness & Healing Karmic Contracts

From deep in my heart, I send great blessings to everyone I know.... including myself.... to my friends.... to my foe...... as I now remember to let it all go. To everyone who may think harmfully of me, I see your force and I raise you with my love bombs! Pew pew pew! I shower you with explosions of rainbow light love like fireworks melting into our hearts, healing everything we think, touch and see. I forgive your childish ignorance and mine equally. It's all right. We just forgot to share love, so here, have some of mine. As my Highest Ascended Self I speak to you as Your Highest Ascended Self. May we drink fromthe endless fountain of abundance. Together, karmic contracts healed with ease and grace for the greatest and highest good of all. Master Source and all our Teachers, thank you for providing us with strong armor and guides. Thank you for helping us grow in awareness and capability. May we learn our lessons well. Help them forgive me for my trespasses. I'm sorry. I now learn to recognize my harmful thoughts which turn to actions. I repenting now with my loving intentions transmuting all attack and defense. God, I trust you'll help them do the same. I call upon a team of volunteer angels to guide, bless, and transmute all our ill willful energies. May their hearts be willing. To you (person/group), please listen to your Higher Reason. I promise to respect myself by respecting you and all living beings. I forgive you as I forgive myself thereby transforming the resistance and carrying it up to the light. Heaven help us.

I'm sorry.
Please forgive me.
Thank you.
I love you. (168)

May this be so. A ho.

DNA Activation

Beloved Ascended Masters, known and unknown, named and unnamed, the most holy of the Holy, I allow my heart to connect with your hearts today and every day. I thankfully, humbly invoke your powers for the greatest and highest good of all for the most benevolent outcomes. Thank you for helping me to receive your gifts. I now download a DNA activation of the most powerful construction with ease and grace. Thank you thank you thank you. I allow this power to flow to me, through me, as me, defragging and reconstructing me. Remind me of the whole, one with the Truth of all that I AM. Thank you thank you thank you.

I ask that you infuse your secrets into the very fiber of my DNA finding all, cleaning all, and clearing all for the greatest and highest good of all. I allow you to activate those aspects of my power which were previously hidden, due to my irresponsibility, amnesia, or lack of faith, and I

accept abundant magical transformational strength as the foundation of my now... current.. abundant reality.

I am open to be free from all genetic programing which no longer serves. I allow for the graceful unfoldment of this new reality within me to be reflected outwardly. Please heal my DNA and that of my family reaching back to my ancestors and extending forward to my successors. Do that now throughout all worlds, times, spaces and dimensions. Thank you thank you thank you.

Abundance

Please fill me with your grace, so that I may only act and react from within my highest intuition. I agree to allow my life to be easier, happier, and healthier. I cancel the limiting beliefs like , 'It's too good to be true.... You have to take the good with the bad... Money doesn't grow on trees.' et cetera. I replace those lacking paradigms with new ones such as, 'I'm such a powerful co-creator, when I allow Source to flow through me. I CAN have everything my heart desires. It's awesome to know that things are always getting better for me. I CAN have my cake and eat it too. I CAN have exactly what is wanted. Money and abundance flow to me easily. In ways I understand and in magical ways, tam bien. These new truths and more, I allow, accept, surrender to, and relax within.'

Willful Alignment

Source, help me listen to my body; this vehicle I have chosen for the expansion of consciousness and co-creation. May my will be in obvious synchronicity with Thy Will. May it be obvious when I am not in alignment so that I can easily find peace and joy in the middle path. May I quickly steer myself back on course through your guidance. Thy Will be done, and only Thy Will. I now download programs for Divine knowledge on how to treat my newly activated DNA, what to eat, how to move, how to breathe, when to sleep, how to speak reverently and remove the non-serving vocabulary. May thy peace be on my tongue.

Releasing Doubts

One by one, I hold up to you all my doubts recognizing that these are not Me. I am divine and pure. Therefore, I am free to release these back to

Source for healing. I am a being of truth, light, and grace. Each and every worry or concern, I now let it be blazed back to Source transmuted by your radiant divine unconditional loving energy. Blaze blaze blaze the violet fire transmuting all lack within this misqualified consciousness. Thank you thank you thank you.

BOOK LINKS & REFERENCES

To access this list of hyperlinks visit this link
https://EnlightenTheFuckUp.Org/
or
http://CarinaCarinosaStore.Guru/Book-Resources
Or use the QR CODEDISCLAIMER:

(1) **Buddha Quote:** https://fakebuddhaquotes.com/believe-nothing-no-matter-where-you-read-it/

FOREWARD:

(2) **Melanie Koulouris:** https://www.google.com/search?q=Melanie+Koulouris&tbm=isch&tbo=u&source=univ&sa=X&ved=2ahUKEwjA7MC3uOveAhUkTt8KHSeLAcwQsAR6BAgAEAE&biw=1680&bih=859#imgrc=tdal75tV-UFzLM:(3)

(3) **Tanya Murkel:** https://thugunicorn.com

(4) **Silver Ra Baker:** http://www.rudracenter.org/events/

(5) **May you be protected and safe:** https://www.amazon.com/gp/product/0553380540/ref=as_li_qf_sp_asin_il_tl?ie=UTF8&camp=1789&creative=9325&creativeASIN=0553380540&linkCode=as2&tag=tommysplaceme-20

INTRODUCTION:

(6) **Orwell's 1984 was coming to fruition:** https://www.cliffsnotes.com/literature/n/1984/book-summary

(7) **Baphomet:** https://rationalwiki.org/wiki/Baphomet

(8) http://www.carinacarinosastore.guru

CHAPTER 1: Accepting The Power

(9) **Some of us carry the shame of our conquered ancestors who converted to the Roman Catholic church to avoid death during the conquests of the 16th century:** https://www.youtube.com/watch?v=2l_eVdplODI

(10) **Map of Human Consciousness:** https://www.youtube.com/watch?v=AW51o9Z--_Y

(11) **Power vs. Force:** https://www.amazon.com/Power-Force-David-Hawkins-Ph-D/dp/1401945074/ref=sr_1_1?ie=UTF8&qid=1504383285&sr=8-1&keywords=power+vs.+force+by+david+r.+hawkins

(12) **We can use kinesiology to calibrate this level of truth just by sticking out our arm and pressing on it until the arm goes weak:** https://www.youtube.com/watch?v=e_sxIBejKZk

(13) **shamanic chakra balancing:** https://carinacarinosastore.guru/product/shamanic-chakra-balance/

(14) **enlightenment integration:** https://carinacarinosastore.guru/product/enlightenment-integration-sessions

(15) **Ramana Maharshi Quote:** https://www.brainyquote.com/quotes/ramana_maharshi_160485

CHAPTER 2: Understanding 'Sin'

(16) **Don't miss what Dr. David Hawkins has to say about the lower realms seeking to subvert truth:** https://www.brainyquote.com/quotes/ramana_maharshi_160485.

(17) http://thespiritscience.net/2014/06/16/what-a-shaman-sees-in-a-mental-hospial

(18) **This YouTube link is quite insightful explaining the glow represented in religious artwork as it depicts holy persons who are transmuting carbon. The glow is caused by an excess of carbon 7 neutrons:** https://www.youtube.com/watch?v=ajZ6KsLoHXk

CHAPTER 4: Diving In

(19) **In fact, evidence from the Roseta Stone suggests that this 'blood of Christ' actually came from the amanita muscaria mushroom:** https://www.youtube.com/watch?v=J7MYEpCl5zo

(20) **I'm talking about etheric implants which are the result of being born into the matrix:** http://galacticconnection.com/want-clear-controlling-matrix-implants/

BOOK LINKS & REFERENCES

CHAPTER 5: Developing Compassion

(21) **explore the truth that "God is omnisexual." and that Jesus had sex:** https://www.youtube.com/watch?v=rTX6ANOspvl

(22) **"control drama":** https://www.youtube.com/watch?v=StaHKOLVm_A

(23) **The Celestine Prophecy:** https://www.youtube.com/watch?v=StaHKOLVm_A

(24) Andrew Boyd, Daily Afflictions: The Agony of Being Connected to Everything in the Universe

(25) **Read Cameron Day's revelations entitled 'Tell the 'Lords of Karma' That You Are Sovereign-Why I'm No Longer a Lightworker":** http://www.delightfulknowledge.com/tell-the-lords-of-karma-that-you-are-sovereign-no-longer-a-lightworker-part-2

(26) **Watch 'The Truth About Angels' by Tobias Lars:** https://www.youtube.com/watch?v=SL_kCBcr5jE

(27) **3D, 4D, 5D- Spiritual Judgement Against Body, Sex, and Emotions:** https://www.youtube.com/watch?v=A6nTYT5X7Mo

CHAPTER 6: Forgiving Ignorance

(28) **etheric implants:** http://galacticconnection.com/want-clear-controlling-matrix-implants/

(29) **Android:** https://play.google.com/store/apps/details?id=com.conduit.app_cfb18a09e47c4a168017d0427a8496d9.app

(30) **iTunes** https://apps.apple.com/us/app/carina-carinosa/id867503943?ign-mpt=uo%3D4

CHAPTER 7: What To Do?

(31) **'flawsomeness** https://www.youtube.com/watch?v=2ShWd6vkj04

(32) **Psycho-Cybernetics** https://www.amazon.com/dp/1593979304/?tag=mh0b-20&hvadid=3524379160&ref=pd_sl_4gjn5gcl6v_b

(33) **control dramas** https://www.youtube.com/results?search_query=control+dramas

(34) **pivot up into a higher feeling feeling** https://www.ebay.com/p/30532451?iid=380540068680

(35) **This link shows a list of ailments and their metaphysical cause** http://paganspath.com/healing/ailments.htm

CHAPTER 8: Karma

(36) **Appreciation avalanche** https://www.youtube.com/watch?v=SWLXKk50F94

(37) **shrouded in history using intoxicants, like hallucinogens, to induce spiritual experiences** https://www.youtube.com/watch?v=J7MYEpCl5zo

(38) **The Pharmacratic Inquisition** https://www.youtube.com/watch?v=J7MYEpCl5zo

(39) **religious leaders** https://www.theguardian.com/science/2017/jul/08/religious-leaders-get-high-on-magic-mushrooms-ingredient-for-science

(40) http://www.CarinaCarinosaStore.Guru

(41) **I can calibrate that moment of consciousness at 567 out of a possible 1000 on Dr. Hawkin's clinically proven Scale of Human Consciousness** https://freedom-within.org/Scale_of_Consciousness.pdf

(42) **The I-Ching Handbook: Getting What You Want** https://www.amazon.com/Ching-Handbook-Getting-What-Want/dp/0943015316/ref=sr_1_1?ie=UTF8&qid=1425030814&sr=8-1&keywords=the+i+ching+handbook+by+wu+wei

(43) **A chakra balancing will help immensely** https://carinacarinosastore.guru/product/shamanic-chakra-balance/

(45) **highest feeling feeling** https://www.youtube.com/watch?v=P4bkIoBBWLk

CHAPTER 9: Beware of Television

(46) **Powerful Energetic Medicines** https://www.facebook.com/powerfulenergeticmedicines/

(47) **Forbidden Cures** https://www.youtube.com/watch?v=gWLrfNJICeM

(48) https://CarinaCarinosaStore.Guru/Cure-Cancer

(49) **Ho'oponopono** https://upliftconnect.com/hawaiian-practice-of-forgiveness/

(50) **Mujin Choi** https://www.facebook.com/mujin.troi

(51) **Rick Simpson Oi** https://www.zamnesia.com/content/361-the-difference-between-cbd-oil-and-rick-simpson-oil?__cf_chl_jschl_tk__=b13e4cc9fe0e620dad6b-b531cadf63f771ebec3b-1579567620-0-AYy33c-MC5euLA2UFIg_8AVDTRKrD6os-SEiKTRsmbyW3RYspg7U03WJAfeRzAJ6wuR0yxeGdTj5SIEssWobMJBHjYTE-f8aifJ-eT6YsDgW-jKSlNfow21GsbKyuEdYFZ68WqWWtlOwC5ktIcNtpw2xe2ZCW-1G3QmfQJG6IDWha2pkdJiVlRd1HERQskZQZiieJFK_z3qLectNUUtq8hrq4D3E-gkz-JIGwQTCJwYPWG5bKoSjFOaghmXG6EjaXqAUlmXJtPeyATqOychrgdqKiUBI2r6KJj-50eVpbQKfocGfxl-xAU3zJ0l4dS_hrFy93KqH6gUK442oay3Bh-EsjTLWtYvWoPRmNi-uwEqzBWVlsW

(52) http://carinacarinosa.com/release-fat/

CHAPTER 10: What is an Empath?

(53) **The Book of Life** https://lifehopeandtruth.com/prophecy/revelation/the-book-of-life/

(54) **Akashic Records** https://lifehopeandtruth.com/prophecy/revelation/the-book-of-life/

(55) **The Empath's Connection** https://www.empathconnection.com

(56) **ionic detox machine** http://carinacarinosa.com/ionic-detox/

(57) **The I-Ching Handbook by Wu Wei** https://www.amazon.com/Ching-Handbook-Getting-What-Want/dp/0943015316

(58) **pre-recorded enlightenment integration CD** https://carinacarinosastore.guru/product/pre-recorded-enlightenment-integration-meditation-lecture/

(59) **Wolfgang Arndt** http://www.crownsandwandsbyheartsongs.com/free_videos.html

BOOK LINKS & REFERENCES

CHAPTER 11: Trust

(60) **Thrive: What On Earth Will It Take?** http://www.thrivemovement.com/the_movie

(61) **consider attending a surrender ceremony** http://carinacarinosa.com/surrender-2-guru-within/

(62) **"All things are possible for those who believe all things are possible." — Wu Wei** https://www.amazon.com/The-Ching-Handbook-Getting-What/dp/0943015316/ref=sr_1_1?ie=UTF8&qid=1387840120&sr=8-1&keywords=the+i-ching+handbook+by+wu+wei

CHAPTER 12: Sharing is Caring

(63) **The Scale** https://www.youtube.com/watch?v=k6xaE38R-o0

CHAPTER 14: Becoming Your Higher Self

(64) **The Eye of the I: From Which Nothing Is Hidden** https://www.amazon.com/Eye-Which-Nothing-Hidden/dp/0964326191

(65) **This link describes the scientific benefits of meditation for your brain** https://www.mindbodygreen.com/0-12793/how-meditation-changes-your-brain-a-neuroscientist-explains.html

(66) **Map of Human Consciousness** https://www.google.com/search?q=dr+david+hawkins+scale+of+consciousness&rlz=1C1AVFB_enUS769US769&tbm=isch&tbo=u&source=univ&sa=X&ved=2ahUKEwiOvevIyZjdAhUJIKwKHUmGAAMQsAR6BAgEEAE&biw=1920&bih=925

CHAPTER 15: Energetic Healing

(67) **ionic detox** http://carinacarinosa.com/ionic-detox/

(68) **Violet Flame** https://www.saintgermainfoundation.org/SGF_09_TheAscendedMasters.html

(69) **All events are perfectly designed for me to grow in awareness and capability." Wu Wei, The I-Ching Handbook** https://www.amazon.com/The-Ching-Handbook-Getting-What/dp/0943015316/ref=sr_1_1?ie=UTF8&qid=1387840120&sr=8-1&keywords=the+i-ching+handbook+by+wu+wei

(70) **Love It Forward** http://carinacarinosa.com

(71) CarinaCarinosa.com

(72) CarinaCarinosaStore.Guru

(73) **The above rates at 977 on The Scale** https://www.google.com/search?q=the+scale+of+consciousness+david+hawkins&rlz=1C1AVFB_enUS769US769&tbm=isch&tbo=u&source=univ&sa=X&ved=2ahUKEwjJq5mH6IPeAhXHz4MKHa8nAeMQ7AI6BAgEEA0&biw=1920&bih=889

(74) www.CarinaCarinosa.com

(75) **HelixileH** https://www.youtube.com/watch?v=KStDRQcV-Nc

(76) **HelixileH** https://www.youtube.com/watch?v=A4VzXGbFdmg

(77) **HelixileH** https://m.facebook.com/helixileh/?sk=info&refsrc=https%3A%2F%2Fm.facebook.com%2Fhelixileh&_rdr

CHAPTER 16: Shamanism and Karma

(78) **Emotional Guidance System** https://www.youtube.com/watch?v=YviTDEw-0GhY&feature=youtu.be

(79) **I-Ching Handbook** https://www.amazon.com/Ching-Handbook-Getting-What-Want/dp/0943015316

(80) **Murphy 's Law** https://en.wikipedia.org/wiki/Murphy%27s_law

(81) www.GuideSpeak.com

(82) **Karma** http://guidespeak.com/chapters/the-law-of-karma/

(83) **Hawaiian** https://en.wikipedia.org/wiki/Hawaii

(84) **reconciliation** https://en.wiktionary.org/wiki/reconciliation

(85) **forgiveness** https://en.wikipedia.org/wiki/Forgiveness

(86) **South Pacific** https://en.wikipedia.org/wiki/Oceania

(87) https://en.wikipedia.org/wiki/Hawaii

(88) **Samoa** https://en.wikipedia.org/wiki/Samoa

(89) **Tahiti** https://en.wikipedia.org/wiki/Tahiti

(90) **New Zealand** https://en.wikipedia.org/wiki/New_Zealand

(91) **Indigenous Hawaiian** https://en.wikipedia.org/wiki/Native_Hawaiians

(92) **New Age** https://en.wikipedia.org/wiki/New_Age

(93) **Wikipedia** https://en.wikipedia.org/wiki/Ho-oponopono

(94) **I know kung fu!** https://www.youtube.com/watch?v=6vMO3XmNXe4

(95) **indigo children** https://www.bibliotecapleyades.net/ciencia/ciencia_indigo30.htm

(96) **Abraham-Hicks** https://www.facebook.com/Abraham.Hicks/posts/because-others-cannot-vibrate-in-your-experience-they-cannot-affect-the-outcome-/572885982838061/

(97) **What we resist will not only persist but will grow in size** https://www.purposefairy.com/1747/what-you-resist-persists/

(98) **Lesson 248 ~ Whatever suffers is not part of me** https://acim.org/workbook/lesson-248/

(99) http://www.greatgenius.com/different-levels-of-power-for-healing-and-miracles

(100) http://www.delightfulknowledge.com/tell-the-lords-of-karma-that-you-are-sovereign-no-lo nger-a-lightworker-part-2

CHAPTER 17: Love Yourself by Loving Others

(101) **Wu Wei's I-Ching Handbook** https://www.amazon.com/Ching-Handbook-Getting-What-Want/dp/0943015316/ref=sr_1_1?ie=UTF8&qid=1511223636&sr=8-1&keywords=wu+wei+i+ching+handbook

BOOK LINKS & REFERENCES

(102) **Psycho-Cybernetics** https://www.amazon.com/Psycho-Cybernetics-Updated-Expanded-Maxwell-Maltz/dp/0399176136/ref=sr_1_1?s=books&ie=UTF8&qid=1511223671&sr=1-1&keywords=psycho-cybernetics+by+maxwell+maltz

(103) **Ram Dass explains in a very interesting way: Suffering as Grace** https://www.ramdass.org/?s=suffering+as+grace

(104) **Ho'oponopono** https://www.psychologytoday.com/us/blog/focus-forgiveness/201105/the-hawaiian-secret-forgiveness

CHAPTER 18: The Magic of Crystal Intuition

(105) **Mujin Choi** https://www.facebook.com/mujin.troi

(106) http://www.crystals-gemstones.com/2013/04/about-opal-stone-benefits-brings-luck.html

CHAPTER 19: Healing The Prostitute Lives

(107) **Lesson 268 ~ Let all things be exactly as they are** https://acimdailylesson.com/268

(108) **Teal Swan would say the isolation, born of enmeshment, is inauthentic** https://tealswan.com/resources/articles/do-you-need-space-if-so-you-are-being-inauthentic-r264/

(109) **Did you know her IQ was an astonishing 168? "Imperfection is beauty, madness is genius and it's better to be absolutely ridiculous than absolutely boring." — *Marilyn Monroe*** https://www.indiatoday.in/education-today/gk-current-affairs/story/marilyn-monroe-10-astonishing-facts-most-popular-actress-332487-2016-08-04

(110) **2150 A.D** https://www.amazon.com/2150-D-Thea-Alexander/dp/0446356492

(111) **Christian Lord's Prayer** https://en.wikipedia.org/wiki/Lord%27s_Prayer

(112) **Polynesian Ho'oponopono** https://en.wikipedia.org/wiki/Hoʻoponopono

(113) **Law of Attraction** https://en.wikipedia.org/wiki/Law_of_attraction

(114) **Patricia Cota Robles** https://www.youtube.com/user/PatriciaCotaRobles

(115) **Rachel Kirkland** http://themodernshaman.net

(116) **Cure Cancer At Home** https://carinacarinosastore.guru/cure-cancer-home-remedies/

(117) **blog post about throat and neck problems** http://www.heartsongs-crystal-wands-crowns.com/throat_problems.htm

(118) **Ingrid Arna** https://themilliondollardivas.com/main/full.php

CHAPTER 21: Forgiveness

(119) **Dave Diamond** https://www.facebook.com/david.diamond.140/posts/2284242478261233

(120) **Psychologist Tara Brach** https://www.amazon.com/dp/0553380990?pd_rd_

i=0553380990&psc=1&pd_rd_w=btMFi&pd_rd_wg=LLKxR&pd_rd_r=90cd779b-f4cb-4171-80c3-ee669a84bd40&ref_=pd_luc_rh_top_sim_01_01_t_img_lh

(121) **healing the mother wound** https://www.bethanywebster.com

(122) **A Course in Miracles** https://acim.org/workbook-lessons-overview/

(123) **Lesson 62** https://acim.org/workbook-lessons-overview/

(124) **Rachel Kirkland** http://themodernshaman.net

CHAPTER 22: Prosperity & Abundance Through God's Will

(125) **Maslow's Hierarchy of Needs** https://almarose.wordpress.com/2008/07/20/sister-alma-rose-is-enchanted/

(126) **Rachel Kirkland** http://themodernshaman.net

(127) **this article** http://www.crownsandwandsbyheartsongs.com/throat_problems.htm

(128) https://carinacarinosastore.guru/bitcoinbeginners/

(129) **Kimberly Maska** https://www.kimberlymaska.com

(130) http://www.greatgenius.com/gods-covenant-of-prosperity-is-what-blesses-you

(131) **The Bible says we are the "royal priesthood" of God (see 1 Pet. 2:9).** https://bible.org/seriespage/9-marks-people-god-1-peter-29-12

(132) **School of the Supernatural (Ryan Watt)** https://www.greatgenius.com/page/75

(133) **"By the sweat of your brow you shall eat"** https://www.greatgenius.com/page/75

(134) **"The wages of sin is death"** https://www.greatgenius.com/page/75

(135) **"The whole creation groans and travails in pain together until now… waiting for the adoption, to witness, the redemption of our body."** https://www.greatgenius.com/page/75

(136) **Psalms 1:1-3** https://www.greatgenius.com/page/75

(137) **Enoch Mind Reality** https://www.greatgenius.com/page/75

(138) **Enoch Mind Reality** https://www.greatgenius.com/page/75

(139) **Enoch Mind Reality** https://www.greatgenius.com/page/75

(140) **Enoch Mind Reality** https://www.greatgenius.com/page/75

(141) **Enoch Mind Reality** https://www.greatgenius.com/page/75

(142) https://carinacarinosastore.guru/product/remember-grounding/

(143) https://carinacarinosa.com

CHAPTER 23: Children vs. Career and Getting Clear

(144) **Wikipedia** https://en.m.wikipedia.org/wiki/Gloria_in_excelsis_Deo

(145) https://www.youtube.com/watch?v=UWcGwCyUviE&feature=emuploademail

(146) **Leave It To Beaver** https://en.wikipedia.org/wiki/Leave_It_to_Beaver

(147) **the Midas touch** https://www.youtube.com/watch?v=3zdTjVrbjKl

(148) **Master Mujin Choi** https://www.facebook.com/Telepathic-Healing-Clin-

ic-893039850768649/

(149) **I also just discovered that PayPal's founder just got an FDA approval for research using psilocybin to treat depression** https://thefreethoughtproject.com/the-fda-just-approved-paypal-founders-project-to-use-magic-mushrooms-to-treat-depression/

(150) **Federation of Damanhur** https://www.google.com/search?q=damanhur&rlz=1C-1GIGM_enUS826US826&oq=Damanhur&aqs=chrome.0.0l8.879j0j7&sourceid=-chrome&ie=UTF-8

(151) **Hawaii Nature Retreat** http://www.hawaiinatureretreat.com

(152) **The Right To Try** http://righttotry.org/rtt-faq/

(153) **Kirillian photography** https://www.google.com/search?q=Karilian+photography&rlz=1C1GIGM_enUS826US826&oq=Karilian+photography&aqs=-chrome..69i57j0l7.959j0j7&sourceid=chrome&ie=UTF-8

(154) http://internationalschoolofexorcism.org/

(155) https://www.boblarson.org/webstore/product-category/special-offers/

(156) **Windsong Movement** https://www.youtube.com/watch?v=KcotiUy7k4c

CHAPTER 24: The Exorcism Part 2

(157) **Star Wars Rise of the Skywalker** https://www.google.com/search?q=star+wars+rise+of+skywalker&rlz=1C1GIGM_enUS826US826&sx-srf=ACYBGNT0yHlcabyyb4knVp9oiwlY0RvJig:1578472760671&source=l-nms&tbm=vid&sa=X&ved=2ahUKEwjOpb-hzfPmAhVOVc0KHVLxDbYQ_AUoA-noECBlQBA&biw=1680&bih=858 (158) Moloch Owl Deamon (159) Signal

CHAPTER 25: Surrender Ceremonies

(160) **Violet Flame. Saint Germain is the gatekeeper of the violet flame** https://www.youtube.com/watch?v=lv9tqY0sPMo

(161) **Patricia Cota Robles** https://www.youtube.com/watch?v=_7LWmmmZUjk

CHAPTER 26: Prayers

(162) The Wisdom of Yoga: A Seeker's Guide to Extraordinary Living https://www.amazon.com/gp/product/0553380540/ref=as_li_qf_sp_asin_il_tl?ie=UTF8&-camp=1789&creative=9325&creativeASIN=0553380540&linkCode=as2&tag=tom-mysplaceme-20

(163) **The next four prayers come from Ernesto Ortiz, author of The Akashic Record: Sacred Wisdom. References: pg 162-164, Balboa Press** https://www.amazon.com/The-Akashic-Records-Exploration-Consciousness/dp/1601633459/ref=sr_1_1?ie=UTF8&qid=1406855491&sr=8-1&keywords=the+akashic+re-cords+ernesto+ortiz

(164) **our store** https://carinacarinosastore.guru/cd-discount/

(165) **If I defend, then I am attacked** https://acim.org/workbook/lesson-135/

(166) "God Eternal Within The Body" http://www.abovetopsecret.com/forum/thread301378/pg1

(167) I'm sorry. Please forgive me. Thank you. I love you. http://www.ancienthuna.com/ho-oponopono.htm

(168) 'Calling all divine powers' Is a modified method taught in-session by mentor Wolfgang Arndt. His videos are available at no cost and his work is offered by donation. Please support this amazingly humble and powerful teacher. https://www.youtube.com/channel/UCmSqLz5hr4AsmnZVlkkMNvw/videos

HELPFUL LINKS:

Healing with Flower remedies http://www.bachflower.com/original-bach-flower-remedies/

CDs:

— **Discounted 6 Pack Enlightenment Audios** https://carinacarinosastore.guru/product/6-pack-enlightenment-audio/

— **Remember Grounding** https://carinacarinosastore.guru/product/remember-grounding-cd/

— **Pre-Recorded Enlightenment Integration** https://carinacarinosastore.guru/product/pre-recorded-enlightenment-integration-meditation-lecture/

— **Relationship Harmony Lectures** https://carinacarinosastore.guru/product/relationship-lectures/

— **Relationship Harmony Meditation** https://carinacarinosastore.guru/product/relationship-harmony-meditation-cd/

— **Looking Inward** https://carinacarinosastore.guru/product/looking-inward-lectures-and-meditation/

— **Goddess Guidance** https://carinacarinosastore.guru/product/goddess-guidance-conversation-and-meditation-cd/

Work Book:

— **Manifest Your Ideal relationship Work Book** https://carinacarinosastore.guru/product/workbook/

Healing Services:

— **Spiritual Counseling And Follow Up** https://carinacarinosastore.guru/product/spiritual-counseling-2/

— **Intuative Healing Session** https://carinacarinosastore.guru/product/psychic-healing-session/

— **Shamanic Chakra Balancing** https://carinacarinosastore.guru/product/shamanic-chakra-balance/

BOOK LINKS & REFERENCES

- **Enlightenment Integration Session** https://carinacarinosastore.guru/product/enlightenment-integration-sessions/
- **Breaking Bonds, Chords, Hooks, & Attachments** https://carinacarinosastore.guru/product/breaking-bonds-chords-hooks-attachments/
- **Black Magic, Curse, And Demon Removal** https://carinacarinosastore.guru/product/black-magic-curse-and-demon-removal/
- **Ionic Detox** http://carinacarinosa.com/ionic-detox/
- **Surrender Ceremonies** http://carinacarinosa.com/surrender-ceremonies/
- **Guided Meditation** http://carinacarinosa.com/guided-meditation/
- **Heart Opening & Chakra Balancing** http://carinacarinosa.com/heart-opening-chakra-balancing/
- **Love Touch Reiki** http://carinacarinosa.com/love-touch-reiki/
- **Nutrition** http://carinacarinosa.com/nutrition/
- **Group Activities** http://carinacarinosa.com/other-activities/

Divine Wisdom:

- **Shamanism How To Videos** http://www.crownsandwandsbyheartsongs.com/free_videos.html
- **Sacred Geometry DNA Activations** http://thetemplateorg.com
- **Spirit Science Animations** http://thespiritscience.net
- **Mantras: 21 Days Free** https://devapremalmiten.com/temple/lyrics-chords/
- **Guru TV** https://www.gaia.com
- **Universal Laws & Principles** http://guidespeak.com/?o=sections&section=1&entry=4880
- **Young Hindu Guru Nithyananda** http://www.nithyananda.org/?__cf_chl_jschl_tk__=8617f1ce63b6b96a3f7e0c864a4c294ec6525e15-1579651965-0-AZJ8Vo9XP-ZL0ncQbSw6OxknaUJDPE1_jtxw2aAoKROdEhDV3V-xsrnpaYtSXe6gtxFTYicQw-B4WHBYfG_peE442J5HE6RhD0ILCdBpNHMwvUTY-lmPgGQhJIjJpB1QlyfQoU-Fy7x9Flf5PVo7gHxES1GylW8HfKgDf1noRCva1dZRMcyRBxLvsuTy2Fi6A5ykmXf-daRvGYDvuNkMOdr4UgT9nXTlyMyt4C7bn4bf0US1t3qbCrMNOk2zTVUb0tMe-ztL-J7v5M6ZCrbe8jsGnjzg#gsc.tab=0
- **Numerology: Easily Understood** https://www.gaia.com/article/life-path-number-report
- **Empath Connection** https://www.empathconnection.com
- **Empath Guide** https://psychicsupport.net
- **Free Empath Guide Book** https://psychicsupport.net/teg/

Video Meditations:

- **Self esteem hypnosis** https://www.youtube.com/watch?v=lSclSYmJetw
- **Self-confidence subliminal** https://www.youtube.com/watch?v=ngOlPBSrNdc

— **Attract love subliminal** https://www.youtube.com/watch?v=uoSNo3HtTcQ
— **Attract love subliminal theta** https://www.youtube.com/watch?v=PEJRmo6QubY
— **Meditation for attracting love** https://www.youtube.com/watch?v=W4EEqaDaHSI
— **Open to love and abundance** https://www.youtube.com/watch?v=m6PZqX1mA74
— **Opening the flow of abundance** https://www.youtube.com/watch?v=m6PZqX1mA74
— **New Angels prosperity & abundance** https://www.youtube.com/watch?v=deizDQks-vDM

OTHER WORKS & PRODUCTIONS BY THE FOUNDATION

AlternativeCancerCures.Org
Cure Cancer At Home Digital Directory
Cure Cancer At Home Exotic Fruit Supplements
Delicious Cancer Tea

PowerfulEnergeticMedicines.Com
Download the App to your SmartPhone & Visit our Farmacy
Magic Microdose Nutritional Supplements
Kambo/ Sapo Jungle Vaccine
Custom Detox Supplements
Ionic Detox Therapy
Bufo & Jaguar Method Medicines

EnlightenTheFuckUp.Org
Secure your Digital Copy to easily access Carina's
Spiritual Supermarket of Resources & Education

SpiritualEvolutionSchool.Com
Enlightenment Integration Workshops Online
Find & Build YOUR Tribal Community or Join One of Ours!

AustinSecretSpa.com
Discover an array of effective alternative health & wellness services.

The Revolution Of Self-Love: A Yearlong Journey Of Self-Love
52 Authors, Stories, and Exercises

FreedomEquityLenders.Pro
Private Real Estate Investing that solves the affordable housing & mortgage crisis.

CPSIA information can be obtained
at www.ICGtesting.com
Printed in the USA
LVHW061109230420
653479LV00001B/1